GARDENING IN THE SOUTH
— with —
Don Hastings
TREES, SHRUBS & LAWNS

TAYLOR PUBLISHING COMPANY
Dallas, Texas

All illustrations property of Taylor Publishing
Company; new illustrations created for this work by
Anne Irene Hurley.

Photographs by the author with the exception of a few
graciously supplied by his father.

Designed by Bonnie Baumann

Library of Congress Cataloging in Publication Data

Hastings, Don.
   Trees, Shrubs & lawns.

   (Gardening in the South with Don Hastings)
   Includes index.
   1. Shade trees—Southern States.   2. Flowering
trees—Southern States.   3. Flowering shrubs—
Southern States.   4. Ornamental shrubs—Southern
States.   5. Lawns—Southern States.   I. Title.
II. Title: Trees, shrubs, and lawns.   III. Series:
Hastings, Don. Gardening in the South with
Don Hastings.
SB435.52.S67H37 1987   635.9′0975   87–7062
ISBN 0-87833-522-6

Printed in the United States of America

9 8 7 6 5

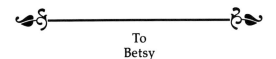

To
Betsy

Whose knowledge and love of the English language and its proper usage has made writing this book possible and the results infinitely more readable. Without her help this book would still be in my mind and not on paper.

And
to
Don III and Chris

For their constant support during the two years of writing this material. A good family is the richest of all blessings and is a gift of God.

Acknowledgements

No person is an island, and knowledge is seldom gained from one's efforts alone. My life has been enriched by others, and my horticultural knowledge gained through the free flow of information from those who have preceded me and from my friends who have shared their horticultural expertise. Without them, this book would be nothing but empty words.

With deepest appreciation and gratitude I acknowledge their contributions to my horticultural life and thus to the preparation of this book:

Donald M. Hastings, Sr. who has always encouraged my horticultural interests and has shared his superlative photographs as well as his extensive horticultural library, and for his critique of many chapters of this book.

Louise B. Hastings, whose love of plants and the beauty which they offer was instilled in me from my earliest days and who offered every encouragement and more than one gentle shove toward the completion of this work.

Kathy Henderson, my radio and TV partner and valued horticultural associate, whose extensive knowledge has been such great help.

John Huyck, the best farmer I have ever known, who made the desert of Egypt extraordinarily productive and shared his tremendous knowledge of vegetables with me.

Bernardino Ballesteros, an extraordinary research director, who introduced me to many tropical plants and helped me bridge the gap between the tropics and our temperate zone.

Special thanks go to Bobby Pierce, Manager of Green Brothers Nursery, Alpharetta, Georgia, for his help with many of the products discussed and shown.

And my eternal thanks to the following academicians and friends who have given of their horticultural knowledge. Though, sadly, some are no longer with us, I will always remember and appreciate their contribution to my knowledge and understanding.

H. O. Buckmann	Jacques Legendre
Henry Chase, Sr.	George W. McClure
John Cornman	Hubert Nicholson
Nelson Crist	James Patterson
O. F. Curtis	Tony Roozen
Fred Edmunds	Tom Sawada
W. Elbridge Freeborn	Hoskins Shadow
Paul Johnson	Rosa Weems
George H. M. Lawrence	John Wight, Jr.

And my special thanks to my editor, Freddie Goff, whose constancy, encouragement and help in the writing and publication of this book have been invaluable.

Grateful appreciation is also given to Anne Hurley for her drawings, which have added so much to this book, and to designer Bonnie Baumann, who made a lot of words and pictures look like a book.

CONTENTS

PLANT NAMES

Sweet Bubbie Bush, Monkey Grass, Banana Shrub, and many similar names are commonly used in gardening circles. Perhaps you have visited a friend who shows you a delightful shrub which you would like in your garden. But a subsequent trip to a nursery is frustrating. Since they have never heard of Banana Shrub, they show you a real, live dwarf Cavendish Banana from Central America in their house plant department, which is not the same plant at all.

Plant names vary from place to place. A South Georgia Pin Oak is very different from the Pin Oak of South Carolina or the Pin Oak of Kentucky. The names of plants can be confusing to both the homeowner and the botanical scholar. Even scholars disagree on the correct botanical name of a plant. Is the commonly-grown shrub Cleyera correctly named *Cleyera japonica* or *Ternstroemia gymnanthera?* Who is the final arbiter? Should an author try to give the most widely-used common and botanical name or the one which is recognized as the most valid?

I have had to decide who my authority will be. Out of deep respect for the institution and its reputation for accuracy and research, I have chosen as my authority the work of the Liberty Hyde Bailey Hortorium at Cornell University. My authority for the plant names found in these books will be *Hortus Third*, prepared from the original works of Liberty Hyde Bailey and his daughter Ethel Zoe Bailey, and expanded and updated by the staff of the Bailey Hortorium.

In some instances I even disagree with them, as with their insistence that Scuppernong and Muscadine are one and the same. Nevertheless I have followed their names, especially their use of the unfamiliar term "cultivar," which they use in place of the commonly-used horticultural term "variety." Once we all get used to this term, it will help tremendously in the proper identification of plant materials by making names uniform throughout the country from growing nurseries to plant sale centers.

My rule has been to use the common name which I have grown up with and which seems to be the most widely used throughout the South. You will also find with each listing the botanical name found in *Hortus Third*. Between the two, I am confident you will somehow know which plant I am referring to.

The botanical name includes the Genus and the species in most cases, followed by cv., which indicates that the plant under discussion is a cultivar. After cv. the cultivar name is given. A plant with a name enclosed by single quotes, such as *Ilex cornuta* cv. 'Burfordii,' is a botanical cultivar under our new rules, and not a variety in the usual way of listing when I grew up. Though this may seem like much ado about nothing, it really is important so that each of us can find exactly the plant we want and identify correctly one we think we might want.

As an example, Pin Oak will be listed as follows:

PIN OAK
Quercus palustris

As for Sweet Bubbie Bush, it is known by most of us as Sweet Shrub and will be listed as follows:

SWEET SHRUB
Calycanthus floridus

Banana Shrub will be listed with our evergreen shrubs in this same format, but you will have to wait for the third volume to find out about Monkey Grass!

INTRODUCTION

Gardening is not a study; it is an experience. Therefore, no matter how much an author might try to be scholarly (and perhaps try to impress the reader), the summation of a work such as this is from his total experience. If my chapter on shade trees is too long for your likes, it is because I have such a deep feeling for these personal friends of mine. If I dismiss your favorite plant as being minimally important, our experiences and preferences have merely diverged.

I started this effort as a single volume which was to cover the basic principles of gardening in our region. As the page numbers increased it was evident that I must either reduce the information, especially about the plant material which I consider so important, or increase the size of the book. The publishers were forbearing and suggested this format which is to produce a three volume work. I hope that you will be as forbearing and will enjoy this more extensive study of the Southern Garden.

This first volume covers how to get started and some of the peculiarities of our area as well as shade trees, flowering trees, shrubs and grasses.

The second volume will cover vegetables, fruits, starting seed for plants to set in the garden, and a lesson on tools for the garden.

The third volume will cover vines, groundcovers, a more extensive look at roses, herbaceaous flowering plants as well as those plants grown from bulbs, tubers, corms and other underground storage organs. I will also try to teach you more about pruning for different purposes and how to be a good detective and search for the answers to your garden problems.

Fortunately for both you and me, there is never the exactness in gardening found in most other subjects. No two plots of ground, even on the same property, are exactly alike. Every garden is unique with its own peculiarities and good and bad characteristics. Also, in many respects plants are as variable as people. Therefore, one may approach the end result of beauty and fruitfulness in different ways.

I expect you are familiar with the expression "it's six or one-half dozen," meaning you can look at the same number in two different ways. In many countries like Egypt, where we lived for two years, the idea is expressed as "six or two threes". The same thought is expressed accurately and correctly in two different ways.

The more we learn about and practice gardening, the more our one approach turns to two, then three, then four, then on and on. Fortunately the approaches are almost ad infinitum.

Dr. O.F. Curtis at Cornell University, a great plant physiologist, taught us over and over "never to say never" and "never to say always." A wise gardener takes this advice also, and sticks to it.

These thoughts are my caveat to protect my integrity if you find something herein with which you violently disagree. I write only from my own experience, which I hope is adequate to make this effort useful to you.

The garden is a living, growing, ever diverse mini-world. These books are written to provide you with the basic tools to begin the experience of expanding your mini-world into something which is rewarding to you, your family and your friends. You may find that much of what you do will be a compromise. Perhaps your Rhododendron bed has never been successful because of poor drainage. Here you face the "six or two threes." You can move it to a more suitable place, which is not where your landscape design calls for it, or you can spend a great deal of time and effort to make the desired spot suitable.

Many of you have moved to the South from other areas, and this work is also designed for you, to help you alter the knowledge you acquired elsewhere so that you, too, can have the best possible results. You will probably try to grow many beloved plants which are not a part of our general garden plantings. My grandmother moved here from Ohio where she grew beautiful lilacs and peonies. Not knowing that they were never planted here, she grew both very successfully despite the fact that "they wouldn't grow in the South." Don't just give up your favorites from other areas but try them in a limited way and you might be successful.

For you who are old-time Southern gardeners, I hope you will gain from another gardener's experience. Don't change a successful practice just because mine is different. Try any new plant or practice in a limited way, and if it suits you better, adopt it.

Gardening is now and always has been "six or one-half dozen" or "six or two threes."

CHAPTER 1

THE GARDEN

The air is still, soft, and cool after the heat of the day. The call of the Chuck-Will's-Widow is answered, and the call and answer repeated, again and again. The air has the sweet scent of honeysuckle. Busy bees are in their hives, their work finished after a frantic day of buzzing from one flower to another. It is the best time of the day, perhaps of the year, in the Southern garden. This is the time when we as a family walk through our flowers and vegetables, with a basket for cutting a bouquet or gathering the fruits of our labors in the vegetable garden. It's hard to keep Betsy from dropping to her knees and extracting a belligerent weed from among her sultana. We examine our garden, give a carrot to each of our horses Milkshake, Princess, and Pokey, and feel deeply grateful for what we have.

The perfect garden at Kensington Palace in London, the magnificent plantings of Longwood Gardens in Kennett Square, PA, the truly Southern gardens of Middleton Plantation near Charleston, what is left of King Farouk's opulent gardens at the Montazzah Palace in Alexandria, Egypt, even the wonderful terraced gardens my mother and father built at Floweracres near Lovejoy, Georgia, where I grew up—none of them can hold as much meaning for me as the simple country gardens and plantings we have here at our place at Sweet Apple. These are ours, not magnificent like many I've seen, but they are extensions of our family's personality and they are the most meaningful to us.

1

Azalea Trails, Callaway Gardens, Pine Mountain, Georgia

Kensington Gardens, London, England

Small cottage garden at the author's home, Sweet Apple, Georgia

Formal Gardens at Floweracres, the home where the author grew up, in Lovejoy, Georgia

Philodendron climbing a large tree in a garden on the island of Mindanao, Republic of the Philippines

Plants surviving in the desert in Upper Egypt

THE SOUTHERN GARDENING HERITAGE

A plantsman looks at growing things no matter where he is at that moment and marvels at the diversity of creation. There are only a few places on this planet where no plant grows at all. From the tundra of the far North and far South to the jungles on the Equator, plants grow and reproduce their kind. In its benevolent state, nature needs no help in these forests and plains.

William Bartram wrote in the 18th century about the groves of dogwoods found in Georgia where the growth overhead was so thick that little light reached the ground. That was the same Georgia where now I struggle to enrich the soil sufficiently to grow my plants well. But this is also the same area where cotton, with its rapacious needs, was grown year after year, depleting the soil which Bartram had seen, depriving it of the benevolence it once gave to produce the groves of dogwoods which impressed him so much. Now that cotton has disappeared from most of our farms, the villains are the bulldozer and the grader, which slice away the topsoil from the land on which new houses are to be built. Away goes the topsoil which has taken eons of time to make. Off go trees which have grown perhaps for a hundred years. It is easier to remove them than to take the time and effort to save them.

A dying oak, victim of grading

The historical significance of the Southern garden has been written about time and again. Gardens seem to epitomize the South of old: the Arlingtons, the Mount Vernons, and all the other gracious plantations which had, as an integral part of their plans, a garden or perhaps many gardens. Gardens were something of great value to the land owners of that day.

And for every Arlington or Mount Vernon there were perhaps a thousand, or even ten thousand, gardens more like mine. Gardening has been a vital part of Southern existence ever since Europeans settled here. During the hard post-Civil War period and perhaps even harder times of the cotton depression of the 1920's and the great depression of the 1930's, Southern mothers planted flowers to make life happier for the family. Whether just a patch of pink thrift, or a bed of lemon lilies or cannas, the love and care were there to make sad and depressed times bearable.

Gardening in the South has always been different from gardening elsewhere, and always will be. It is different not just because of the wonderful assortment of plant materials which can be grown, but also because of the climate, the depleted soil, the long growing season, and the heritage.

A GARDENER'S CHOICE

I have studied gardens in many different climates and have grown vegetables in what had been desert until a few years ago. I have coveted the soils and climate of England, where I think there are the most beautiful gardens in the world. I have seen the parks of Oregon with roses as big as saucers, and the remarkable gardens of Glengarriff in Ireland where Australian tree ferns grow under the shade of Norway Spruce, and where our own Camellias grow close to the most luxurious Daphne imaginable.

I have wanted to live in each of the places I have seen and to have the opportunity to grow things like that. Yet, like you, I have chosen to stay in the South and be a gardener. Though I happen to have been born into this

Pruned heather,
Gardens of
Glengarriff, Ireland

Colorful flower gardens in London, England

particular world of gardening, I know that there are many more who, like my grandfather, chose this to be their land. He always said that he was a Southerner by choice and not by birth.

I found in Egypt that my background and knowledge served me well. There was Bermuda grass, purslane, nut grass, white fly, powdery mildew, soil to amend, climate to work with, and all sorts of cultural problems which were in my horticultural background. The key was adapting past experiences to new conditions. That is what my grandfather did when he chose the South, just as each newcomer should do as he or she chooses to garden here.

A small, enclosed garden in Alexandria, Egypt

E. A. A. Co. fresh vegetable project in West Nobaria, Egypt

A GARDENING JOURNEY

I want to take you with me on a journey through the Southern garden, stopping from time to time to look at the soil, the plants, the practices, and my experiences. It takes a lot to garden here, or for that matter, anywhere. Knowledge, experience, and faith are perhaps the most necessary ingredients. It takes knowledge to know what to do, experience to do it, and faith to foretell the results.

Have you ever thought how much faith it takes to be a gardener? Look at the seed of lettuce. Can you see any embryonic head? Not even the scientist with a high-powered microscope can see the head of lettuce which will come from that tiny seed. Yet you and I know that properly planted and properly grown, that seed will produce for us a beautiful head of lettuce. That takes faith!

Yes, it snows in Georgia! Savannah Hollies (below) and Boxwood (right) are shown bending under the weight of the snow.

Camellia japonica buds and leaves killed by extreme cold

Nandina, severely damaged by extreme cold

Japanese Beetles devouring rose flowers

It is rather popular in today's society to equate nature with God, our Creator. Do not be tempted to succumb to this modernism. What disappointment comes and what damage to faith occurs when the droughts and freezes, which nature sends, kill our plants and ruin our gardens! Nature, like you and me, is only a creature of God and not God Himself. God is perfect; we and nature are not.

"We've had a fail!" is a country expression I have heard and respected all my life. Parts of gardening are often a failure. There is no shame necessary when a crop does poorly. The shame is when the same mistake is made the next time.

Our journey through the Southern garden will show many variances from what you may have been accustomed to in other parts of the country. We plant roses more shallowly and prune them later than is done farther north. Bermuda grass may be a friend here sometimes, and not always an enemy. This journey will take us through gardens of dogwoods and flowering crabapples, Azaleas, Rhododendrons, and Camellias; and, of course, in the next volume, we will spend a long time where I spend so much of my time, growing squash, melons, tomatoes, beans, Silver Queen corn, and maybe even some peanuts and okra.

We will start on our knees, looking at that soil which has been abused so badly, and we will try to make it more like Bartram found it in the 18th century, before the plagues of man arrived.

Perhaps, most of all, we will learn to have fun while gardening. Gardening with a vengeance is all right if there is a big smile on your face. But deliver me from a dour, sad-faced, grumpy gardener. It is impudence to God and nature to be grumpy in a garden. Time spent growing things must either be a happy time, or in these days of so much activity it will never be done. Even if the tiller won't start or the fertilizer is lumpy, still, kick a clod in frustration and then smile. The garden is a place to be happy while you're being productive.

THE NATURE OF A GARDEN

Those of us who love to garden are in good company. After all, God placed the first man and woman in a garden, and with this scene from the Old Testament, our appreciation of gardens began.

The definition of a garden is simple. It is a place to grow trees, shrubs, grass, flowers, fruits, and vegetables near a home. It is also considered to be any place planted for enjoyment with trees, shrubs, grass, and flowers. A garden, however, is whatever you wish it to be, for there are few things in life as personal as your garden.

In the Holy Land and the areas surrounding it, a garden always had great meaning. This bleak and unwelcoming terrain needed man's intervention into nature to make a blessed, restful place where one was surrounded

St. Fiacre, patron saint of gardens, Floweracres, Lovejoy, Georgia: in summer (left) and in winter (right)

An English garden in Kenya

Formal gardens, Powerscourt, Ireland

with beautiful growing things rather than sand and rock. The garden became man's highest achievement in this area of harsh landscape. The Hanging Gardens of Babylon were more famous, I think, for *where* they were than for *what* they were. The idea of making a Garden of Eden in such an unlikely spot was one of the great wonders of the world.

In other less foreboding parts of the world, gardens have been developed to enhance the wonders of nature and personalize them. The garden has become an extension of the personality and lifestyle of its creator.

I want to clarify from the beginning that gardening and landscaping are two different subjects. Gardening is the growing of the plants; landscaping is the planning of the use of materials. I will not intrude upon the territory of the landscape architects and landscape designers.

Our gardening experience in this book will be to introduce various types of plants as the building blocks of a garden or a landscape. I shall leave it to others to prescribe the combinations of color, texture, height, balance, placement, and intermingling of structures which make for a good landscape design. Obviously, there is a lot of crossover between the world

Rest house and small garden in the Nile Delta, Egypt

Garden being tended by Egyptian boys at the E. A. A. Co. compound in West Nobaria, Egypt

of horticulture and the art of design. After all, the plants of the horticulturist are the building blocks of the designer. Unfortunately, not all designers and landscape architects are as familiar with their building blocks, plants, as they should be. I will give you the use of plants from a growing standpoint and not from a design standpoint. It will be up to you to decide how these building blocks should be added to your own garden and landscape, using as a guide the plan which you or your landscape architect or designer has prepared.

Knowledge of your garden conditions will determine whether a Rhododendron or a rose, a maple or an ash, can be planted and grown successfully in your landscape. You will have to judge whether the suggested building blocks are horticulturally suitable for you and your property.

THE CREATIVE GARDENER

The reasons for having a garden have always been very personal to its creator. The ingredients of happiness, beauty, serenity, and enjoyment of nature result from proper planning, good techniques, and knowledge of materials.

A tranquil area, Powerscourt, Ireland

Gardens at Floweracres,
Lovejoy, Georgia

Common Snowball in a
Southern country yard

Another ingredient is often significant: a love of plants as plants and not just as building blocks. Plants can become very personal friends to the creator of a garden. In the country, I have heard comments so many times about Momma's Phlox or her Cape Jasmine or some other prized plant. I have known gardeners who were noted for their roses or perennials or fruit trees or whatever. As we take our journey through the Southern garden, I hope that you will find a plant or group of plants which excites you enough for you to adopt it as your specialty. This is really a rewarding aspect of being a gardener.

From what I have said, you might think that the only reason for a garden is serenity and beauty. But there is another reason, and that is the productive part of our gardening experience. Beauty, serenity, and pleasure

The author's vegetable garden

Monte Carlo tomatoes in the author's vegetable garden

are most important in our high-pressure society, but so is productivity. One of the stops in our gardening journey will be in the vegetable garden and fruit orchards and vineyards. When we get there, in the next volume, stop and consider all the benefits of adding these to your property. What a great sense of accomplishment one has when the table is filled with your own harvest!

When our journey is complete, you will stop at your own garden, for that will be your creation. You will decide what plants to grow, what plants to adopt as your specialty, where each plant will be set, whether your emphasis will be on beauty or on fruitfulness, and how to make your landscape a pleasing and happy place for those you love.

When my wife Betsy and I were married, we went to England and Ireland on our honeymoon. While in London, she took me to the beautiful garden at Kensington Palace on the west side of Hyde Park. I will never

Kensington Gardens, London, England

Powerscourt, Ireland: the gardens (upper left); a circle bed of Dahlias and marigolds (upper right); and the view from across the lake (above)

A city doorstep planting in London, England

Anthurium planting in a garden on Mindanao, Republic of the Philippines

An informal garden in Kenya

forget that absolutely perfect small garden. The use of materials, the design, and the layout were so exquisite that it is always in my dreams when I start a new plot. Of course, I can't have the setting or the pools or the arbors, but I have adapted the ideas about color and mixtures of plants to my own garden. From London we went to Ireland where we visited the magnificent gardens at Powerscourt. I know that I will never have such a garden, but when I look down to my small lake, I still see the vista at Powerscourt leading to that lake with its swans.

You will also see gardens wherever you go. Try to learn from each you see and adopt a plant, a view, a structure, or a design for your own garden.

Our journey through the Southern garden is not exactly going to be like a stroll through Hyde Park in London, or Middleton Gardens near Charleston, or Longwood Gardens in Kennett Square, PA. If you and I were walking together in one of those places, we would observe each area as a whole and be pleased at the combinations of plants which we see. But since this is a learning journey, we must examine each group of plants separately so that you can make decisions as we go, important decisions about the growth characteristics of the plants, the soil that they need, proper spacing when planting, hardiness, and many other characteristics which will help you not only choose what is appropriate but also know how to grow it.

PLANTS AS DESIGN BUILDING BLOCKS

The South is fortunate in the wide range of plant materials which may be grown. Nowhere else are the broadleaf evergreens so magnificent. Our trees are sturdy and of great variety, from small to monstrous. Flowering

Massive oak shading a country house in the South

Forsythia in the spring

Photinia and white azaleas

shrubs range from the bursts of bloom found in the deciduous types to the long-blooming Camellias. Azaleas are spectacular, enhancing our spring as in no other area except Japan. Annuals can be grown easily for summer color. Perennials, when carefully grown, come back year after year with their continuing show.

Despite this extraordinary range of materials, many Southern landscapes are just plain boring. A friend from Europe arrived in Atlanta one April and was overwhelmed with the beauty of the Azaleas, dogwoods, flowering cherries, and flowering peaches. Several years later he came during July. "Where are all the flowers?" he asked. "Your city looks like a sea of green." Since then I have been conscious of how very boring many of our landscapes are with green grass, green shrubs, and green trees. Where is the color?

Landscapers insist that this is what most people want. A myriad of summer leisure-time activities, as well as the summer heat, make the spring

Oakleaf Hydrangea in early summer

Althaea 'Paeoniflora' trained as a tree

Althaea 'Paeoniflora' flower cluster

our major gardening period. For most people, it is too much trouble to be colorful in the summer. However, I don't agree in the slightest. If annual beds are too time-consuming, there are many summer-flowering shrubs. I am afraid that there is a notion that in the South, if it isn't evergreen, it's not worthwhile, and we miss the opportunity to have beauty from many flowering shrubs, trees, and, of course, annuals and perennials.

Don't overlook the opportunities before you to have the beauty of many types of plants that are different from those so common in the landscape today. Altheas, rejected by many as being too common, now are found with huge colorful single blossoms much more beautiful than the older doubles. Crape myrtles don't have to be hot red or pink; some of the most beautiful are the soft pinks. Buddleias are still worthwhile, and so is the Vitex or Chaste Tree. All of these summer-flowering plants can add tremendously to your landscape if you will just use them.

Double Flowering
Pomegranate

'Near East' Crape Myrtle,
pale pink to white

My plea is that you read and study the plant lists and descriptions to be found in the next chapters and consider some of these less-used, less-run-of-the-mill plants. Dream a little of the beauty which you have seen in other places and add to your landscape the ideas which you have encountered, not necessarily with the same plant material, but with similar plants which do well in our climate. The South does not have to change from a place of spectacular spring beauty to a summer sea of grass.

CHAPTER 2

GETTING STARTED

There is no more satisfying time for me as an inhabitant of the South than when, during the winter, I talk on the telephone with an associate of mine in Connecticut. He is worried about getting to the post office because of the snow while I am sitting in my shirt sleeves enjoying one of the warm periods of our winter. It is hard not to remind him in an ugly way that he doesn't have to live there.

The four years I spent at Cornell University convinced me that cold weather was not for me, despite the dire warnings of my agronomy professor who pleaded seriously with me not to go back to the South where, according to him, nothing was ever accomplished because the hot weather made the brain work too slowly.

Living in Egypt and traveling to many North African and Caribbean countries has convinced me that even the South may be too cold for my true liking. My son Chris says that his dad is allergic to cold weather. I agree!

But for the most part, here in the South we enjoy an extraordinary climate for living and for growing things. Despite the sudden drops to near zero, not too much of the winter is really miserable for most of us, except perhaps me.

THE SUNNY SOUTH

The sunny South is really a remarkable place to garden. Plants from much farther north and plants from farther south all commingle happily, side by side with our own

19

Red Horse Chestnut, commonly grown in the North, can also be grown in much of the South.

Banana Shrub grows through much of the South when protected from severe cold.

native plants. We have the advantage of many deciduous flowering shrubs and trees which depend on the changes of the seasons for their cyclical existence, while enjoying the extraordinary broadleaf evergreens for which the South is noted.

The study and understanding of climate and weather is of great importance to all people dealing with plants. Farmers of old days followed many signs: banks of clouds at a certain point on the horizon, how the birds and animals were acting, and even how the farmer was feeling. "It's going to rain because my trick knee is hurting," he would say.

The following are some of the old-time weather sayings I grew up hearing:

- If the cows are under the trees when the rain starts, the rain will not last long.

- If the cows are in the open when the rain starts, it will be a long rain.
- If the raindrops are large, the rain will not last long.
- Heavy corn shucks at harvest mean there will be a cold winter.
- When the squirrels are active burying nuts, winter and bad weather will soon be here.
- When birds are feeding heavily at the feeder, a storm is approaching.
- Plant seeds of beans on Good Friday because the last frost of spring occurs between Good Friday and Easter.
- When the sky is blue in the west during a storm, the storm will soon be over.

Though these popular notions may have been replaced by the TV weatherman, the old-timers were often more accurate. As a boy working in the nursery, I listened eagerly for morning thunder because "thunder before seven means rain before eleven." And rain meant we wouldn't have to work that afternoon!

THE SOUTHERN CLIMATE

Climate is the overall; weather is the specific. We must understand and work with both in order to be successful gardeners. The climate of the South is rather mild, fairly moist, and has a long growing season of around 220 days. The last killing frost of spring is around April 10 and the first killing frost of fall is around November 1. In our area, there are between 45 and 50 inches of rain per year, with the highest amounts in the winter and early spring, and the lowest amounts in May and October. The highest temperatures are about 100° F. and the lowest about 10° F. That is the general climate in which we grow things. Each specific area of the South has its own micro-climate. The closer to the mountains one lives, the lower the highest temperatures, the lower the lowest temperatures, the more the rain, the shorter the growing season, and the more the frost dates will change. Even within a micro-climatic zone there are variances. I live 30

January Jasmine (left) and *Camellia japonica* cv. 'Lady Clare' (right), midwinter-flowering shrubs in the South.

miles north of Atlanta. On a still cold night the temperature at my house may be as much as 10 degrees lower than in the city. My last frost date is almost May 1, and my first frost date is late October.

Each gardener should gradually establish a micro-climatic zone for his land through personal observation. Understanding your micro-climate will help you with plant material selection, proper plant placement, and timing of crops. There is nothing as disappointing as planting too early and watching plants being killed by late frosts or trying to grow plants which die during the winter.

Every garden location has its own peculiarities. A low garden will be colder on a still, clear night than one on a hill or rise. A garden protected from the cold west wind will support plants which cannot be grown in the open. Some plants which are susceptible to heat, like peonies, may grow successfully in morning sun but do very poorly in hot afternoon sun. Be aware of these idiosyncrasies. These special features of your garden will determine when and where each group of plants can be grown.

WEATHER CONDITIONS

The weather is another matter. The weather is the single most important uncontrollable factor with which gardeners must deal. Everybody talks and worries about the weather, and truly nobody can do anything about it. Thank goodness! If we could control the weather we would probably mess it up.

There is a wonderful story about fruit growers in the Pacific Northwest who were experiencing an extended drought. They hired a group to seed the clouds and make it rain. The plan worked and the rains fell, only to ruin the cherry crop. The sudden rain caused the cherries to split and the growers lost huge amounts of money. Man had best stay out of the weather-making business. Instead, he had better learn to deal with weather.

The climate is something which we work with by planning properly. We plant tomatoes, Salvia, Zinnias, and other tender crops late enough to avoid the frosts. We make cuttings of Begonias, Impatiens, and Coleus, we dig Dahlia tubers and sweet potatoes, before the first killing frost of the fall. We grow squash and sweet corn in hills or on beds to avoid the cold, wet water in a furrow during the heavy spring rains. We study which plants will withstand what amount of cold and abide by those findings. We learn to garden within the climatic conditions which we find in the South.

On the other hand, we learn to work with the weather. Rainfall, or the lack of it, is a bothersome factor but we can work with it by irrigation or watering. Proper irrigation or watering of plants is essential to good growth.

Other weather factors with which we learn to contend are how to protect plants when sudden hard freezes occur, how to overcome the tenderness of some plants' roots by using mulches, and how to use wind protection and fertilizing practices which allow plants to become dormant on the best schedule.

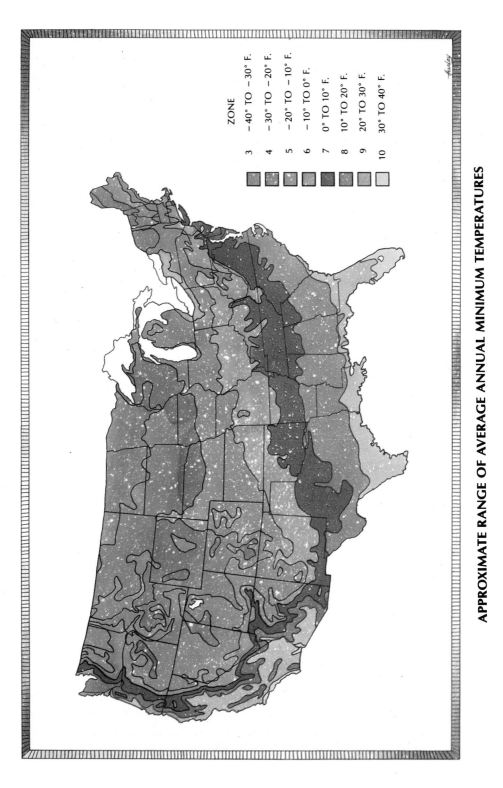

ZONE

3   −40° TO −30° F.
4   −30° TO −20° F.
5   −20° TO −10° F.
6   −10° TO 0° F.
7   0° TO 10° F.
8   10° TO 20° F.
9   20° TO 30° F.
10   30° TO 40° F.

APPROXIMATE RANGE OF AVERAGE ANNUAL MINIMUM TEMPERATURES

PLANTING ZONES

It is important, as a gardener, to understand plant zones and how they help us to grow the right plants. The map shows that the South is primarily in zone 8 (low temperatures between 10° F. and 20° F.), though our area may also include zone 7 (low temperatures between 0° F. and 10° F.). Every gardener should be aware of the general lows so as to grow plants which have the hardiness to take the temperatures found in their area. At Sweet Apple, which is north of Atlanta, we have lows 5 to 10 degrees below those in the city or at the airport where the official figures are recorded. I grow plants like White Pine quite successfully while my father and mother, living south of Atlanta, cannot grow them successfully. They grow Gardenias, and I cannot. In my micro-climatic zone there are even variances which determine which plants I can grow.

You should choose plants according to the zone map at first, and then adjust the map to fit your own locale after you have observed the lows for a few years. Neighbors and gardening friends are also useful advisors in choosing plant material. Plants grown successfully within a few blocks should do well for you.

The plant zones seen on the map are very important to know and to follow, but not every plant listed with a particular zone number will thrive in that zone. These zones are hardiness zones and do not take into consideration other climatic factors which affect plant growth such as heat, length of the growing season, and rainfall. You will find that many vegetables which are not generally possible to grow in other areas farther north prosper here because of our long growing season. Likewise, many plants like Brussels Sprouts are not really satisfactory for us because their best crops are in the fall; being long-season plants, they must grow during the highest temperatures of our summers, which are not conducive to their proper growth.

The Silver Maple is a fine tree in New England, but in our long growing season and high temperatures it grows too rapidly and becomes weak-wooded. I remember planting a 'Crimson King' Norway Maple many years ago. After nearly a decade of being pampered, the tree had increased in size only a few inches, while a neighboring Red Maple had grown over 12 feet during the same period. Norway Maples simply do not like our heat and long growing season.

We must consider plant zones when choosing what plant material has the best possibilities for our area, but hardiness is only one of many factors which determine how successful a plant will be. All factors must be considered.

SOUTHERN SEASONS

Before we move from the subject of climate and weather, we should look at the seasons here in the South. For all practical and gardening purposes, the seasons in the South follow the calendar fairly well. The winter or coldest part of the year starts in January and continues until the spring equinox.

Spring really starts about the time of the spring equinox and continues through mid-May. Summer and hot weather go from mid-May until mid-September. Fall starts about the time of the autumnal equinox and lasts until December. December is in limbo, sometimes mild, sometimes cold.

There is almost always a cold snap at Easter; mid-January to mid-February usually has the lowest temperatures of the year; May is often a time to be concerned with the lack of rain on young plants; and August is a time for rapid insect and disease development due to the hot, muggy weather.

Growing plants is an introduction into nature. Since we cannot change the natural order of things, we must work within its parameters. The winter of 1984–85 saw record low temperatures throughout much of the South. Plants which had survived happily for dozens of years were killed completely. The last time plants in this area were killed so widely was the Thanksgiving freeze of 1950. It took 34 years for a freeze of such disastrous proportions to strike again. My father has the best philosophy. He has stated after each of these natural disasters that if we gardeners chose our plant materials according to the anomalies, the only plants we would grow would be junipers and spruce.

As we journey through the Southern garden we will learn a lot about plant materials. We will also see what measures to take when there is a sudden drop in temperature, and what factors cause a zero cold snap to kill certain plants one year and not the next.

Frigid weather occurs but is short-lived.

Winter storms give way to mild weather which makes gardening in the South a year-round activity.

Spring storms are often accompanied by high winds or even a tornado.

For centuries, I suppose, farmers and gardeners have looked to the phases of the moon for planting times. Crops which mature their edible portions above ground were planted on the wax of the moon, the time from the new moon until the full moon. Plants which mature their edible portions underground were planted on the wane of the moon, the time from the full moon until the new moon. I have never done my gardening according to these signs. I have known very fine gardeners who did. Scientifically, there may not be a grain of truth in these signs, but by regarding them as accurate methods of computing planting and even harvesting times, the gardener stayed on a strict schedule which contributed very greatly to his success. Gardening goes best with strict adherence to schedules, and when the farmer followed the signs, he put himself on a schedule. Success was probably the result of a schedule's being followed, and probably not the result of the signs themselves.

CLIMATIC FACTORS AFFECTING PLANTS

The requirements of any particular plant determine the effect of climate and weather upon them. The most common climatic factor governing the ability to grow is the depth of cold. Other limiting factors are rainfall, length of growing season, length of the day at a particular period in the plant's development, high temperatures, humidity, and amount of light.

A view of the green English country side from atop Windsor Castle; the mild, misty climate makes England an almost perfect gardening spot.

The Sahara Desert in Egypt; where there is no water, plants cannot survive.

RAINFALL

Rainfall or the amount of water available to a plant is critical. Deserts are devoid of plants because the climate of an area prevents rain. The Sahara, where I worked; the Mojave in this country; the Atacama Desert in northern Chile, one of the driest areas of the world; and the huge 500,000-square-mile Gobi Desert in Mongolia and northern China are areas of little natural plant growth because of little, if any, rain. The lack of rain is in itself not limiting; the problem is the lack of water. When dams, canals, and irrigation schemes are designed and built to bring water into these regions, they may then become highly productive.

Even in areas of normally sufficient rainfall, the wise gardener will develop alternatives to rainfall so that plants may flourish even when the weather is dry. Bed planting with deep middles to hold water, home drip irrigation systems, and sprinklers can prevent disaster from occurring if the rainfall is insufficient.

LENGTH OF GROWING SEASON

The length of the growing season determines whether many plants will produce to their full capability. Cotton takes many months to produce a crop. Thus it must be grown in the areas of the world with enough frost-free days to mature. Most tomatoes take about 90 days or three months to produce a crop. In Finland and Sweden, where the growing season is barely this length of time, almost all tomatoes are grown in greenhouses or imported from farther south. We are fortunate to have a very long (220-day) growing season in most of our area. This means we may grow a wide range of vegetables, flowers, and fruits. But it is most important to understand the maturing time for each plant which we attempt to grow. No plant should be started so late in the season that it fails to mature and produce to our satisfaction before the end of the growing season.

LENGTH OF DAY

The length of the day (or night) has an important effect on plants. Have you ever wondered why Chrysanthemums bloom in the fall, or Poinsettias bloom one year and not the next when grown inside the house? It is because some plants grow and set their bloom buds under a given number of light or dark hours. The Chrysanthemum has vigorous vegetative growth during periods of long days, and sets its buds during periods of short days. Poinsettias are similar. Their vegetative growth comes during long days and they set their buds during short days. Since they are very susceptible to cold, they will not set buds or flower here in the South before the frost in the fall kills the plant. They are grown as a house plant, but if they are given artificial light during the bud development time, the buds will not initiate since the plant's vegetative growth cycle continues indoors.

TEMPERATURE

High temperatures may be very detrimental to some plants. Peonies, lilacs, and some other plants we will discuss as we journey through the Southern garden do not grow well in the heat of the South. Often this poor growth is due not just to the heat on a given day but to the accumulation of days of high temperatures. High temperatures affect soil fungi, insects, and diseases also, which may prevent the proper growth of these plants.

HUMIDITY

Humidity is important in two ways. Very low humidity can retard plant growth by removing water from the plant faster than the roots have the ability to replace it. Desert plants are often modified to be able to hold water for long periods of time. Cacti and succulents have a strange "different" look to their foliage. These structures are there to prevent excessive water loss under very low humidity. The gardener should be aware of these differences and plant cacti and succulents in areas of good air movement because in humid, stagnant air they will do poorly. Santolina is a popular plant which is excellent for hot, dry locations in the garden but which will grow poorly and look very bad in the wetter, shadier areas where the humidity is too high.

LIGHT CONDITIONS

There are plants for shade and plants for sun. Nature has provided us with a range of plants for almost all conditions. If you are aware of the natural growing conditions each plant requires, you will have much better results. When Impatiens (sultana) are noted as shade plants, don't put them in full sun. When geraniums or roses are said to require sun, don't plant them in the shade.

Shade plants, such as this Mahonia, do poorly when planted in too much sun.

Over millions of years plants have evolved to accept the conditions of their natural habitat. Gardening is the art of taking plants from other places and growing them under whatever conditions we have on our property. If we use only plant materials that are native to our particular spot, our gardens would be very uninteresting, perhaps even boring. It is the introduction of materials native to other conditions and places that makes gardens unique. The gardener must know, however, that by introducing plants from other areas and other climates into this area, we may have to alter our conditions to accept them. That is what gardening is all about—learning to provide the most natural conditions for each plant we grow.

SOUTHERN SOILS

In 1791 William Bartram wrote in his *Travels* about the fertile plains, huge forests, and abundant plant life he had found in South Carolina, Georgia, Florida, and Alabama. He described the pristine rivers and herds of wild animals which were common throughout the whole area.

Then the settlers came and took the Indians' land. The fertile soils were planted over and over with the same or similar crops to bring in cash. My father wrote in *The Southern Garden Book,* published by Doubleday & Company, Inc. in 1948, "The tillers of the soil did not see the coming destruction of that rich land. . . . They kept planting those same fields year after year with crop after crop without putting anything back in the ground. It was not long until those once-rich lands began to show unmistakable signs of starvation."

Agricultural leaders like my father, grandfather, and many others watched the disaster reach its height with the abandonment of farm after farm and the onslaught of terrible erosion. The fertile lands found by the early settlers no longer supported the crops for which the South had been so famous.

Looking back, it is easy to criticize. But the Civil War, the depressions, the boll weevil, and all the other economic factors which made our families slaves to the land contributed to the destruction of the fertility which the settlers had discovered.

The disregard for the future productivity of our land still exists. Even though agricultural technology has taught us how to preserve and rebuild the land on which crops are grown, an even more deadly threat has arisen. This is the builder, who shows the same kind of disregard for tomorrow and for who or what will exist on the land in the future. The subdivision, the shopping center, and the office complex are placed for convenience and economics and not because of land configuration. If the land is not right, the bulldozer and grader will make it right. Trees that held the soil in place with their massive roots fall to the chain saw. Soil that could support our lawns and gardens, commercial plantings, and natural cover is pushed into low areas to make the land flat. What is left is even worse than land worn out from years of cropping. A grader can destroy in an hour what it took cotton

Heavy grading kills many plants, such as this old oak tree.

fifty years to destroy. A bulldozer can undo in a day what it took nature perhaps millions of years to make.

Some say it is greed; I call it egotism. We live only for ourselves. Today what is ours is ours, not held in guardianship for future generations but used to extract our pleasures and profits with little regard for the consequences.

This is what we find as we "settle" our land. The modern "settler" may not have to clear the land with an axe and have a house-raising to carve a life out of the wilderness, but his task is no easier. His task is to take graded land with little, if any, life-giving topsoil and make it into a garden spot.

When I told you that our journey through the Southern garden would start on our knees, I was saying that we must begin by looking at the disaster man has wrought upon this land and by taking steps to correct it. We must start our gardening experience by realizing that the good earth can be bountiful and productive. Man's greed and egotism have taken much of the good from the earth and we must work hard to return to the soil the ingredients which once made it bountiful.

SOIL CLASSIFICATIONS

Technically, our Southern soils are extremely varied. There are rather strict classifications of soils and each soil area has a name. There are Davidson, Fullerton, Sequoia, Coosa, and Colbert soils and many others with wonderful names taken from the regions where they are found. Then there are the general soil types: clay, sandy, loam, calcareous, and many others, as well as mixtures of these.

It is helpful to the gardener if he knows his soil class, but it is not generally necessary to go to the trouble and expense of finding more exact information. The farmer who is economically dependent on his soil may

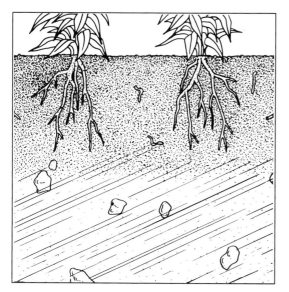

The root zone (topsoil or furrow slice) and the subsoil

vary crops or even change locations to have the best soil type for the crop he wants to grow. But we gardeners must learn to work with what we have.

The soil of any area is made of many components. The mineral composition may be classified as clay, sandy, clay-loam, etc. This material will vary from the surface to the subsoil and from place to place on the property.

The vertical composition is divided into the furrow-slice or topsoil and the subsoil. The biggest problem for us comes when the furrow-slice or topsoil has been removed, leaving the subsoil as the growing area for plants. Our effort now becomes the making of topsoil out of subsoil. In other words, we must accomplish in a very short time what nature has taken thousands, perhaps millions, of years to do.

Besides the mineral structure of the soil (and subsoil), the major ingredient is organic matter. This is referred to as the humus content of the soil. Humus gives life to the soil, binds together the soil particles, and, in the proper amount, keeps the clay soil from feeling slick and sticky when wet. Humus also gives the soil greater moisture-holding capacity and allows excess moisture to drain through the soil. The constant replenishment of the soil with organic matter is an absolute need in gardening. Otherwise our gardens are no better than the one-crop farms which died and eroded away.

PREPARING THE SOIL TO PLANT

Think of your land as being like the earth was millions of years ago. Through the addition of humus you bring it through the ages until it is the way it was when Bartram traveled through the South. Unless you keep adding humus, your garden will become like starved farmland which can support little growth. Then you or the next gardener on your land must start all over again.

Humus alone, however, cannot make the land as fertile as you wish. You must also add nutrients or plant growth minerals. I will constantly refer to fertilizers, but these are not foods for your plants, despite what the bag might say. Fertilizer adds chemical nutrients to the soil to support the growth of the plant. Through the process of photosynthesis, the plant makes its own food. We can only add the major and minor nutrients which are necessary for the plant to grow properly; we never "feed" plants because they do that for themselves.

Gardeners are constantly bombarded with all sorts of advice about the role of organics and inorganics in their gardens. Should one use only organic materials or only inorganic materials? There is a whole system of growing things using only organic materials for fertilizers and sprays. Then there are those who would have you believe that you can achieve the Garden of Eden with various inorganic materials. I am a firm believer in balance. Organic material is an absolute necessity for a good garden. In Egypt we used fifteen tons of manure per acre per year on our desert sand. What a difference a few years of this addition made! On the other hand, inorganic fertilizers are also, in my opinion, absolutely necessary. They are the quickest, easiest, and most sensible way to add the needed nutrients, both major and minor, to our soils. The enormous productivity of American farms has been achieved to a large extent by the use of relatively inexpensive inorganic fertilizers. In Egypt, we used huge amounts of inorganic fertilizers to grow our crops. That was an absolute necessity in the desert sand which had supported virtually no living matter for thousands of years.

Desert lands need huge amounts of organic matter and inorganic fertilizers to support plants.

EVALUATING SOILS

Most of our homes are on land which has either just been graded or has been worn out by improper care over many years. Very few of us are fortunate enough to settle on land which has been properly cared for. We must make do with what we have.

Start by looking at your soil and what plant life it is supporting. Newly-graded areas show characteristics different from areas which have been planted for many years and which have declined in fertility. The fertility of the soil is what needs to be determined and perhaps corrected.

Newly-graded areas have a light, poor look. Plants grow slowly and are not deep, rich green in color. Grass is weak, light green, and sparse. Evergreen shrubs are not full and healthy; trees seem to be stagnant without any signs of bursting forth into heavy leaf.

Old plantings have the look of decline. Leaves may be smaller than normal and lawns filled with weeds. Trees seem to be the only plant material which is thriving.

Now look at the soil itself. Dig a hole about a foot deep and a foot across. Remove the soil, laying it carefully beside the hole. Take some of the soil in your hand, smell it, feel it, break up the clumps, and recompress them into a ball in the palm of your hand. Then try to break the ball with your fingers. If the ball breaks easily into crumbles, the structure is good; if the soil is hard to break up and feels slick, it needs humus. Look at the hole you have dug to remove the clump of soil. The side of the hole will show the soil in layers. Inspect these carefully. How deep is the dark, perhaps rich-looking area beginning at the surface? This is your topsoil. Note the condition of each layer and what the bottom-most layer is like. Many soils of our region lie on a sandstone base. This crumbling stone makes planting difficult and moisture a real problem.

Presence of moss indicates an acid condition and poor surface drainage.

In newly-graded areas, there will be very little demarcation between the topsoil and the subsoil. The whole profile will have a light, perhaps yellow, look. Soil which has declined may have a demarcation, but the extent of the topsoil may be rather shallow.

A test for drainage should be made. Fill the hole with water, and leave it until all of the water has been absorbed. Then fill the hole again and observe how long it takes for all the water to be absorbed. A good indication of poorly drained soil is when it takes several hours for the second filling to disappear.

Make these tests in several different areas of your property. Very soon you will discover the good and bad characteristics of the soil in each area.

The soil profile and drainage tests are not the only things you should observe. Note other symptoms of poor soil:

- Presence of moss indicates an acid condition and poor surface drainage.
- Sour-smelling soil indicates very poor drainage.
- Light red or yellowish soil indicates low humus content.
- Late afternoon wilting of weeds or grass indicates poor moisture-holding capacity.

WET AND DRY SOIL

The expression "dry" or "wet" areas will be found in many writings including these. The tests you make may or may not uncover these characteristics of your soil. A "dry" area is one which drains excessively or is so tight and hard that water cannot penetrate and be held in the topsoil. Within a day or two of a hard rain or heavy watering the soil is dry once again. Such an area needs humus and enriching to develop the ability of the soil to take moisture and hold it without becoming and staying so moist that plant roots do not develop and grow properly.

"Wet" soil is that which holds too much moisture. The rain or water which is applied stays in the topsoil for long periods of time. The test for drainage suggested above will help you determine if a particular area is a wet area. Loosening the soil with humus and sand or perlite will increase the drainage and keep the area from being a "wet" area.

MOISTURE-HOLDING CAPACITY

You will also read about moisture-holding capacity. This term is important to understand as you strive to make plants grow better. "Dry" soil has very little moisture-holding capacity, "wet" soil has too much. Soil which has been properly conditioned with humus has a greater capacity to hold the right amount of moisture while allowing excessive amounts to percolate through the topsoil and away from the root zone of the plant. The addition of drainage-improving materials like perlite or sand will increase the percolation of water through the soil and will help prevent too much moisture in the root zone.

ENRICHING THE SOIL

The observatins and tests help you to identify the good and bad characteristics of your sil. After identifying these features you will need to begin the process of coricting the major areas of weakness and building the soil to its greatest produdve capacity. There are several major ways of making your soil highly producve and supportive of good plant growth.

HUMUS

Throughout this book I am going o stress over and over the need for using humus on a regular basis. It is absuitely essential to a good growing program. For one thing, humus in the sil does not last forever. It must be added on a continuous basis. Here in th South our long growing season and high temperatures increase the bacterih action and the breakdown of humus. Since it is rapidly removed from thesoil, adding it once is not sufficient.

For many years, we had a beautiful flower be outside our window. In it we grew an assortment of flowers that brightly colced our lives. While we were out of the country the bed was never worked, no umus added, no flowers planted. When we returned, I tilled the area and plated a new bed without much thought of rebuilding the soil. What a failure we ad! The soil which seemed to work well soon baked hard and dry. When it rined the water stood on the surface and the bed stayed sticky. In only fou vears, the soil of my prize flower bed had reverted to the bad soil which I fund when we moved here. I had to start a whole new rebuilding program to pt life back into this area.

Humus does a great deal for the soil. It not only adds life by binding the clay particles together to make the soil loose and friable, but it also adds

The author's Impatier suffered from poor development aftr soil lost its hur

some nutrients, increases the beneficial bacteria in the soil, and allows organisms like earthworms to live and develop good aeration. You can use many forms of humus, including peat moss, ground bark, rotted leaves and herbaceous plant residue (compost), manures, and green plant material. Let's look at these.

Peat moss is a dried bog material found in several parts of the world such as Canada, Ireland, and Germany. This material is in the process of evolution toward becoming coal, but at this stage it has many excellent qualities for building the soil. Since it is acid in nature, it should be used with caution on high pH plants. Do not confuse peat moss with peat. True peat of Ireland is a material which is burned in place of coal and is not suitable for soil building. There is also a black, soil-like material which is bagged and called *peat* here in the U.S. I find it too heavy and of little use in gardening, either outside or while potting plants. So always ask for *peat moss*.

Ground bark is literally some type of bark, usually pine, which has been ground into a fine material. It is an excellent soil amendment because it lasts much longer than peat moss and is much less expensive. Ground bark has a less acidifying effect on the soil than peat moss and should be used on areas where the plants requiring a higher pH are to be grown.

Compost is a free and superlative way to add humus continuously to the soil. It consists of plant material like tree leaves, herbaceous stems and leaves, and grass clippings which have been decomposed by bacteria to leave a wonderful residue that is excellent for soil conditioning.

Manures from grain- and grass-eating animals are an excellent source of humus. These give the same good soil-building characteristics and they are much higher in plant nutrients than the other forms of humus mentioned. But it is important to let manures age before you use them. When they are fresh the large amounts of ammonia which they contain will damage plant roots.

Be sure you ask for peat moss; peat is not the same.

Ground bark is an excellent soil amendment.

Green plant material is one of the best continuing methods of adding humus to the soil. These are referred to as green manure or sometimes cover crops, planted for the purpose of plowing or tilling them into the soil to add humus. In the South we use green manure crops which are also legumes, a class of plants which have the ability to harbor nitrogen-producing bacteria on their roots. This allows the addition of nitrate nitrogen fertilizer at the same time the soil is being improved with the green manure crop. Austrian winter peas, Crimson Clover, and cowpeas are commonly-used green manure crops which are also legumes.

One of the difficulties in using humus in the garden is that after plants are growing, it is hard to add humus to the soil on a continuing basis. Flower beds and vegetable gardens which are basically restarted each year are easy; new humus may be added at planting time each year. Lawns are more difficult, because humus can be added only as a top dressing which, with some grass types, is not wise. Shrubs and trees are deep-rooted, and in many instances piling humus on top of the roots may be harmful. Therefore, alternative methods of adding organic matter to the soil must be found.

Fortunately, plants produce a large amount of humus themselves. The sloughing-off of roots as they penetrate the soil adds humus. Good nutrient levels will encourage soil bacterias which in themselves are organic matter, and other soil organisms like earthworms develop large amounts of humus. The fertility level of all garden and landscape areas should be kept high to encourage natural humus regeneration in planted areas which are not tilled or replanted each year.

Another way of adding organic material to the soil is through the use of organic fertilizers like dehydrated cow manure, fish oil emulsion, blood meal, cottonseed meal, and chicken manure.

FERTILIZERS

Strictly speaking, fertilizers are materials which add the nutrients to the soil which plants must have for growth. These may be organic materials or inorganic materials. They may be natural or manmade. They may be in many forms, some quickly available to the plants, and some very slowly available. No matter what the form or what the availability, they are absolutely necessary to good plant growth.

In some parts of the world the soil is rich enough to grow plants without fertilizing. The South is not one of these places. To grow plants, we must add fertilizer. The form which is used is the result of the particular needs of the given plant during its growth cycle, not the general need for the nutrients.

Fertilizers are identified with numbers indicating the percentages of the major nutrients which all plants need, nitrogen-phosphorous-potash, and always in that order. A 10-10-10 fertilizer contains 10% nitrogen, 10% phosphorous, and 10% potash. A 12-0-6 contains 12% nitrogen, no phosphorous, and 6% potash. You will always know what you are buying by looking at these numbers.

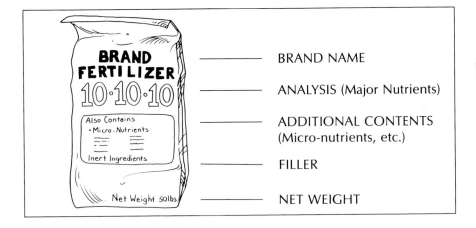

BRAND NAME

ANALYSIS (Major Nutrients)

ADDITIONAL CONTENTS
(Micro-nutrients, etc.)

FILLER

NET WEIGHT

In addition, plants have a need for certain other nutrients in very small amounts. These are called micro-nutrients or trace elements. The label will show if trace elements have been added to a bag of fertilizer. The better brands also list the names and amounts of trace elements in the bag. This is important, for you should know what you are buying. These trace elements will generally be listed not on the front of the bag but on the analysis label on the back.

It is also very important to know about fertilizer forms. Basic fertilizers with nitrogen, phosphorous, and potash are generally very inexpensive and are composed of ammonium nitrate, phosphoric acid (from superphosphate), and muriate of potash. The nitrate and potash are very soluble, quickly dissolving in the soil moisture, readily available for growth, and rapidly moving down through the root zone into the subsoil and outward in the soil water away from the feeder roots. Generally speaking, their useful time for the plants is about six weeks.

There are other forms of nitrogen, which become soluble and available much less quickly. These are generally found in materials derived from manmade urea. These materials require bacterial action to turn them into a usable form for the plant and thus are called slow-release nitrogen materials. These are somewhat more expensive and are widely used in lawn fertilizers where a long time of availability is more desirable. Other forms of fertilizers which are generally slower in becoming available to the plants are derived from organic matter. Some fertilizers are combinations of various manures, blood meal, bone meal, and cottonseed meal as well as other organic materials. These are slow-acting and often very expensive.

LEGUMES

Along with fertilizers, there is a most interesting and practical way to add nitrate nitrogen to the soil. There is a class of plants called legumes which contain many widely used and common plants of the garden. These include peas, beans, clovers, alfalfa, and even some ornamentals like lupines and sweet peas. These plants harbor a bacteria on their roots which has the ability to take free nitrogen from the air and turn it into nitrate nitrogen, the form plants can use.

The legumes have long been an important part of good farming practices, being used to add nitrogen for the economically important cash crops on which the farmer's income depended. They are no less important today even though the ready availability of low-cost nitrate nitrogen fertilizers has made commercial inorganic nitrogen fertilizers the prime source of this mineral nutrient. Today, the legumes are used in farming and gardening for the dual purpose of providing green manure to the soil and providing a bonus of nitrate nitrogen.

The South is most fortunate in having several leguminous crops which may be grown in the winter while gardens are mostly bare. This practice, called cover-cropping, literally means putting a cover of plants over the bare garden to hold and build the soil during this unused time.

Our two major leguminous cover crops are Crimson Clover and Austrian Winter Peas. There are others which are good but do not produce the amounts of green manure which these two hardy plants do. Though almost all clovers, many other peas, and some beans are suitable for the purpose, here in the South the Crimson Clover and Austrian Winter Peas are ideal because of their hardiness and heavy growth. Crimson Clover is planted in late August or early September; Austrian Winter Peas may be planted in October and until the first hard freeze in November. Both produce large amounts of nitrate nitrogen, heavy top growth for turning under as green manure, and deep roots for holding soil in the winter.

Another group of legumes which are used in the spring, summer, and early fall for cover-cropping is the cowpea. These are excellent to broadcast over bare areas which have been tilled but on which no crop is to be planted. Cowpeas grow rapidly in the heat of our Southern summers and may be turned under while young and succulent for green manure or may be used as a nitrate-producing crop while allowing the plants to mature for harvestable peas.

Legumes are most often used in vegetable areas and I will discuss them further in the volume on vegetables and fruits. However, legumes can be just as important in the building of a good lawn and keeping good flower areas.

Crimson Clover is one of the South's best green-manure legumes.

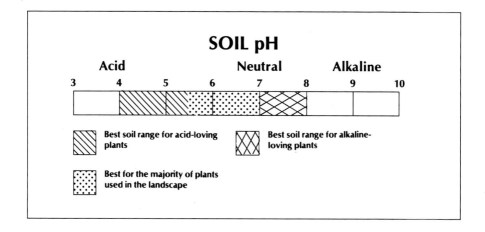

SOIL pH

In developing your soil into a suitable planting area, it is important to know its pH, which is the indication of the acidity or alkalinity of a given soil. Many plants such as our broadleaf evergreens and Azaleas must have low pH soil or soil that is quite acid, while other plants like lilacs, peonies, and many grasses need higher pH soils to grow properly.

A soil test is an essential part of gardening and the pH test is perhaps the most important part of that soil test. Most of our Southern soils are mildly acid, ranging in pH from 5.5 to 6.5. In this pH zone a broad range of plants will flourish. However, many garden plants will need a raising of the pH, which is done by adding the alkaline material lime. If by chance your pH is too high, you may lower it by adding aluminum sulphate to the soil.

RAISING THE pH WITH LIME

Lime is an extremely important ingredient in gardening. Our low pH soils may need lime to raise the pH and to supply calcium to some plants. It also contributes to the binding of the clay particles, giving better texture to heavy clay areas. Liming the soil is a yearly ritual for many of us because this addition helps vegetable gardens and lawns immeasurably. But not all plants or garden areas should be limed. Azaleas, Camellias, Rhododendrons, hollies, laurels, boxwood, centipede grass, and other broadleaf evergreens need an acid soil. Before liming any areas containing these types of plants, do a pH test. Never lime areas to be planted in Irish potatoes because it encourages attacks of scab disease on the tubers. All other areas of the garden will respond very positively to the application of some form of lime.

The form of lime which gardeners generally use is agricultural limestone, a very finely-ground limestone. In the South, the most commonly-

Pelletized limestone is fast-acting and easy to apply.

found limestone is dolomitic limestone which contains magnesium, a necessary minor nutrient.

Pelletized limestone is a new form which you may see in your supply outlet. It has the advantage of being faster-acting and easier to apply, especially when using a fertilizer distributor.

Occasionally, hydrated lime is found in garden shops and nurseries. Much faster-acting than ground limestone, this lime form is often used in preparation for planting tomatoes, which need a quickly-available source of calcium, or plants like clematis and lilacs which need a rapid change in the pH.

Never use builder's lime, which may be called burnt or slaked lime. This form absorbs water rapidly, producing high amounts of heat which will burn the roots of plants.

When applying lime, remember that agricultural limestone is really finely-ground rock and is slow-acting. Plan ahead when using agricultural limestone, applying it well ahead of the time of planting. Apply hydrated lime when you need calcium or a pH change in a hurry.

Calcium may also be added to garden areas by using bone meal which is rapid-acting and also has some nitrate nitrogen.

CORRECTING HIGH pH

Occasionally our soils may be too alkaline to grow many of the acid-loving plants which are such an important part of our landscape material. Many of these plants grow best when the pH is below 6.5. Higher pH soils may be treated with aluminum sulfate to lower the pH. The use of acid-forming fertilizers will also help to lower the pH and keep it in the right range for these acid-loving plants.

High pH conditions are often discovered when acid-loving plants are chlorotic, a condition indicated by yellowing between the veins of the leaves. Chlorosis is most often due to a lack of iron in the plant. Soil which is too alkaline has the normally available iron bound in compounds which are not usable by the plants. These plants should be fertilized with an acid-forming fertilizer or the soil treated with aluminum sulfate, both of which will reduce the pH and free the iron for use.

You may correct the immediate problem of chlorosis by the use of an iron compound applied as a spray or as a drench around the roots. However, this is a temporary solution, and if the chlorosis returns, undertake the more permanent solution of lowering the soil pH with acid-forming fertilizers or aluminum sulfate.

GARDENING TOOLS AND SUPPLIES

The excitement of owning your new home has not fully worn off when the reality of gardening begins. Perhaps you have just moved to the South or perhaps you have been living in an apartment and now own your first home. There is a shock when you look at your new property and realize there are certain shrubs, trees, and grass which are now a part of your life.

These new members of your family are in need of help, just like a new baby coming home from the hospital. In the case of a baby, you have spent much time purchasing a new bed, a changing table, and many other baby needs. You have also begun to learn the basics of caring for this new addition to the family.

Though it's not really fair to equate a tiny, wonderful, helpless baby with a newly-acquired oak tree or boxwood, still your new plants do need attention and you do need materials and equipment like fertilizer, chemicals, pruners, spades, shovels, hoes, rakes, and other useful equipment.

My best advice to you is to move slowly. Purchase only the essentials at first. As your gardening horizons expand, you will begin to know what you like and need. In the next two volumes of this book, I will show you the equipment and implements for each specialized part of your gardening experience. For now let's look at the basic needs.

4-cycle rotary push mower with grass catcher

Lawn tractor with mower or riding mower for large lawns

MECHANIZED EQUIPMENT

I will start with the heavy investment items, which include the power equipment that makes life so much easier. I will list my suggestions for buying each item.

The Essentials

A GOOD LAWN MOWER

Look for the following features when buying a lawn mower:
- 4-cycle engine—so you do not have to mix the oil and gasoline.
- High cut—the cutting height should be adjustable up to 3 $1/2$ inches.
- Blades which are easily removed for sharpening.
- A catcher for grass clippings.
- Consider a riding lawn mower if you have large lawn areas.

A NYLON FILAMENT WEED TRIMMER
- Gasoline-powered for larger, electric for smaller properties.
- Purchase a unit with a brush cutter if you have wooded, brushy areas.

A BICYCLE-TIRED CART
- A well-balanced large-wheel cart will take much of the drudgery out of gardening.

Nylon filament, gasoline-powered trimmer

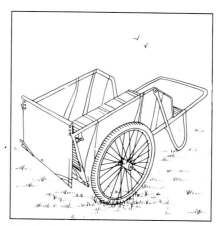

Bicycle-tired cart

Secondary Items

ROTO-TILLER

A roto-tiller is one of the most useful pieces of home garden equipment you can have. However, do not purchase one until you have gardened for a while. The size and the capability you will need will be determined by your total gardening program. Rent one until you have really started your garden

Rear-tine roto-tiller

Power edger

program, then purchase one when you know exactly what you will need. The following suggestions are based on many years of owning a tiller:

- Purchase a rear-tine tiller *only*.
- I recommend at least a 6-hp tiller.
- Study the optional attachments carefully before purchasing the tiller. Many of the newer models have attachments which will greatly aid your garden program.

POWER EDGER

- A very helpful power tool which helps keep lawn edges, flower beds, and walks neat and trim.

POWER TRIMMER

- A rechargeable trimmer is a blessing when you have extensive jobs to do.

LONG-HANDLED TOOLS

Tools are expensive but they are necessary. Choose only a few and buy the best. There is nothing worse than breaking the handle of a shovel when you have a big job ahead of you.

RAKES

There are two types of rakes for the garden. Neither will do what the other can, so buy both types:

- **Leaf rake:** Buy a leaf or broom rake (also called a "spring tooth" rake) for raking leaves and other plant material.
- **Bow rake:** You will also need a garden rake, often called a "bow" rake or "sharp tooth" rake, for working and smoothing soil.

SHOVEL

- Purchase a long-handled shovel with a slight point.
- It should be a straight-shank shovel with a fire-hardened wood handle.

LOPPERS

- Buy *only* a lopper with knife-cut blades.
- Loppers with strong, tubular steel handles are best.

SMALL HAND TOOLS

- These are necessary but very personal, and you will have to choose the ones you like.
- Be sure to include a good, sturdy trowel and a hand cultivator.

SPRAYERS

- You will need two sprayers: one for weed killers and one for insecticides and fungicides.
- Mark them clearly so that you will never use insecticides and fungicides in the one with which you have sprayed herbicides.
- I prefer either compression sprayers or trombone sprayers over "hose end" sprayers.

Mark your sprayers.

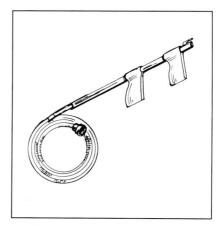

Trombone sprayer, best for reaching high into trees

WATERING EQUIPMENT

HOSE

- A $3/4$-inch heavy, corded hose is the best.
- Be sure your hose has brass fittings.
- Purchase a cut-off valve for the end. This helps when connecting two hose pieces together and when attaching sprinklers and other watering equipment.

SPRINKLERS

- The impulse sprinklers are the best type to buy.
- Purchase an impulse sprinkler made of brass. Plastic sprinklers do not last.

Impulse type sprinkler

Root watering rod

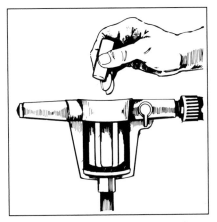

Pellets are available for fertilizing with a root watering rod.

Water breaker

ROOT WATER WAND

This is a most practical instrument which puts water at the roots of plants.

- Excellent, especially for trees and shrubs which have been growing for over three years.
- Saves water since there is little evaporation from the surface.
- Pellets may also be used in the instrument for fertilizing.

WATER BREAKER

How can you break water? Look at the little nozzle on your kitchen sink faucet. Gardeners can buy the same type of nozzle for the end of the hose. I have three. They are inexpensive and very necessary.

- Softens the stream of water so that you do not have heavy gushes and washout.
- Necessary when planting seedlings in trays or transplanting small plants into the garden.

- I prefer the metal ones rather than the plastic models.
- Purchase the larger size.

FERTILIZER

Your first trip to a nursery or garden supply store will be an eye opener with all the stacks of fertilizer and soil amendments. I get confused, after all these years. You will read in a book like this that you should buy a specific formula fertilizer. You look and look for a bag or sign that says "10-10-10 Fertilizer." You may not find it, but don't give up; ask the salesman. There may be a 20-20-20 formula which is the same ratio but stronger so that you can use half as much.

I will tell you much more about fertilizers as we proceed, so keep reading. Here are a few tips as you get started:
- The ratio of the numbers is very important.
- I will often recommend slow-release nitrogen fertilizers. The bag may say "long-lasting," "slow-release," or "Uramite nitrogen." These are all the same type and are what I am talking about.
- Acid-forming fertilizers are often referred to or sold as "Camellia-Azalea-Rhododendron Fertilizer."

Not all fertilizers are in bags. There are other forms with which you should be familiar.

Soluble fertilizers are made to be mixed with water and applied as a liquid. They are a very good way to start seedlings, to fertilize transplants, and to fertilize plants in tubs, planters, and pots. They are widely used for fertilizing houseplants. Soluble fertilizers are much more expensive for the amount of nutrients which you receive than are dry, granular fertilizers. Also, their being soluble may be a disadvantage when applications are made on plants growing in the ground. The soluble fertilizers move quickly through the root zone and are wasted when there are heavy rains.

Drop-type spreader

Cyclone-type spreader

Liquid fertilizers are similar to the soluble ones except that they are already partially mixed. There are some excellent fertilizers like fish oil emulsion that come only in liquid form. The liquid fertilizers have the same disadvantage of fast movement in the soil as do the soluble ones.

Fertilizer spikes are excellent for use around established shrubs and trees, especially larger ones with deeper roots. These are driven into the ground and into the root zone of the plant.

FERTILIZER SPREADERS

There are two kinds of spreaders, the drop type and the cyclone type. There is not much difference in action, and I have had both kinds.

- The drop type is better for applying dry weed-killers since there is less chance for drift.
- The cyclone type is excellent for seed distribution and most other jobs.

CHEMICALS

Another thing you will notice in the nursery or garden supply store is the shelves and shelves of chemicals for controlling insects and diseases, killing weeds, fertilizing plants, rooting plants, starting plants, and almost every other garden chore.

I am not going to mention many specific chemicals because I hope that this book will last you for a long time, and the chemical part of gardening is ever-changing. The chemicals found in books only a few years ago are no longer found on garden supply shelves. My rule here has been to mention chemicals by name only when they have survived many years without taint of being a carcinogen or dangerous in any way.

Discuss your problem with a nurseryman or garden supply dealer and with your county extension service. They can give you up-to-date information, and that way I won't have to write a revised version of these books every year or two.

Chemical labels should be read and understood before using the material. Follow directions carefully and use a chemical only in the manner specified on the label. Apply a material only on the plants which are shown on the label.

Which is easier, spraying or dusting? I don't know. It is really up to you. I spray most ornamentals and dust most vegetables. Whichever you do, be careful and do it safely. Wear a long sleeve shirt and heavy rubber gloves when mixing and when spraying. Wear a mask to prevent inhaling the material. Stay out of the drift of the material when spraying or dusting.

A FINAL WORD

The best advice I can give to you about "getting started" is to buy well-made tools and equipment even if you restrict yourself to just the very basics. The list is long even though I have listed what I consider only the basics. Remember, however, the above list covers all the different parts of the garden. You may be interested in only one or two.

Start slowly and buy the best.

CHAPTER 3

PLANTING TREES AND SHRUBS

Southern soils, as we have seen, usually need a great deal of attention before plants can thrive in them. The soil in flower beds and vegetable gardens may be improved over a number of years. A lawn will grow beautifully for a long time if it is properly installed and given enriching materials and sufficient fertilizer. But preparing the soil in which to plant individual trees and shrubs is a different story because it has to be done once and for all, when they are planted. So it should be done correctly.

The ideal would be to prepare the whole landscape the way a vegetable garden or lawn is prepared. Of course, this is impossible. Therefore, each tree or shrub must be planted in a specific area which has been well prepared. This is called spot planting. However, spot planting is not the only way to plant shrubs. Bed planting is extremely important, especially with Azaleas and Rhododendrons.

We will be looking now at the general principles of planting trees and shrubs, with the admonition that these are general rules. There are many plants which have variations in their planting procedures. Whenever these occur, I will note the special planting techniques in the text covering that particular plant. This is especially true with plants which have varying drainage, pH, moisture, and planting depth requirements.

53

Bare-root Plants

Balled and burlapped (B&B) plants

Container-grown plants

When you go to a nursery or read a catalog to order a plant by mail, you find that the same tree or shrub may be purchased in one of several different states. It may have been grown in some type and size container (container-grown); it may have been dug from the growing nursery with a ball of earth around its roots (balled and burlapped or B&B); or it may have been dug with no soil around the roots (bare-root). Each of these must be planted in a slightly different manner. Large trees are almost always balled and burlapped. Evergreen shrubs may be either container-grown or balled and burlapped. Deciduous shrubs and smaller sizes of deciduous trees are usually bare-root with some type of moisture-holding material wrapped around the roots to keep them from drying out.

PLANTING BARE-ROOT PLANTS

Trees and shrubs which have been dug without soil around the roots, or bare-root, require the most care when planting. These should have been dug and shipped to you or to a nursery during the time when they are dormant.

Almost always these plants are deciduous because evergreen plants seldom survive bare-root digging. You will find many of these plants in nurseries and in mail-order catalogs for shipment during the winter months while their roots are mainly inactive and before their leaves appear. Their chances for survival are greatly diminished if you plant them after they leaf out.

The time you plant is very important for dormant, bare-root shrubs and trees. Late fall and early winter planting is generally the best. The closer to the growing season you plant the tree, the poorer its first-year growth will be because the roots will not have had sufficient time to develop before they have to meet the demands of the new top growth. Remember that the roots will grow even in very cold weather, and the better the root system, the better the first year's growth. There are a few exceptions to this rule. Plants which are marginally hardy like figs and blue or pink Hydrangeas are best planted after the coldest part of the winter has passed.

Bare-root mail-order plants may be shipped with no packing material around the roots.

Soak the roots, overnight if possible.

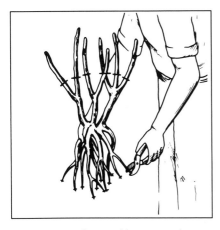

Prune roots and tops of bare-root plants before planting.

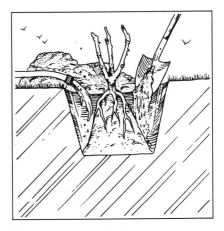

Planting bare-root plants

Though bare-root plants are dormant, they are still alive and must be treated carefully. After you take them home or receive them by mail, prepare them for planting as soon as possible. First, examine the material around the roots carefully to see if there is still moisture in the packing material. If it seems to be dry, pour a cup or two of water into the package to freshen the roots before planting. Nowadays many mail-order nurseries will ship plants which are laid in a box with a plastic wrap around the roots and no packing material. Even though this is quite satisfactory, you should never leave such plants in the sun or in a hot place. If they look particularly dry, use a mister to spray a small amount of water to freshen the roots while you are preparing to plant. Remember that excessive moisture may cause rotting to begin.

Try to be ready when you get your bare-root plants. Do not buy them at a nursery on the spur of the moment. It is difficult to hold these plants at home for long, so why take a chance? Since one never knows when a mail-order package will arrive, get everything ready soon after you place your order.

I always plant the day after receiving or picking up the plants. The night before planting I take the plants out of the package, remove all the packing material, cut any broken or excessively long roots, and place the root system in a bucket of water overnight. This allows the roots to absorb moisture and freshens them considerably.

Now you are ready to plant. Dig a hole larger and deeper than the root system. Make a good soil mixture out of the soil taken from the hole. Use $1/3$ peat moss or ground bark, $2/3$ soil (from the hole), and a large handful of cattle manure (dehydrated is much better than composted). Do not add any fertilizer to the mixture. Now check the feeling of your mixture. If it still feels

A young dogwood

tight and slick, add more humus and perlite to loosen it up. If the pH of the soil needs to be corrected, add lime or aluminum sulfate to the mixture.

Next, observe the bottom of the hole. If the soil layers are particularly tight, sticky, and damp, dig the hole a little deeper and place some fine gravel, sand, or chunks of bark in the bottom to allow drainage.

Take the plant out of the bucket of water and position it in the hole. Begin filling the prepared soil around the roots. Be sure that the planting depth is the same as it was in the nursery. *Do not plant too deeply!* Continue filling the prepared soil around the roots, packing it down as you do. I water larger plants thoroughly when half the hole is filled. This settles the soil around the roots and prevents air pockets from forming in the root zone. Continue filling the hole until it is full, and water again. Now make a collar of dirt around the outer edge of the hole to hold water as growth begins or during any dry periods during the first growing season.

Mulching new trees and shrubs is always helpful. A good pine-straw or bark mulch will keep weeds under control and prevent excessive water loss.

Small trees up to 6 feet in height should not need staking. However, larger trees do need to be staked to prevent the swaying of the tree in the wind from breaking the young feeder roots.

Some gardeners prune the tops of the plants rather severely after planting. This may be very helpful, especially if the roots were damaged or dry when you planted. However, shade trees should not be pruned except to remove any broken or damaged limbs. The main trunk should never be pruned. Altering the growth habit of a shade tree by pruning the main leader may ruin its natural shape.

After new growth starts, fertilize on top of the ground in a circle at the outer edge of the hole and on top of the mulch. For starting new trees and shrubs, I use a tree and shrub fertilizer which is formulated with a slow-release nitrogen, or a 10-10-10 fertilizer. Always water after adding fertilizer.

Bare-root trees and shrubs should be cared for regularly during the first spring. Water during periods of drought, prune out any branches that die, and keep them well mulched. If a plant is slow to come out in the spring, prune it back to reestablish the proper root-top balance. This will usually force the new growth quickly. However, *do not* cut the main stem (leader) of a shade tree. This will ruin its shape.

To recapitulate, then:

1. Plant early, as soon as dormant in the fall, or in the winter.
2. Obtain plants when you are ready to plant (the day before actual planting).
3. Handle plants carefully.
4. Soak roots in a bucket of water overnight.
5. Dig hole larger and deeper than the root system.
6. Mix soil taken from the hole.
   a. Use 1/3 peat moss or ground bark.
   b. Mix with 2/3 soil from the hole.
   c. Add a handful of dehydrated cow manure.

d. Add more peat moss or bark plus perlite if it still feels tight and sticky.

e. Add lime or aluminum sulfate to the mixture if the pH of the soil needs to be corrected. (See pages 40–42)

7. Put small gravel or chunk bark in bottom of hole if drainage is poor.
8. Plant at the same level as the plant was growing in the nursery. Do not plant too deeply!
9. Pack prepared soil tightly around roots.
10. Water when the hole is half full to settle soil.
11. Fill the hole and water again.
12. Make a collar around the outer edge of the original hole to hold water.
13. Mulch the newly planted tree or shrub to conserve moisture.
14. Prune back tops if roots were badly damaged. Do not, however, prune the main trunk (leader) of a shade tree.
15. Fertilize your new plants when the growth starts in the spring. Place a good tree and shrub fertilizer or 10-10-10 in a band at the outer edge of the original hole which you dug and on top of the mulch. Water thoroughly.
16. Keep well-watered during dry periods after growth starts.

PLANTING BALLED AND BURLAPPED PLANTS

Digging and selling balled and burlapped plants is an old practice. Early horticulturists found that very large plants like evergreens, which do not go into a true dormancy, survive much better if they are dug with as much of the root system as possible still intact. Since this practice is prevalent today, gardeners find many plants in nurseries which are labeled B&B or balled and burlapped.

The digging of a large amount of soil around the roots of a plant keeps these roots in good condition and ready to start new growth when replanted if weather conditions are proper. This practice extends the time of planting past the leafing-out time which generally signals the end of the bare-root planting season. With proper care, B&B shrubs and trees may be replanted throughout most of the year. However, the digging of B&B plants is best done during the dormant season because the roots are least active and foliage and stem growth are at a minimum.

B&B shrubs and trees are still best planted during the dormant season. As with bare-root plants, the late fall, early winter, and early spring are the best times for setting B&B plants. Much better growth will occur during the first growing season if they are planted at a time that allows the roots to become well-established before the new growth starts.

Handle B&B plants carefully, especially when you take them from the nursery to the place in the garden where you will plant them. Here are a few rules which should help:

• Never grab the plant by the stem or top. The heavy ball will pull away from the roots, breaking many of the feeder roots. Always carry the plant by the ball.

Never lift and carry B&B plants by the stem; handle carefully by the ball as shown.

- Do not drop the ball.
- Plant as soon after purchasing as possible.
- If planting is not immediately possible, place the plant in a protected place in case of freezing temperatures. Never leave a plant in the hot sun. If it will be several days before planting, pull a mulch of pine-straw, peat moss, or ground bark around the ball and keep it damp.

The basic principals of planting B&B plants are almost the same as for bare-root plants:

1. Dig a hole larger and deeper than the ball.
2. Mix soil taken from the hole.
   a. Use $1/3$ peat moss or ground bark.
   b. Mix with $2/3$ soil from the hole.
   c. Add a handful of dehydrated cow manure.
   d. Add more peat moss or bark plus perlite if it still feels tight and sticky.

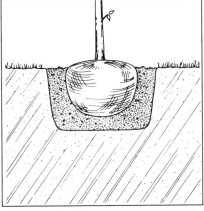

Proper planting in well-drained soil

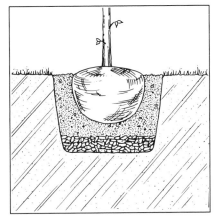

Proper planting in poorly drained soil

    e. Add lime or aluminum sulfate to the mixture if the pH of the soil needs to be corrected. (See pages 40–42)

3. Look at the bottom of the hole. If the soil is tight, damp, and seems to be poorly drained, dig the hole deeper and place gravel, sand, perlite, or chunks of bark in the bottom for drainage.

4. Measure the ball of earth and place enough of the prepared soil in the bottom of the hole so that when the ball is placed in the hole, the top of the ball will be at or slightly above the surface of the surrounding soil. Do not plant too deeply!

5. Place the plant in the hole, turning it until it is positioned correctly and sitting straight.

6. *Do not try to remove the burlap from around the ball.*

7. Begin filling the hole with the prepared soil. Tamp it tightly so that there are no air pockets in the soil being packed around the roots.

8. When half full, water thoroughly to settle the soil against the ball.

9. Undo the ties that hold the burlap tightly around the ball. These ties are usually made around the base of the stem. Remove them and the burlap from around the stem and off the top of the ball. I cut the burlap with a knife and remove that which is on top of the ball rather than laying it back into the hole as some do. The treated burlap used today rots very slowly and may cause air pockets.

10. Continue filling the hole with the prepared soil until the hole is full. *Do not put soil on top of the ball or against the stem.*

11. Ideally, the top of the ball should now be exposed and about $1/2$ to 1 inch above the surrounding surface.

12. Make a collar around the outer edge of the original hole to hold moisture.

13. Soak the newly planted shrub or tree. Place the hose nozzle at the stem and let the water run very slowly into the ball until the hole will not accept any more water and the cup within the collar begins to fill.

14. Mulch the newly planted tree or shrub to conserve moisture. *Do not let the mulch touch the stem.*

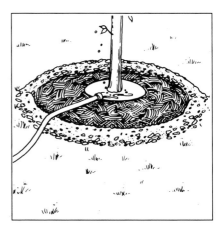

Mulch and soak plant after planting; note that the top of the ball is left exposed.

15. Keep the ball of earth around the roots moist by soaking as in step 13, especially during periods of dry weather.
16. Prune out any broken or damaged stems or twigs.
17. When the new growth starts, apply fertilizer in a band around the outer edge of the hole but inside the collar and on top of the mulch. Water thoroughly.

PLANTING CONTAINER-GROWN PLANTS

Nursery growers have discovered that plants grown in containers have definite advantages over balled and burlapped or bare-root plants. The roots of a container-grown plant remain undisturbed when the plant is put into your garden. There is no cutting of the roots as the plants are taken from the ground, and the plant should start growing immediately. Theoretically, a container-grown plant should survive just as well when planted in June as in December because it does not suffer root shock. No matter when a B&B or bare-root shrub is dug, there is going to be some shock because some roots are always damaged.

I wish it were that simple. Container-grown plants do offer tremendous advantages over the two other types we have looked at, but they also have problems which must be overcome.

First, the soil mixture used by nurserymen is very light in order to prevent root rot while the plant is growing. This light mixture dries out very quickly, and these plants must be handled carefully by the retailer as well as by you when you take them home. Container-grown plant material must be watered thoroughly if it is not to be planted immediately.

Second, the root systems of the plants are extensive and the plants are usually pot-bound. When removing the plant from the container, you must pull these roots away from the ball of earth so that they can start growing into your soil rather than continuing to grow inward into this light mixture.

Third, after planting, this soil mixture has a tendency to dry out very rapidly. Soak the newly planted container-grown shrubs often, especially during periods of dry weather. Keeping the root ball damp is much more difficult with container-grown plants than with bare-root or B&B plants.

Here are the basic principles for planting container-grown plants:

1. Container-grown plants may be planted during the entire year. For best results, however, avoid the hottest and the coldest times.
2. While preparing to plant, soak the container thoroughly.
3. Dig the hole larger and deeper than the ball.
4. Mix the soil as you do for B&B plants.
5. Inspect the bottom of the hole you dug and correct the drainage as you did for B&B plants.
6. Remove the plant from the container and inspect the roots. Pull the outer mass of roots away from the ball with your fingers or with some instrument like the back of your pruning shears.

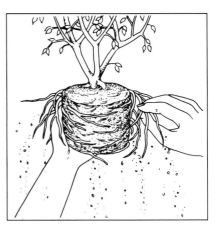

Loosen the roots of container-grown plants before planting.

7. Plant the same as with B&B plants, being sure that the top of the ball is slightly above the surface of the surrounding soil.
8. Pack the prepared soil tightly around the ball, watering once when half full. Continue filling until the hole is full, and water again.
9. Make a collar around the outer edge of the original hole; water and mulch the same as with B&B plants.
10. Keep newly planted container-grown shrubs and trees well-watered during the first summer after planting. Soak slowly with the nozzle at the stem.
11. Fertilize new plants the same as was suggested for B&B shrubs, except that during spring and summer planting the fertilizer should be applied at the time of planting.

There are many plants which have particularly bad root systems and which transplant much better if they are container-grown. The following is a list of plants which are best bought in containers:

Dogwoods	Sourwood	Most hollies
Native Azaleas	Franklinia	Mountain laurel
Rhododendrons	Camellia japonicas	
Some oaks	Camellia sasanquas	

BED PLANTING

In the beginning, I mentioned that spot planting was the accepted way to plant large trees and shrubs. I also mentioned that one should do bed planting whenever possible. This is particularly true of foundation plantings around a house, background shrubs, hedges and screens, bank cover plantings, and borders.

The rule should be spot planting for individual specimens and bed planting for mass or row plantings. There are some plants which almost demand bed planting. Azaleas, Rhododendrons, boxwoods, and the box-leaf hollies are some that respond very poorly, over the long run, to spot planting, but do well with bed planting.

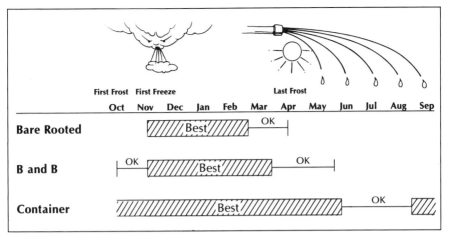

	Oct	Nov	Dec	Jan	Feb	Mar	Apr	May	Jun	Jul	Aug	Sep
	First Frost	First Freeze					Last Frost					
Bare Rooted		////// Best //////				OK						
B and B		OK	////// Best //////				OK					
Container		///////// Best /////////							OK			////

When to plant bare-root, B&B, and container-grown plants

Prepare a bed for shrubs in the following way:

1. Mark off the area to be planted.
2. Inspect the area for drainage problems. Poorly drained soil will need correcting as the bed is being made. Till deeply. Then remove the soil from the bed to a depth of 12 inches. Line the bottom of the bed with 4 inches of coarse bark or gravel, and fill the bed with the soil which has been laid aside.
3. Till the bed as deeply as possible with a roto-tiller.
4. Work peat moss, ground bark, and any other humus into the entire bed area.
5. Work any organic fertilizers like cow manure, cottonseed meal, or blood meal into the bed.
6. Inspect the soil for a heavy or a slick feeling. Add perlite to loosen it further.
7. After soil preparation, plant the same as for spot planting except that you do not need to prepare the soil taken from the hole.
8. Water and fertilize as you do with spot planting.
9. Mulching, however, should cover the entire bed.
10. Do not plant too deeply or mulch tightly around the stems of the plants.

Foundation planting at a country home in Sweet Apple, Georgia

CHAPTER 4

SOUTHERN SHADE TREES

I have a thing about trees. Perhaps it is because I grew up before air conditioning; perhaps it is because I have spent so much time in desert countries; perhaps it is because two of my horticultural mentors, John Cornman and Nelson Crist, taught me that trees were to be revered more than almost any other garden plant. Then, too, common sense, observation, and a lot of study have shown me the value of a sturdy oak or a stately maple in the landscape.

Not too long ago, the location for a house was chosen for the presence of a tree or group of trees. If you drive through the rural South, you will see home after home situated under an oak or maple or amongst pecans. These trees were the natural air conditioners in the days when none of the mechanical contrivances were available.

Today we live in a new era. Most builders, at least those doing subdivisions, hate trees because trees make building more difficult, work more laborious, and grading impossible. The prevailing theory is that it saves money to wipe them all out, have the freedom to grade and work, and then plant some more. When you finish reading this chapter, go out and look at what your builder planted around your house. You will probably be appalled at the cost-cutting measures he took when he chose the trees for

Deciduous trees allow the sun to warm a home during the winter.

your new home. Unfortunately most home buyers find themselves redoing what the builder has done.

Trees are important in the landscape, and they are expensive. A good tree of a reasonable size will probably be the most expensive plant material you will invest in. In fact, trees should be considered one of your major capital investments, along with the house, drive, and retaining walls. They are also most important in the economics of running your house. A tree is a natural air conditioner in two ways. First, its foliage blocks the sun and absorbs a tremendous amount of heat which would otherwise affect your house. Second, the huge amount of evaporation from its foliage cools the air around and underneath the tree. The people who built their houses under huge oak trees in the deep South knew what they were doing.

If the natural cooling were not important enough, a deciduous tree is also of economic value in the winter. When the leaves are gone, the sun comes through and the cold house is warmed.

When we moved into our rebuilt country farmhouse, the entire west side was plate glass. The heat coming through those windows in the summer made the rooms almost unbearable without running the air conditioner full-blast or pulling down blinds to shade them. One of the first things I did was to plant two American red maples and one sugar maple across that side of the house. Now, except on rare occasions, the air conditioner is not needed and the blinds are long gone. My trees have made a huge difference in the electricity usage in the summer, and that side of the house is just as pleasant in the winter as in the summer.

There is no clear-cut delineation between a shade tree and a flowering tree. Many authors lump them together, but for the sake of clarity I list them separately. This is an arbitrary decision but, to me, their major use dictates how you will be making your choice.

The author's Red Maples were planted sixteen years ago to shade the hot western side of the house.

Before the maples were planted, the heat was so great that heavy blinds were needed.

The flowering trees which will be discussed later have a very useful place in the landscape design and should not be overlooked, but they would not be considered as candidates for the one or two spots in the landscape where shade is of the greatest importance. The flowering peach, for instance, would certainly be eliminated as a suitable shade tree but may be used quite well as a spectacular flowering tree. And there are shade trees, like the Bradford Pear, which do flower very well, but because of their size, are more suitable as shade trees than as flowering trees.

CRITERIA FOR CHOOSING A SHADE TREE

The choice and placement of a shade tree is one of the most important things which you will do in planting the landscape. When the sun is beating down upon the house and the draperies must be drawn to keep the boiling

The Tree of Heaven is a fast-growing but weak-wooded tree which provides much less cover than more desirable trees.

sun from ruining the furniture and making a room unbearable, the advertisement of a tree which grows 15 feet per year is appealing. The Tree of Heaven sounds like exactly that: something sent from heaven to relieve the house of its burden from the hot sun. Would that these "miracle" trees were the answer! Speed of growth is one of the lesser characteristics of shade trees which should enter into your choice. There are many other criteria which are far more important.

Trees should be considered as a permanent part of the home. Think of them as being as permanent as the driveway or carport. They are just as long-lasting and a whole lot harder to have in a useful size. Consider the following important characteristics when thinking about planting a shade tree:

- Length of life
- Strength
- Depth of roots
- Insect and disease resistance
- Foliage
- Rate of growth
- Shape and head size
- Color in the spring, summer, and fall
- Rate and time of foliage drop
- Availability in the size wanted
- Cost
- Flowers and fragrance

Let us look at each of these and see why they are so important.

LENGTH OF LIFE

Trees involve a heavy investment in time, money, and energy. Even the largest tree which can be moved is relatively small and lacks the usefulness of a tree which has been growing for many years. Therefore, it is important to have a tree which will last for many years after it has reached the size where it is providing what the gardener is seeking. It is frustrating for the owner suddenly to find, after many years of struggling with a tree, that its usefulness is negated by die-out or die-back. Many of the highly-advertised "miracle" trees are relatively short-lived, since the unfortunate fact is that the faster the growth of the tree, the shorter its life span.

STRENGTH

This characteristic is important and is often directly related to the rate of growth. Fast-growing trees are generally weak-wooded. Slower-growing trees are generally longer-lived and very strong. The wood strength is important in preventing breakage and damage to the property. Areas where the wind is often high are areas where wood strength is most important. Throughout the South, high winds are a possibility during summer thunderstorms. Weak-wooded trees can break easily if their foliage is wet and heavy when the wind comes up.

Strength of the wood is also important during ice storms, which occur upon occasion in the South. These devastating storms cause extreme damage to property when weak-wooded trees break and fall on roofs and power lines.

The fast-growing Chinese Elm provides little shade (left); it is also weak-wooded and subject to breakage during ice storms or high winds (above).

This Bald Cypress is a very deep-rooted tree which has not buckled the adjacent sidewalk.

The root system of a tree may be huge, as shown by this tree which toppled during a very high windstorm.

DEPTH OF ROOTS

This characteristic is crucial when planting trees in lawn areas or near shrubs, flower beds, or vegetable gardens. The deeper the root system, the better chance there is of growing grass, flowers, and vegetables in the area. Trees have massive root systems to anchor the plant in the ground and hold it upright. The deeper the anchor, the less chance there will be of the tree toppling over in wind or ice and damaging the property. Also, the deeper the main root system, the fewer surface feeder roots there will be to deprive the topsoil of moisture and nutrients which grass, flowers, and vegetables need. Remember that in the competition for moisture and nutrients, the tree always wins because it is bigger.

A good rule of thumb in planting trees is that the roots will be competitive outward from the tree approximately $1/3$ to $1/2$ the height of the tree. Consider the ultimate height of the tree and use this rule of thumb when placing the tree near buildings, drives, walls, and other manmade structures, as well as near planting areas.

I am frequently asked about the pressure of roots against the foundations of houses. When the tree is planted too close to a structure, the roots will cause problems. All of you have seen driveways lifted and walls pushed over. On the other hand, if given some leeway, tree roots will grow toward moisture and away from areas which are dry.

Another consideration is the danger to water and drain lines from roots penetrating while searching for moisture. I lived for a number of years in a place which was built during the 1920's with terra-cotta drain lines. Every spring the lines had to be reamed out, or they would clog. However, drain lines have been much improved and now are made of impenetrable cast-iron pipe. What a blessing this is to homeowners! There is no danger of water lines being penetrated since they are also watertight and impenetrable.

A type of Wooly Aphid is a serious pest of Silver Maple.

INSECT AND DISEASE RESISTANCE

Shade trees are not immune to pests. Many have serious insect and disease problems which are costly and bothersome to control. Large trees are hard to spray and commercial spraying can be very expensive. It is better to choose a tree which has minimal pest problems to prevent a continuous need for spraying. Many trees have pests which are neither unsightly nor particularly harmful, and can be ignored. But you should avoid buying trees with bothersome or destructive pests.

FOLIAGE

Shade trees are almost always planted to eliminate the sun from an area. The heavier the foliage, the more the sun will be blocked by a combination of the size of the leaf and the number of leaves. Many very large-leaved trees do not provide the shade of smaller-leaved trees. The number of branchlets and the number of leaves per branchlet, as well as the size of the leaves, determine how good a tree is for shade.

RATE OF GROWTH

Most homeowners mistakenly consider this the most important criterion. Advertisements feature trees which will grow extraordinarily fast to appeal to the poor homeowner who has a serious sun problem. As can be seen from the previous criteria, there are many reasons not to buy a tremendously fast-growing tree. However, there are trees which combine enough good qualities with a reasonable growth rate to be planted in the home landscape for quick results.

Another important growth factor is growth density. A tall skinny pine offers little help in blocking the sun, while a much smaller Sugar Maple will afford a great deal of shade. Very fast-growing trees usually have long internodes, which are the areas between the leaves. Slower-growing trees have shorter internodes and are thus more dense, blocking more of the sun.

The Weeping Willow adds an unusual form to the landscape.

SHAPE AND HEAD SIZE

This is somewhat the same idea as was described on the previous page when discussing density. Trees which have long arching branches will grow wider and provide more shade. An American Red Maple, for instance, is a much wider-growing tree than a Sugar Maple. It will block the sun off a larger area of the house than its cousin the Sugar Maple will because it reaches farther. The Sugar Maple, however, has a very tight and dense head and as a young tree may block the sun from a specific window before it attains much size.

The shape of the head of a tree is also very important in developing the artistic aspect of the landscape. Weeping Willows, which might be rejected for their numerous problems, are often used because of their unusual form. The landscape would be extremely boring if only thick oval-headed trees were used. One of our great new trees is the Bradford Pear, but it seems that every office park, every street association, every highway project is lining up these trees like soldiers. The overuse of these armies of Bradford Pears has made this beautiful tree a real bore, unfortunately.

COLOR IN THE SPRING, SUMMER, AND FALL

Trees need not be green all the time. We assume that a shade tree is going to be a cool-looking specimen in the landscape, but we should never overlook the interesting advantage that colorful trees afford.

Trees which bloom enough to be seen in the spring will add much interest to the landscape. An American Red Maple is bright red as it blooms

FALL COLORS

Red Maple

Sugar Maple

Sourwood

Pin Oak

Sweet Gum

FALL COLORS

Ginkgo

Bradford Pear

early in the spring before the foliage comes out. The cloud of white which covers a Bradford Pear and the bull's-eyes of white which lie on the mass of green covering the *Magnolia grandiflora* are assets which you should consider when choosing a tree.

We usually think of summer tree color as always green, but there are also choices here. The Purple Beeches, though not always happy in the South, give a pleasant reprieve from the inevitable green of most trees. Some of the newer red-leaf Norway Maples (really more purple than red) will grow in the northernmost part of our area, though they are not too satisfactory elsewhere in the South. The purple-leaf plums make attractive small trees for the landscape, and so do the red-leaf Japanese Maples.

Let's drive to the mountains and see the fall color! The reds, the flames, the yellows, the golds adorning the hardwood trees of Appalachia are like looking at an artist's palette. No city area or suburban subdivision will ever match this wonder of nature, but we should try to improve our landscapes by growing things which change with the season. The careful choice of shade trees which do change color well adds a lot to any property.

RATE AND TIME OF FOLIAGE DROP

In my mind, leaf-raking is about as unhappy a chore as comes around each year. I want trees to shed and get it over with—none of this waiting around until spring for the last one to come tumbling down. Leaf pick-up can be tolerated for a few weeks in November, but it is ridiculous in March. The best tree of all in this regard is the Ginkgo. This lovely creature is pure gold one day and bare the next. Zip, zip with a rake, off to the compost pile, and no worries for twelve months. That is a near-perfect friend.

I have never understood why nurserymen grow and sell Chinese Elms. This poor tree has every problem a tree could have. It is fast-growing, weak-wooded, shallow-rooted, low-density, and attracts a myriad of insects. A worm laces the leaves in the late spring. After regrowing its foliage, the poor tree is attacked by a mildew in the late summer which causes premature drop. When the hot days of August are crying for shade, this poor tree is almost bare. We should avoid trees like this! The idea is to have shade all summer, not just part of it.

On the other hand, a Water Oak can drive you bananas with its incessant leaf drop all fall and even into the winter.

Ginkgo leaves all drop within a short period of time.

AVAILABILITY IN THE SIZE WANTED

It is discouraging to decide upon a tree for a particular location and then be unable to find one. Many very fine trees for the Southern garden are not widely grown by nurserymen. They are sometimes grown only by specialty nurserymen in small quantities and sizes. Many of the more unusual trees may be obtained only from mail-order houses where the sizes are restricted by postal and UPS limits.

Your choice of a tree, therefore, may have to be a compromise if a large-sized tree is needed. But don't give up on whatever unusual or unique trees fascinate you. Go ahead and get them in whatever size is available and plant them for the future. Many uncommon trees will add tremendously to the future landscape. Though they cannot be purchased in a large size, they should not be forgotten.

The ideal size to purchase, in my opinion, is a 2- to 2 1/2-inch caliper tree (diameter of the trunk, measured 3 feet above the ground). These can be handled with some help, are available in the better nurseries, and will begin growth quickly without much setback.

But don't reject the smaller trees outright, because many will be quite satisfactory in just a few years.

COST

Widespread availability and relatively low cost are a result of nurserymen growing large quantities of a given type of tree. Otherwise, cost is directly proportional (in almost all cases) to the age and size of the tree to be purchased. Faster-growing trees are less expensive since they are not in the nursery as long as slower-growing types of the same size.

A tree is a capital investment and should be considered in a different light from buying a shrub. Since only one or two trees may be all you need, give great care to your choice of the type and the size, with cost a secondary consideration.

FLOWERS AND FRAGRANCE

Fall color is an added benefit which may sway your choice to a particular tree; likewise, flowers and fragrance may influence your decision. The European Linden is a fine tree which you might not choose without knowing

Flower of Fraser Magnolia

The flower of a Tulip Poplar

Bradford Pear in flower

The European Linden spring blossoms are extremely fragrant.

of its particularly sweet-smelling blossoms which perfume the late spring air. The Bradford Pear might not be your choice until you see its magnificent blossoms in the spring.

PLACING A SHADE TREE PROPERLY

Here sits a nice new home on a lot with three skinny pines carefully saved, so it is advertised, by the builder. The couple really feels that this is their dream home. Everything about the house is ideal: many closets, a wonderful playroom, a family room with a huge fireplace, a great modern kitchen with the newest microwave oven, a bedroom with a bath for each child, and central air-conditioning. The huge glass window across the side of the family room gives a light, open feeling to the house.

It is March when the closing occurs and the family moves in. In April all is well. On the first 85-degree day in mid-May, the wonderful family room is an oven. The air-conditioning system is running full blast but doing very little good. The east side of the house is cold; the family room on the west side is hot. The dream is turning into a nightmare. A trip to a nursery to look at trees isn't really reassuring. "They are so small!"

I've worked through this scenario many times, not only as a nurseryman, but also as a home owner. I told you about my own sun problem. The answer is a good shade tree. It can restore the dream for you just as it restored mine for me. But don't expect results overnight.

When purchased, shade trees do look small. It is very hard *not* to place them in the wrong spot. Follow the rules and don't let a tree's present size cause you to place it too close to the house or in a spot which ruins the landscape.

Consider the several ways in which trees can help:
• Blocking the sun.
• Shading the area.
• Cooling through evaporation.

This Red Cedar had grown into the power lines and required topping, which has ruined its shape.

Give a tree the correct amount of space when you plant it or there will be trouble when it matures.

Now consider the future.

- How large will this tree be in 10 years?
- How large will it be in 20 years?
- Where are the limbs going to be by then?
- Where will the roots be by then?
- Can the top growth interfere with utility lines by then?

Now consider your problem. Observe at the time of day when the sun is causing the most problem. See for what period of time direct sun comes through the windows. Is it an hour? Is it more?

If the situation is bad for only a short time, a tree may be planted in a certain spot away from the house to block the sun. In this case, a round-headed densely-growing tree, like a Bradford Pear, may be suitable. If shade for many hours is needed, then a wide-headed tree like a Red Maple may be desirable.

CRITERIA FOR PLACING A TREE

Do not plant too close to the house, no matter how great the temptation might be. Consider what the tree will be in just a few years. Also consider your landscape design. A tree in the middle of the line of the house may look terrible. Consult with a landscaper. If the design calls for a tree which seems too far away to be useful, choose a tree with a very wide head and long arching branches. You will want to consider your present and proposed planting areas. Remember, tree roots may ruin a prospective lawn or garden spot. The presence of walks, driveways, walls, or other structures are features that deserve attention. Avoid planting too close to them. Finally, plant trees so that the branches do not come over the roof of the house, if possible. Limbs may damage roofs.

CHOOSING THE RIGHT TYPE OF TREE

There is a tree to fit almost every kind of situation. There are trees with long arching branches, tight oval heads, tall pyramidal shapes, broad evergreen forms, and even long, weeping branches. Fortunately for us in the South, the choice of trees we can grow is very wide.

Our forests are filled with gorgeous trees. We see huge beeches, massive oaks, hickories, elms, and many others. Not all, however, are suited to the landscape, unless they are there already. Many transplant poorly or have other characteristics which keep them from being favorable trees to purchase and plant.

Everyone has his favorites, and the following list contains mine. After you have chosen several that seem to fit your criteria and your landscape design, be sure to read the detailed descriptions which follow. You should be well introduced to the tree which you will plant. This is going to be a long-time association and you want to be certain that you will be friends for life.

THE BEST SHADE TREES FOR THE SOUTH

COMMON NAME	CULTIVAR NAME	BOTANICAL NAME
ASH, AMERICAN	'Autumn Purple'	Fraxinus americana
ASH, GREEN	'Marshall Seedless'	Fraxinus Pennsylvanica lanceolata
BALD CYPRESS		Taxodium distichum
BEECH, EUROPEAN		Fagus sylvatica
BEECH, PURPLE	'Purpurea'	Fagus sylvatica
BIRCH, EUROPEAN WHITE		Betula pendula
BIRCH, JAPANESE WHITE	'Whitespire'	Betula platyphylla japonica
BIRCH, RIVER		Betula nigra
BUCKEYE, RED		Aesculus pavia
CEDAR OF LEBANON		Cedrus libani
CEDAR, EASTERN RED		Juniperus virginiana
CEDAR, INDIAN		Cedrus Deodara
CHERRY LAUREL		Prunus Caroliniana
CHESTNUT, CHINESE		Castanea mollissima
DAWN REDWOOD		Metasequoia glyptostroboides
GINKGO		Ginkgo biloba
HACKBERRY		Celtis laevigata
HEMLOCK, CANADIAN		Tsuga canadensis
HOLLY, AMERICAN		Ilex opaca
HONEY LOCUST	'Green Glory'	Gleditsia triacanthos
HORSE CHESTNUT	'Briotii'	Aesculus carnea
LINDEN, EUROPEAN	'Greenspire'	Tilia cordata
LOBLOLLY BAY		Gordonia lasianthus
MAGNOLIA, BIGLEAF		Magnolia macrophylla
MAGNOLIA, CUCUMBER		Magnolia acuminata
MAGNOLIA, FRASER'S		Magnolia fraseri
MAGNOLIA, SOUTHERN		Magnolia grandiflora
MAGNOLIA, SWEET BAY		Magnolia virginiana
MAGNOLIA, UMBRELLA		Magnolia tripetala
MAPLE, RED		Acer rubrum
MAPLE, BLOODLEAF JAPANESE	'Bloodgood'	Acer palmatum
MAPLE, JAPANESE		Acer palmatum
MAPLE, LACELEAF JAPANESE	'Dissectum'	Acer palmatum
MAPLE, RED	'October Glory'	Acer rubrum
MAPLE, RED	'Red Sunset'	Acer rubrum
MAPLE, SUGAR	'Green Mountain'	Acer saccharum

COMMON NAME	CULTIVAR NAME	BOTANICAL NAME
MAPLE, SUGAR		Acer saccharum
OAK, CHESTNUT		Quercus prinus
OAK, PIN		Quercus palustris
OAK, SAWTOOTH		Quercus acutissima
OAK, WATER		Quercus nigra
OAK, WILLOW		Quercus phellos
PEAR, BRADFORD	'Bradford'	Pyrus Calleryana
PECAN		Carya illinoinensis
PINE, EASTERN WHITE		Pinus Strobus
PINE, JAPANESE BLACK		Pinus Thunbergiana
PINE LOBLOLLY		Pinus Taeda
PINE SLASH		Pinus Elliotti
PINE, VIRGINIA		Pinus virginiana
PLUM, PURPLE LEAF	'Newportii'	Prunus cerasifera
POPLAR, YELLOW		Liriodendron tulipifera
SOURWOOD		Oxydendron arboreum
SPRUCE, NORWAY		Picea abies
SWEET GUM		Liquidamber styraciflua
WALNUT, BLACK		Juglans nigra
WILLOW, WEEPING		Salix babylonica

Chris Hastings and his Magnolia tree

European Linden

SELECTING TREES FOR MATURE HEIGHT

We have discussed the criteria; now it is time to see which tree will be the very best for your location. The first consideration is whether the tree will fit your space. The following charts show the trees which I recommend for the South, grouped according to their mature height.

Deciduous Trees

SMALL-GROWING SHADE TREES
Less Than 40 Feet

COMMON NAME	CULTIVAR NAME	HEIGHT
MAPLE, LACELEAF JAPANESE	'Dissectum'	12
BUCKEYE, RED		15
MAPLE, BLOODLEAF JAPANESE	'Bloodgood'	15
CHERRY LAUREL		25
MAPLE, JAPANESE		25
PLUM, PURPLE LEAF	'Newport'	25
WILLOW, WEEPING		30

MEDIUM-GROWING SHADE TREES
40 to 60 Feet

COMMON NAME	CULTIVAR NAME	HEIGHT
HORSE CHESTNUT		40
MAGNOLIA, FRASER'S		40
MAGNOLIA, UMBRELLA		40
PEAR, BRADFORD	'Bradford'	40
HOLLY, AMERICAN		50
MAGNOLIA, BIGLEAF		50
OAK, SAWTOOTH		50
PINE, VIRGINIA		50
ASH, GREEN	'Marshall Seedless'	60
BIRCH, EUROPEAN WHITE		60
BIRCH, JAPANESE WHITE	'Whitespire'	60
CHESTNUT, CHINESE		60
HONEY LOCUST	'Green Glory'	60
MAGNOLIA, SWEET BAY		60

LARGE-GROWING SHADE TREES
65 to 100 Feet

COMMON NAME	CULTIVAR NAME	HEIGHT
OAK, WILLOW		70
CEDAR, EASTERN RED		75
SOURWOOD		75
ASH, AMERICAN	'Autumn Purple'	80
BEECH, PURPLE		80
LOBLOLLY BAY		80
OAK, PIN		80
OAK, WATER		80
HEMLOCK		80
BEECH, EUROPEAN		90
BIRCH, RIVER		100
DAWN REDWOOD		100
LINDEN, EUROPEAN	'Greenspire'	100
MAGNOLIA, CUCUMBER		100
MAGNOLIA, SOUTHERN		100
MAPLE, RED	'October Glory'	100
MAPLE, RED	'Red Sunset'	100
OAK, CHESTNUT		100
PINE, LOBLOLLY		100
PINE, SLASH		100

VERY LARGE-GROWING SHADE TREES
Over 100 Feet

COMMON NAME	CULTIVAR NAME	HEIGHT
HACKBERRY		100
CEDAR OF LEBANON		120
GINKGO		120
MAPLE, RED		120
MAPLE, SUGAR	'Green Mountain'	120
PINE, EASTERN WHITE		120
SWEETGUM		120
MAPLE, SUGAR		130
PINE, JAPANESE BLACK		130
BALD CYPRESS		150
CEDAR, INDIAN		150
PECAN		150
POPLAR, YELLOW		150
SPRUCE, NORWAY		150
WALNUT, BLACK		150

Evergreen Trees

I discussed the value of trees as energy savers. We have seen how deciduous trees serve the cause of energy conservation by blocking the sun when it is hot and letting it through when it is cold. However, there may be a situation where the winter sun is not wanted and an evergreen tree is desirable. The following list shows our best evergreen trees with their mature height.

COMMON NAME	HEIGHT	COMMON NAME	HEIGHT
CHERRY LAUREL	25	PINE, LOBLOLLY	100
HOLLY, AMERICAN	50	PINE, SLASH	100
PINE, VIRGINIA	50	CEDAR OF LEBANON	120
*MAGNOLIA, SWEET BAY	60	PINE, EASTERN WHITE	120
CEDAR, EASTERN RED	75	PINE, JAPANESE BLACK	130
LOBLOLLY BAY	80	CEDAR, INDIAN	150
HEMLOCK	100	SPRUCE, NORWAY	150
MAGNOLIA, SOUTHERN	100		

*Semi-evergreen

SELECTING TREES FOR GROWTH RATE

The new home is ideal in every way except that the sun is burning through the windows. At this time, the Tree of Heaven may seem to be the answer. Fifteen feet of growth a year! It sounds perfect. But is it? Growth rate is an important consideration, but not the most important. The following lists show the relative growth rates for my recommended trees. These trees are all excellent, and if they fit the other criteria, they may be chosen with confidence.

FASTER-GROWING SHADE TREES

COMMON NAME	CULTIVAR NAME	GROWTH RATE
ASH, AMERICAN	'Autumn Purple'	Fast
ASH, GREEN	'Marshall Seedless'	Fast
DAWN REDWOOD		Very fast
HONEY LOCUST	'Green Glory'	Fast
MAGNOLIA, CUCUMBER		Fast
MAPLE, RED		Medium fast
MAPLE, RED	'October Glory'	Medium fast
MAPLE, RED	'Red Sunset'	Medium fast
PEAR, BRADFORD	'Bradford'	Fast
PINE, LOBLOLLY		Fast
PINE, SLASH		Fast
WILLOW, WEEPING		Fast

TREES WITH MEDIUM GROWTH RATE

COMMON NAME	CULTIVAR NAME
BIRCH, RIVER	
BUCKEYE, RED	
CEDAR, INDIAN	
GINKGO	
HACKBERRY	
LOBLOLLY BAY	
MAGNOLIA, BIGLEAF	
MAGNOLIA, FRASER'S	
MAGNOLIA, SWEET BAY	
MAGNOLIA, UMBRELLA	
MAPLE, SUGAR	'Green Mountain'
MAPLE, SUGAR	

COMMON NAME	CULTIVAR NAME
OAK, PIN	
OAK, WATER	
OAK, WILLOW	
PECAN	
PINE, EASTERN WHITE	
PINE, VIRGINIA	
PLUM, PURPLE LEAF	'Newport'
POPLAR, YELLOW	
SWEET GUM	

SLOWER-GROWING SHADE TREES

COMMON NAME	CULTIVAR NAME
BALD CYPRESS	
BEECH, EUROPEAN	
BEECH, PURPLE	
BIRCH, EUROPEAN WHITE	
BIRCH, JAPANESE WHITE	'Whitespire'
CEDAR OF LEBANON	
CEDAR, EASTERN RED	
CHERRY LAUREL	
CHESTNUT, CHINESE	
HEMLOCK, CANADIAN	
HOLLY, AMERICAN	
HORSE CHESTNUT	
LINDEN, EUROPEAN	'Greenspire'
MAGNOLIA, SOUTHERN	
MAPLE, BLOODLEAF JAPANESE	'Bloodgood'
MAPLE, JAPANESE	
MAPLE, LACELEAF JAPANESE	'Dissectum'
OAK, CHESTNUT	
OAK, SAWTOOTH	
PINE, JAPANESE BLACK	
SOURWOOD	
SPRUCE, NORWAY	
WALNUT, BLACK	

American Holly

Fall color of a Red Maple

SELECTING TREES FOR FOLIAGE COLOR

Trees with beautiful fall color are greatly prized. Though this may not be the most important consideration in choosing a shade tree, it is an advantage you should not overlook. A few trees which have a distinctive color all season, and thus can be very desirable in the landscape, are marked in the list with asterisk or double asterisk.

COMMON NAME	CULTIVAR NAME	FALL COLOR
ASH, AMERICAN	'Autumn Purple'	Yellow
ASH, GREEN	'Marshall Seedless'	Yellow
BEECH, EUROPEAN		Gold
*BEECH, PURPLE		Purple/Bronze
BIRCH, EUROPEAN WHITE		Yellow
BIRCH, JAPANESE WHITE	'Whitespire'	Yellow
BIRCH, RIVER		Yellow
CHESTNUT, CHINESE		Bronze
GINKGO		Bright yellow
MAPLE, RED		Red
**MAPLE, BLOODLEAF JAPANESE	'Bloodgood'	Red
MAPLE, JAPANESE		Red
**MAPLE, LACELEAF JAPANESE	'Dissectum'	Red
MAPLE, RED	'October Glory'	Red
MAPLE, RED	'Red Sunset'	Red
MAPLE, SUGAR	'Green Mountain'	Red
MAPLE, SUGAR		Flame
OAK, PIN		Scarlet
PEAR, BRADFORD	'Bradford'	Maroon
PECAN		Yellow/Tan
**PLUM, PURPLE LEAF	'Newport'	Red
POPLAR, YELLOW		Yellow
SOURWOOD		Brilliant Scarlet
SWEETGUM		Red

*Remains purple throughout the season
**Remains red throughout the season

Southern Magnolia blossom

SELECTING TREES WITH SPECIAL FEATURES

We think of fall color or fast growth as outstanding characteristics which may make a certain tree good for a particular location. Some additional noteworthy characteristics to consider when making your choice are listed below.

COMMON NAME	CULTIVAR NAME	UNUSUAL CHARACTERISTIC
ASH, AMERICAN	'Autumn Purple'	Deep purple fall color
BALD CYPRESS		Grows in wet places
BEECH, PURPLE		Purple foliage
BIRCH, EUROPEAN WHITE		White bark
BIRCH, JAPANESE WHITE	'Whitespire'	White bark
BIRCH, RIVER		Tan, flaking bark
BUCKEYE, RED		Red flowers in spring
CHESTNUT, CHINESE		Delicious nuts
DAWN REDWOOD		Red bark
GINKGO		Quick leaf fall
HACKBERRY		Berries attract birds
HOLLY, AMERICAN		Red berries
HORSE CHESTNUT		Nuts
LINDEN, EUROPEAN	Greenspire'	Fragrant flowers
LOBLOLLY BAY		Attractive flowers
MAGNOLIA, BIGLEAF		Very large leaves
MAGNOLIA, CUCUMBER		Attractive flowers
MAGNOLIA, FRASER'S		Attractive flowers
MAGNOLIA, SOUTHERN		Attractive flowers
MAGNOLIA, SWEET BAY		Attractive flowers
MAPLE, RED		Red flowers in spring
MAPLE, BLOODLEAF JAPANESE	'Bloodgood'	Red foliage
MAPLE, LACELEAF JAPANESE	'Dissectum'	Very lacy red leaves
PEAR, BRADFORD	'Bradford'	White flowers in spring
PECAN		Excellent nuts
PINE, JAPANESE BLACK		Grows near seashore
PINE, VIRGINIA		Gnarled growth habit
PLUM, PURPLE LEAF	'Newportii'	Dark red foliage
SOURWOOD		Summer flowers
WILLOW, WEEPING		Graceful habit

ALL ABOUT
THE SOUTH'S BEST SHADE TREES

The preceding lists have given you some insight into the characteristics of different types of shade trees. To choose the right tree for a particular spot, you have seen that it takes more than just being able to recognize a maple or oak or pine. There are often many different species and cultivars of each genus which might be considered. Some maples may be dwarf; others may be tremendous. Study the descriptions before purchasing a tree. You want to know everything possible about this new addition to your landscape. Ten years from now you will not want someone to tell you that the only solution to a problem which your tree has is to prune it with an axe—at the ground!

There is really no way to list trees and avoid all confusion. Common names vary from area to area, and most people are not familiar with botanical names. I am listing them alphabetically by the name commonly used in the South, like ASH, with the botanical name as a sub-title, like *Fraxinus americana*. The cultivar name, like cv. 'Autumn Purple,' is what you may think of as the "variety" name. In order to be accurate, I am using the term cultivar rather than variety since it is botanically correct. When you go to purchase your tree, take with you the common name, the botanical name, and the cultivar name.

Now here is an alphabetical list of the best shade trees for the South:

ASH
Fraxinus sp.

There are two particularly noteworthy members of the Ash family. Both are native to the South, and both do well here. The White Ash (*Fraxinus americana*) is rarely planted in the landscape because there are far better trees for the same situations. It is widely found in forests and its wood is prized for tool handles and baseball bats. Though it is fast growing, it seeds so freely that it may become a pest. But the cultivar, 'Autumn Purple,' is worthwhile for its beautiful deep purple fall color and because it does not produce seed.

The Green Ash is widely grown as a smaller, fast-growing shade tree for the landscape. The seedless cultivars are the only ones to plant since the specie seeds so freely that it can be a nuisance.

AUTUMN PURPLE WHITE ASH
Fraxinus americana cv. 'Autumn Purple'

Mature Height: 70 feet
Growth Rate: Medium fast
Unique Features: Purple fall color; seedless
Best Use: As a medium size, faster-growing tree with good shading potential.
Do not plant in restricted spaces; allow ample room to fully develop.

Fall Color: Consistent mahogany purple
Problems: It is a fibrous-rooted tree which allows for easier transplanting but makes it difficult to grow grass over the roots.

The 'Autumn Purple' cultivar of the White Ash is the only form of this tree which is worthwhile in the landscape. It is a faster-growing tree with a good round-topped head. Autumn Purple does not form seed and thus does not become a pest like the common White Ash.

MARSHALL SEEDLESS GREEN ASH
Fraxinus pennsylvanica lanceolata cv. 'Marshall Seedless'

Mature Height: 60 feet
Growth Rate: Fast
Unique Features: Dense and fast-growing
Best Use: An ideal lawn tree for quick, dense shade, especially in more restricted locations. It is also good over patios and decks since it holds its foliage well into the fall.
Fall Color: Attractive yellow
Problems: Insect and disease resistant, no major problems

The Green Ash is denser and more attractive than the White Ash and better for more restricted spots in the landscape. Its compact habit of growth, combined with its dense foliage, makes it an excellent smaller-growing tree for quick shade. I recommend this cultivar, 'Marshall Seedless,' above all the others. It has proved to be a reliable and sturdy tree for quick shade in the South. It is seedless, eliminating the problem of seedlings sprouting in every nook and cranny, and it is long-lived even though it grows fast.

BALD CYPRESS
Taxodium distichum

Mature Height: 150 feet
Growth Rate: Slow
Unique Features: Grows in wet places
Best Use: Although it is usually only planted as a novelty in home landscapes, it can be most useful in blocking the sun in the summer and letting it through in the winter. It is perfect for planting beside a stream; and since it is a narrow-headed tree with a pyramidal shape, it will grow well among other trees.
Fall Color: Deciduous needles that turn an interesting reddish-tan color
Problems: Despite its slow growth, it is attractive when small and should not be disregarded.

The Bald Cypress is one of the most elegant trees of the South. It is thought to be a swamp tree since it grows at the edge of any wet area, including bogs and streams. This is not always true. The Bald Cypress grows anywhere it can obtain significant moisture for its tremendous growth. Missing in its upland habitats are the extraordinary "knees" which seem to breathe life into the roots of the plant when it is growing in water.

Bald Cypress in its natural habitat

The interesting bark of the Bald Cypress

The unusual seed pods of a Bald Cypress

Two huge Bald Cypress growing between the sidewalk and the street in Atlanta

Purple Beech

There are two fantastic examples of the Bald Cypress growing out of a confined area between the sidewalk and street on McDonough Boulevard in Atlanta. I have personally observed these two huge plants since the early 1950's, and despite pollution, they continue to grow magnificently.

The Bald Cypress is a deciduous conifer or needle tree. Before the needles fall in the autumn, they turn a reddish-tan color. The bark is interesting and the immature cones are laced with interesting, almost geometric, designs.

❧ BEECH
Fagus sp.

There are two beeches which are possibilities for the landscape: the great American Beech, which is native to the South, and the European Beech, which is one of the few European shade trees thoroughly at home in America.

The American Beech (*Fagus grandifolia*) is widespread but is seldom found in nurseries due to the tap root which makes transplanting difficult. If you are lucky enough to have a native beech tree growing on your property, do everything possible to keep it happy. The gorgeous shape, firm gray bark, unusual nuts, and dense foliage make this an ideal heavy, large-growing shade tree.

Those of us who do not have a native beech tree can choose the European Beech. You will find these more frequently in nurseries, for they do not have the tap root problem which makes the native beech hard to transplant.

I will discuss two forms of the European Beech, the specie or regular green type, and the purple cultivar. There are many others which, if found in a nursery, should be considered. Among these are the Copper Beech, the Weeping Beech, and the Fern Leaf Beech.

In general the only significant problem with the beech tree is that it has very fibrous, surface-feeding roots, making it impossible to grow grass or other plants underneath. This problem is best overcome by allowing the lower limbs to sweep the ground, thus eliminating the need for anything growing underneath.

EUROPEAN BEECH
Fagus sylvatica

Mature Height: 80 feet
Growth Rate: Medium
Unique Features: Gray bark
Best Use: Ideal as a large free-standing specimen shade tree. Give it plenty of room to utilize the beauty of its form.
Fall Color: Yellow to bronze range
Problems: Do not expect to grow either grass or ground cover under a beech because the roots are just below the surface.

The European Beech is an ideal shade tree for the home landscape. The leaves are deep green and densely-formed. It is one of the best of the larger-growing shade trees with no insect or disease problems of significance.

PURPLE BEECH
Fagus sylvatica cv. 'Purpurea'

Mature Height: 50 feet
Growth Rate: Medium
Unique Features: Purple foliage all summer
Best Use: As a specimen lawn tree. Allow it to grow without restriction, with its limbs sweeping the ground.
Fall Color: Changes from a purple in the summer to a bronze before the leaves fall
Problems: The root system is surface-feeding and grass will not grow underneath. Do not plant in dry soil. The leaf color will not be satisfactory and the growth rate will be miniscule.

The Purple Beech is one of the few large-growing trees with unusual summer color which can be grown satisfactorily in the South. This cultivar grows more slowly than the green form but is worthwhile where a colorful-leaved tree will add to the landscape. Though listed as a medium-growing tree, this may not be accurate if the tree is grafted rather than grown from a selected seedling. The grafted trees will grow slower and will attain less size.

BIRCH
Betula sp.

To me, there is nothing as beautiful as a birch. I can remember on trips to Canada seeing the fantastic Paper Bark or Canoe Birch with the extraordinary exfoliating bark. In Europe and in the Pacific Northwest, the European Birch grows into enormous and spectacular trees which make you wonder why they are not in our landscapes.

Most white birch are not happy here because they need cooler climates and more misty summer rain. I have seen the Canoe Birch planted many times in our area, but growing poorly and never performing satisfactorily. Many years ago I planted a European Birch on the dam of our pond. Fifteen years later it is still growing, with its bark of a definite white cast and without (yet) an attack of the dreaded birch borer. In Tennessee these are grown quite frequently and seem to survive nicely. So the upper part of our region could well be suited to this beautiful tree.

Perhaps the best of the white birches for the South is the Japanese White Birch. These have been growing for many years without borer injury. The cultivar 'Whitespire' seems to be the best.

We do have a birch which does exceptionally well—the River Birch. These native trees grow wild along streams and other damp areas, even surviving spring floods. As age creeps upon them, the paper-thin bark begins to exfoliate and makes a rare and attractive sight. This is the birch for us, even though the bark is light tan, not the beautiful white which is so appealing.

The Canoe Birch in the forests of the Northern United States and Canada are almost always found in clumps. Nurserymen do plant three or more of the small European White Birch together to give this same clump effect. I do not think this is good, because it crowds the plants as they become mature, and if one of the single plants should die the clump becomes lop-sided. These plants are so beautiful as single-stemmed trees that I think this abnormal clumping is unnecessary.

Our native River Birch trees are seen in clumps in the wild, resulting from a number of stems coming from a single root system. However, most of the clumps purchased from nurseries are several individual plants grown together. Once again, this is a poor way to get a clump of birch trees and it should be avoided for the reasons given above.

EUROPEAN WHITE BIRCH
Betula pendula

Mature Height: 60 feet
Growth Rate: Slow
Unique Features: White bark
Best Use: As a spectacular lawn specimen tree. It is best when grown on the east side of the house in morning sun to avoid hot afternoons.
Fall Color: Bright yellow
Problems: Hot dry soil reduces vigor and keeps the plant growing poorly. Keep watered in dry weather or plant near a stream. Also, the Bronze Birch Borer is always a threat. Spraying is difficult because the borer attacks the top of the tree first, and by the time die-back is noticed, control measures are ineffective.

The European White Birch grows better in the South than the more spectacular Canoe Birch. However, it is still not as vigorous as the native River Birch nor as long-lasting as the Japanese White Birch. It should be planted only in the upper part of our region and always as single-stem plants. Though listed as growing to 60 feet at maturity, it rarely reaches that size in the South except, perhaps, in the mountains. In the rest of the South, one should feel lucky if the tree matures at 35–40 feet.

WHITESPIRE JAPANESE WHITE BIRCH
Betula platyphylla japonica cv. 'Whitespire'

Mature Height: 60 feet
Growth Rate: Slow
Unique Features: White bark; heat and borer-resistant
Best Use: As a specimen lawn tree planted in the open for best effect
Fall Color: Yellow
Problems: Its only faults are slow growth and bark that does not become spectacularly white until the plant is older.

The Japanese White Birch is a relatively recent introduction into the American landscape. It has excellent white bark and is much more tolerant to heat than any of the other white birches. 'Whitespire' is the best of the cultivars of the Japanese White Birch and the one which should be used. It seems to be completely resistant to the Bronze Birch Borer.

River Birch

The unusual bark of River Birch

European White Birch
in Tennessee

European White Birch
in Salem, Oregon

RIVER BIRCH
Betula nigra

Mature Height: 100 feet
Growth Rate: Medium
Unique Features: Exfoliating tan bark
Best Use: Grown for its unique appearance. Its pyramidal shape makes it quite useful as a small shade tree near a patio or outdoor living area.
Fall Color: Normally yellow, but not as colorful as white birches
Problems: No serious problems

Our native River Birch has been neglected because the bark is not white like the beautiful birches of farther north. This is a pity and proves that something common is often ignored. Yet, of all the birches, this tree familiarly sighted along rivers and streams is the easiest to grow. In the right place in the landscape, the River Birch will make an outstanding shade and ornamental tree. It is insect and disease-resistant. The light green foliage in the spring appearing against a background of evergreens is a most refreshing sight and a real harbinger of good things to come. The most unique feature is the reddish-tan paper-thin bark peeling in sheets from the trunks of even younger trees.

In its natural state, the tree does arise with multiple stems, but generally nurserymen plant several youngsters in the same spot to form the clump. Since this can lead to problems, it is best avoided. However, if you find a clump in the wild and have permission to move it, the results in the landscape are spectacular.

RED BUCKEYE
Aesculus Pavia

Mature Height: 15 feet
Growth Rate: Medium
Unique Features: Red flowers, large buckeyes
Best Use: Excellent in any restricted location, including large tubs, deep planters, or walled gardens. Keep pruned to a central trunk with limbs removed to a height of 6 to 8 feet.
Fall Color: Yellow in better years, but often has little fall color
Fruit: Typical buckeye
Problems: No major pest problems

The Red Buckeye is not normally considered a shade tree; it is more often classed as a woodland shrub. In its natural state, the Red Buckeye is usually found as a multi-stemmed plant with little tree-like appearance. But there are so few good small-growing shade trees available that I list the Red Buckeye with this qualification: If you keep it pruned to one central trunk, the Red Buckeye will make a marvelous small tree for tubs on decks or patios. It is also excellent for small walled gardens adjacent to many townhouses and condominiums where the only other practical choices are the Japanese Maples. The Red Buckeye grows faster than the Japanese Maples and offers the unusual advantage of its attractive flower in the spring.

I have seen some listings of this easy-to-propagate tree, implying that it is the red form of the great horse chestnut (*Aesculus carnea* cv. 'Briotii') or even the famous Ohio Buckeye (*Aesculus glabra*), both of which grow into much larger and heavier trees. Be forewarned that this plant is nothing like the larger horse chestnuts.

If unavailable, it is very easy to grow from the buckeyes which are readily found in the fall. Take these as soon as they fall, refrigerate in a loosely-capped jar for two months, plant in a 6-inch pot filled with a peat-light potting mixture, and cover the seed about an inch. Place the pot in a sunny window and keep the soil damp. You will soon have a nice Red Buckeye to transplant into a tub after the danger of frost has passed.

TRUE CEDARS
Cedrus sp.

There are three true cedars which may be grown in the South: the Cedar of Lebanon, the Atlas Cedar, and the Indian or Incense Cedar. The Cedar of Lebanon is the cedar from which Solomon's Temple was probably built, and so it has great nostalgic and historic appeal, and the added advantage of being the hardiest of the three. I see no reason to plant the Atlas Cedar since it is very much like the Cedar of Lebanon in appearance but not as hardy. The Indian or Incense Cedar will be discussed primarily for the lower part of our region. Of the three, it is by far the most attractive, being much less stiff in appearance.

CEDAR OF LEBANON
Cedrus libani

Mature Height: 100 feet
Growth Rate: Medium
Unique Features: Large, unusual cones; unique habit
Best Use: Use advisedly. It grows very large and should be allowed at least 40 feet to grow. It is not a tree for shade, but one for beauty.
Fall Color: Evergreen
Problems: This cedar is the least susceptible to the Cedar Bark Beetle since most attacks follow freeze damage and the Cedar of Lebanon is the hardiest.

This tree is mentioned many times in the Bible and is most certainly the tree from which the great Temple of Solomon was built. Thus, it has tremendous appeal as a rare and unique plant with a sense of history and religion. In fact, the first one I had ever noticed was planted in the churchyard of St. George's Episcopal Church in Griffin, Georgia. This magnificent small church of great age was a perfect setting for this stiff but picturesque tree.

Its beauty is in its unique character and not in any softness or gracefulness, for surely it has neither. Nor does it give much shade or block much sun. Rather it is one of those plants which you put in the landscape simply because you want it.

INDIAN CEDAR or INCENSE CEDAR
Cedrus Deodara

Mature Height: 120 feet or more
Growth Rate: Medium
Unique Features: Soft pendulous effect; unusual cones
Best Use: As a magnificent lawn tree. Give it room because its long, pendulous branches are its real beauty. It is dense enough to block the sun and provide plenty of shade.
Fall Color: Evergreen
Problems: Zero cold is disastrous. Cedar bark beetles are a problem when the tree is injured.

I grew up with Indian Cedars. We had several at our home place and I shall always cherish the beauty of this wonderful tree. It is a soft, bluish-green color and the needles are often in bunches, making them most attractive on the drooping branches. The cones are very large and unique. In fact, my mother used to send me to collect them for Christmas decorations.

These trees were widely grown in my early nursery days and were almost a staple of the landscape, being to the South what the firs and spruce were to the North. But the disastrous Thanksgiving freeze of 1950 took its toll. The very top portion of all of them was killed and they never recovered. This cold injury was followed by severe attacks of the cedar bark beetle which further devastated the already damaged trees.

The Indian Cedar was being planted once again when the freezes of 1983 and 1984 took their toll. Perhaps we should forget this tree, but I really hate to. It is certainly acceptable for the lower part of the region, which never gets zero cold. To me, it is worthwhile enough to keep trying to grow.

RED CEDAR
Juniperus virginiana

Mature Height: 75 feet
Growth Rate: Slow
Unique Features: Dense evergreen
Best Use: A good, widely-pyramidal, evergreen shade tree that may be used for blocking the sun, shading when older, and for screening.
Fall Color: Evergreen
Problems: Very slow growing. Also, it is the alternate host for the disastrous cedar-apple rust disease which can ruin many crabapples and fruiting apples. Though the disease does not bother the Red Cedar, the leaf spot stage on the other host can be a serious problem. If apples are close by, do not plant a Red Cedar. If crabapples are to be planted, check to see if the particular cultivar is susceptible; not all are.

Beside our bedroom at Sweet Apple is a huge, mature Red Cedar. In it Mother Nature always seems to be holding forth. Birds come to the feeder hanging on a branch, snakes climb in search of birds' nests, the Mockingbirds delight at perch-

Red Buckeye

Dawn Redwood

Red Cedar

99

ing on its very tiptop and singing their hearts out on moonlit nights. This magnificent tree has withstood heavy wind, ice, and almost everything that nature can throw at it.

Whoever plants a Red Cedar tree? Landscapers belittle its virtues, I suppose, because it grows everywhere and lacks any real "sophistication." Yet it is a tree which can be magnificent, as I think mine is.

Nowadays there are many cultivars of the Red Cedar which embellish the native form. Among the best are:

'Burkii,' which is lower-growing (30 feet) and more dense and narrowly-pyramidal. The summer foliage is silver-green, while the winter foliage has a definite purple tone.

'Keteleeri,' which is correctly a *Juniperus chinensis* cultivar but is listed by most nurserymen as a *J. virginiana* cultivar. It is smaller-growing and has a conical instead of a pyramidal form.

'Columnaris' has a very tight column form and is used for screens.

CHERRY LAUREL or CAROLINA CHERRY LAUREL
Prunus caroliniana

Mature Height: 25 feet

Growth Rate: Slow

Unique Features: The beauty of this plant used as a tree is the arching branches, which form a very wide evergreen head.

Best Use: An ideal, small evergreen that will shade or block sun. Use in restricted places or in half-barrels on patios and decks.

Fall Color: Evergreen

Flowers and Fruit: The blossoms of the Cherry Laurel are individually insignificant, but in mass they are quite attractive. The fruit is small, black, and berry-like.

Problems: As a member of the cherry genus this tree is susceptible to borers. Take care to seal wounds when they occur. It should not be used as a street tree because mechanical injury may be disastrous if left untended.

The Carolina Cherry Laurel has been grown primarily as a huge shrub or screen during the past forty or fifty years. It is certainly noteworthy when used this way and will be discussed under "Shrubs"; but the Carolina Cherry Laurel can also be used as a small evergreen tree. In many of the old gardens of the South you will find magnificent specimen trees of this native plant. At St. George's Church, Griffin, Georgia, I remember two very old ones beside the Rectory which were a good example of what this plant will do when allowed to grow into a tree.

Make the tree form by removing all but the strongest stem, and keep the sprouts rubbed off as they appear during the season. Let the top few branches form the head but keep removing the branches as the tree grows until the main stem reaches the height at which you wish the top to begin spreading. The plant will withstand severe pruning and the head may be shaped into practically any form desired.

Do not confuse this plant with the English Laurel, *Prunus laurocerasus*, which has a much larger, more leathery leaf and is a heavy shrub. Some (non-Southern) authors refer to the English Laurel as Cherry Laurel and it is so listed in *Hortus Third*. To us, there is but one Cherry Laurel, the Carolina Cherry Laurel.

❦ CHINESE CHESTNUT
Castanea mollissima

Mature Height: 60 feet
Growth Rate: Slow
Unique Features: Wide-spreading; good nuts
Best Use: Dual-purpose tree for nuts or for shade. Give it plenty of room, and keep the limbs removed to a height of 6 to 8 feet to restrict its spreading; allow it to branch within 3 feet of the ground if you wish a 40- or 50-foot tree.
Fall Color: Insignificant yellow-brown
Fruit: The nut is worthwhile, but will turn hard quickly.
Problems: No blight or insect problems. The trees are self-sterile; if you want nuts, plant three for good cross-pollination.

The massive American Chestnut was so magnificent to those who can remember them that any chestnut of lesser stature suffers by comparison. To those of us who have come along since the American Chestnut disappeared with the chestnut blight which started in the 1930's and spread throughout the United States, that beautiful tree is only imagined with the help of words and old photographs. Perhaps, one day, a really blight-resistant American Chestnut will be found. But the Chinese Chestnut can be grown upon its own merits and not just as a substitute for its incomparable cousin.

The Chinese Chestnut is a medium, wide-spreading shade tree which, if planted in groups of two or three, will produce many good nuts. Since it is practically self-sterile, a single tree will produce only a few (if any) chestnuts, something which is not all bad if you have ever spent a long evening pulling chestnut prickles out of a small boy's foot. It is listed as a slow-growing shade tree for it takes many years to reach its great size, but it is worthwhile even as a smaller tree, and so its slow growth should not deter you from using it.

❦ DAWN REDWOOD
Metasequoia glyptostroboides

Mature Height: 100 feet
Growth Rate: Very fast
Unique Features: Fast growth, beautiful wood
Best Use: Excellent for blocking the sun
Fall Color: Reddish-tan deciduous needles
Problems: Heavy shade makes it impossible to grow grass or any plant underneath. Allow the limbs to sweep the ground to eliminate the need for ground cover.

The Dawn Redwood is another of those trees, like the Ginkgo, which was first classified from fossil records before it was found growing in China. It is a more recent discovery than the Ginkgo, being described from fossil records in 1941 and discovered in its native habitat in China in 1948. It was introduced quickly into the United States and accepted immediately.

I planted one of these at our nursery in the late 1950's and marvelled at an excess of 5 feet of growth in the second year. Yet it has never been significantly damaged by ice or cold and continues to grow well. A Dawn Redwood planted a few years earlier in one of Atlanta's city parks is now pushing its ultimate height but with a spread of only about 25 feet. This makes it a very suitable shade tree for the home landscape. It quickly starts performing and yet does not cover everything in sight in its breadth.

It seems to be tolerant to a wide range of conditions. The one at the nursery was beside a small stream; the one in the park is on a dry rise.

GINKGO or MAIDENHAIR TREE
Ginkgo biloba

Mature Height: 120 feet
Growth Rate: Medium
Unique Features: Unique foliage, fall color
Best Use: As a specimen in an open area to realize its full potential. It is a beautiful shade tree and can be grown in any moderately good soil if given plenty of room.
Fall Color: Bright yellow leaves make the tree glow.
Problems: Undesirable female fruit; use only one tree if the plants are grown from seed, or purchase asexually propagated males if more than one is to be planted in an area.

The Ginkgo is another ancient plant identified first from fossil records and subsequently found in the wild in China. Fossil formations indicate that at one time it was native in North America, but none has ever been found in the natural state. They were introduced in Colonial times and the tree has achieved remarkable adaptation.

This tree is ideal for cities, being immune to the pollutants which kill so many of our street trees. Perhaps the atmosphere was very polluted from volcanoes and other natural phenomena during the Jurassic Period a hundred million years ago, when the Ginkgo grew abundantly. Maybe we are not so doomed as we are led to believe.

The Ginkgo is a tree for our environment, having almost everything a good shade tree should have. The form is beautiful, limbs arching upward like a vase; the leaves are dense and heavy, giving excellent shade; the roots are deep so that grass will grow underneath; it has no insect or disease problems; the wood is not subject to breakage; and the fall color is perhaps the most beautiful of any of our trees. In addition, the leaves drop almost overnight, making removal much easier than with trees which drop their leaves over months of time.

Nothing, however, is perfect, and the Ginkgo does have one problem. There are male and female trees, and the fruit formed on the female tree has an obnoxious

The tight shape of a young Ginkgo

Fall color of a Ginkgo

The summer leaves of a Ginkgo

A very old Ginkgo in Atlanta

odor like rancid butter. It is best to plant only a male tree or to plant only one tree. If the female tree has no male close enough to pollinate it, there is no problem; if the tree is a male, there is no problem.

Most Ginkgos are grown from seed since the rooting of cuttings and grafting are more difficult and costly. Thus there is a theoretical 50-50 chance of having a male or female tree if they are grown from seed. If more than one is desired, plant only the more expensive asexually propagated male plants.

There are also new cultivars of the Ginkgo which are asexually propagated and have specific properties which might be of interest: 'Fastigiata,' with a pyramidal shape; 'Laciniata,' with deeply-divided leaves; 'Macrophylla,' with very large leaves; and 'Pendula,' with drooping branches.

MISSISSIPPI HACKBERRY or SUGARBERRY
Celtis laevigata

Mature Height: 100 feet
Growth Rate: Medium
Unique Features: Gray, slick bark; sweet berries
Best Use: Excellent for fast shade
Fall Color: Not significant
Fruit: Profuse, sweet berries that attract birds
Problems: This tree is prone to infestation by psyllids which cause no harm but form a visible home on the leaves which looks like strands hanging from the underside of the leaf.

The Mississippi Hackberry should be used more often than it is. The large, round head formed from huge spreading branches makes an excellent shade tree when there is room. The two main features are the slick, gray bark, not too unlike a beech, and the sugarberries which are most attractive to birds.

Some Northern authors scoff at this fine tree, classing it too closely with the common hackberry of the North, *Celtis occidentalis*, which is beset with problems. Our specie, *Celtis laevigata*, is listed as medium in growth rate, but it rapidly makes a serviceable tree for shading problem areas, even when young.

Every time I see a mature hackberry, I envy the boys who live nearby. It is a marvelous climbing tree with heavy branches set close enough together for an energetic young'un to scamper to great heights. This is perhaps not reason enough to plant the tree (unless you are a young'un), but it is worth noting.

The smooth gray bark is attractive and gives a visual effect lacking in most trees. Old hackberry trees are also used to carve names upon, possibly by the climbers as they grew older and found their first girl friend. An ancient hackberry will give the history of an area if the boys were kind enough to add the date along with their girl's name.

CANADIAN HEMLOCK
Tsuga canadensis

Mature Height: 80 feet
Growth Rate: Slow

Unique Features: Of all evergreens, this is the most graceful and the most beautiful.
Best Use: As an outstanding specimen tree for the lawn
Fall Color: Evergreen
Problems: Slow growth and serious scale attacks on old screening-hedge forms

The Canadian Hemlock is one of the most versatile plants we have. It may be pruned and used as a tall screening hedge, or it may be planted as a specimen tree. It is slow-growing, and its use as a tree is confined mainly to those who have infinite patience or to the more affluent who can afford to have a large one moved in with a tree mover.

No matter how you get your hemlock tree, this stately tree is worth either the wait or the price. The huge native hemlocks which hug the banks of my favorite trout fishing stream in the mountains are so magnificent that one can easily lose a lunker while gazing upward.

Hemlocks need well-drained soil which has plenty of moisture, or they will end up like the one I planted years ago to block an old trail leading onto my property. It still isn't much to behold and the height is nothing to brag about.

If you want your hemlock in tree form rather than as a screen, just be sure the one you purchase has one central trunk. You don't need to worry about pruning off the lower limbs to make a tree. The Hemlock will grow upward, naturally losing the lower limbs as it does.

The Canadian Hemlock is sometimes confused with the Carolina Hemlock in nurseries. The needles of the Canadian Hemlock lie flat on the branchlets, whereas the needles of the Carolina Hemlock lie more irregularly. I think the Canadian Hemlock has greater beauty and is the more desirable specie, so be careful to get the correct one.

AMERICAN HOLLY
Ilex opaca

Mature Height: 50 feet
Growth Rate: Slow
Unique Features: Evergreen with red berries
Best Use: As a specimen tree for foliage and berries; also good as a sun block or for shade on a porch
Fall Color: Evergreen
Fruit: Named female cultivars will produce large numbers of berries in the winter.
Problems: Infestation by leaf miners causes premature leaf drop; this can be controlled by Orthene spray. Working flower beds nearby can be hazardous because of the spiny holly leaf.

There is nothing quite like a beautifully-grown holly tree. The stiff pyramidal shape makes a unique specimen tree. Then there are the red berries which cover the trees during the winter.

One seldom thinks of a holly tree for shade but they will actually do an excellent job of blocking sun from a hot window or porch. Though listed as slow-growing, they are handsome when they reach 8 or 10 feet and only improve with time.

Canadian Hemlock

Green Glory Honey Locusts

Since hollies are male and female plants, it is wise to buy a named female cultivar which is known to set berries. I have never seen much need to have a male tree in a planting since hollies are bee-pollinated and our bees always seem to come up with some pollen from a "bo" plant in the woods.

There are many named cultivars from which you may choose a good berrying plant. One of the best is 'Croonenburg,' which always seems to set plenty of berries and has a more pyramidal than conical shape.

GREEN GLORY HONEY LOCUST
Gleditsia triacanthos cv. 'Green Glory'

Mature Height: 60 feet
Growth Rate: Fast
Unique Features: Fast growth, good shading
Best Use: As a fast-growing, medium-sized shade tree
Fall Color: Insignificant
Problems: Spider mites may cause premature leaf drop. Spray with Kelthane and apply Disyston with the late winter fertilizer application.

The best attribute of the honey locust is its rapid growth. This is one of our fastest-growing trees which still offers a denseness comparable to the more moderate trees commonly used for quick shade. And it is long-lived at the same time. They have been grown as street and shade trees for many years but always with a reservation about the free-seeding which made them somewhat of a nuisance and the long thorns which could be very painful if touched. These were poor trees, at best, for play areas or lawns where children were active.

There are, however, several cultivars which have neither seeds nor thorns and these are the ones for us to use. The best which I have observed is 'Green Glory' because it has a darker color and holds its leaflets longer in the fall. It is ideal as a patio tree or for shade over outdoor living areas. I have seen them planted in large half-barrels and placed on terraces with good results for a number of years.

I have seen some of the other thornless, seedless cultivars being stripped of their foliage by spider mites, but so far the 'Green Glory' has not been so adversely affected, at least in my experience.

HORSE CHESTNUT
Aesculus sp.

The horse chestnuts are in general poor trees for the home landscape. They are coarse and messy, and the common horse chestnut, *Aesculus hippocastanum,* is subject to a number of problems.

There is one horse chestnut which might be considered for a special spot. It is the Red Horse Chestnut, *Aesculus × carnea* cv. 'Briotii,' a cross between our native *Aesculus pavia* and *Aesculus hippocastanum.*

RED HORSE CHESTNUT
Aesculus × *carnea* cv. 'Briotii'

Mature Height: 40 feet
Growth Rate: Slow
Unique Features: Large red flowers
Best Use: As an unusual feature in the landscape, perhaps adjacent to a wooded area where other trees can soften its coarse appearance.
Fall Color: Little, if any
Problems: Beware of mowing over the nuts in the autumn.

The Red Horse Chestnut is worth planting only if you are interested in something unusual. The plant is coarse and the growth rate is slow. The huge blossoms stand up like candles in the spring and are a rare sight to behold.

It is on the small side for a horse chestnut, which makes it a little more advantageous for the normal home landscape. There is a very old one, planted in the 1920's in Piedmont Park in Atlanta, which has survived despite the typical abuse in a city park.

GREENSPIRE EUROPEAN LINDEN
Tilia cordata cv. 'Greenspire'

Mature Height: 80–100 feet
Growth Rate: Medium
Unique Features: Fragrant flowers in the spring
Best Use: An ideal lawn shade tree
Fall Color: Insignificant
Problems: No significant problems

The European or Little-leaf Linden is quite happy, here in the South, and is a tree well worth having. It offers as much shade as any tree I know, with its dense, pyramidal head.

I remember the day that Nelson Crist took me on a day-long tour of Atlanta's best trees. Our first stop was the upper drive in Piedmont Park under one of the huge European Lindens. Nelson had been involved in the planting of these trees many years before, and he stood like a proud father showing off his debutante daughter. He said, "This is the loveliest of all shade trees."

Some of these trees remain today, despite bureaucratic neglect, the ravages of a high-density public area, and city pollution. In the spring the fragrant flowers perfume the area, and during the summer the shade is welcomed by all who walk or run underneath.

One of the great boulevards of the world was Unter den Linden in Berlin. This tree-lined avenue was virtually destroyed during World War II, and in the post-war period it became a part of East Berlin. This is unfortunate in many ways since the Communist rule has not had the impetus to bring this famous street back the way others have been restored in the vastly more prosperous West Berlin. The boulevard lined with the elegant European Linden was one of the most beautiful in the world, but like so many things it has succumbed to an ideology which has outlived its usefulness.

Red Horse Chestnut

Red Horse Chestnut blossom

Loblolly Bay

European Linden

The best of all the European Linden cultivars is 'Greenspire.' It is an ideal shade tree for a home because, like few others, it begins to perform while it is still relatively small. Remember, even though it will take a long time to reach its eventual height of 80 or so feet, it should be planted a good 40 feet from the house. Even at that distance it will give good shade in just a few years. 'Greenspire' is dense, compact, and a near-perfect shade tree.

❧ LOBLOLLY BAY
Gordonia lasianthus

Mature Height: 80 feet
Growth Rate: Medium
Unique Features: White, cup-shaped flowers; evergreen
Best Use: A beautiful, evergreen shade tree for lawns or the edge of a woodland area.
Fall Color: Evergreen
Problems: It is a Zone 8 plant, which would indicate possible cold damage at zero; however, they survived the 1950, 1983, and 1984 freezes remarkably well.

The Loblolly Bay is one of the most underused and perhaps underrated trees of the South. If you drive through the coastal plains, you will see these fine evergreen trees growing in their native habitat. In the summer the 2 1/2- to 3-inch creamy-white flowers cover the tree for most of the summer.

Though it is a tree of the low forests, it is at home in any soil which is not too dry. In its native habitat, the Loblolly Bay may be looser than is desirable for a shade tree in the landscape, but when grown without competition from other trees, it forms a dense, pyramidal head which is excellent for shading and blocking of the sun. The leaves are 6 inches long and have a lustrous sheen and leathery texture.

It is seldom possible to find large Loblolly Bay plants in a nursery, so you will probably have to buy a smaller one and grow it into a tree. Many nursery plants are multi-stemmed and should be avoided. Choose a single-stem, straight-trunked plant and keep the branches pruned off, up to a height of 6 to 8 feet, where the head should begin. Allow smaller plants to reach that height before beginning the training into a nicely-shaped tree.

Loblolly Bay makes an ideal tub plant for patios, terraces, and decks, and also responds to espaliering, though eventually it will outgrow either of these uses.

❧ MAGNOLIA
Magnolia sp.

The South is blessed with many Magnolias of great beauty and usefulness as shade trees. In addition, there are many of the "flowering Magnolias" like the Star Magnolia, the Saucer Magnolia, and other Oriental types which do well and will be discussed in Chapter 5, Flowering Trees.

When we think of tree Magnolias, we almost always think of the great, ever-green Bull Bay or Southern Magnolia which is acclaimed as one of the most beautiful trees known to man. There are others which should not be overlooked. These deciduous tree Magnolias are usually very large-leaved and coarse, but because of their leaf size and unusual flowers, they should be considered for that special spot in the landscape where something different is needed.

THE BEST MAGNOLIAS

BIGLEAF MAGNOLIA
Magnolia macrophylla

Mature Height: 50 feet
Growth Rate: Slow
Unique Features: Large, showy flowers, and huge leaves
Best Use: As a medium-height, very large-headed specimen tree
Fall Color: Insignificant
Problems: Leaf removal is a real chore unless you can convince all the ladies of your area that these leaves are prize dried-arrangement material. If you spread the word, maybe they'll pick them up for you.

You will not find this tree in a normal nursery because few have heard of it. This tree has the largest leaves of any tree in the temperate zone, some reaching over 36 inches in length and 10 inches in width. The flowers may be as much as 12 inches across, but lack the perfect shape of the Southern Magnolia.

The most perfect specimen I have ever seen was on State Street in Atlanta in the tiny yard of a simple frame house. It stood there for many years, attracting the curious as well as professional horticulturists and foresters. After my return from overseas I went to find this magnificent plant and to my horror, the little frame house and the rare Magnolia were gone, victims of the bulldozer which had graded a huge area for some damnable building at Georgia Tech. There is nothing so all-consuming as "progress."

This is not a tree for everyone, but a most unusual tree for those who want to have something of real distinction.

SOUTHERN MAGNOLIA or BULL BAY
Magnolia grandiflora

Mature Height: 100 feet
Growth Rate: Slow
Unique Features: Near-perfect flowers that are velvet-white saucers with a tube in the center. They smell like lemonade tastes.
Best Use: As a specimen tree or as a shield against the outside world.
Fall Color: Finest evergreen
Problems: It is impossible to grow anything under a Southern Magnolia. It has a shallow, fibrous root system which takes everything from the soil underneath. Let the limbs sweep the ground and don't worry.

When the great designer of trees sat down to make the perfect tree, the result was the Southern Magnolia. It has outstanding foliage, gorgeous flowers, a beautiful habit of growth, and no particular problems. True, nothing is really perfect; for you can't grow anything underneath it, it is slow-growing, and it is a specimen plant, not a tree to sit under. But who cares? Here is the most beautiful tree in the world!

There are several rules about growing a Southern Magnolia. Give it plenty of room; crowded Magnolias are a travesty. Plant in the mid-spring after the hardest of freezes have passed. Winter planting often causes severe leaf burn and unsightliness. Get a professional to plant any tree over 6 feet unless it is container-grown. And *never* cut back the lower limbs, which should sweep the ground majestically. Be forewarned that if you prune off the lower limbs of a Southern Magnolia to make a high-headed tree, I will personally come back from the next life and haunt you.

The Southern Magnolia needs good, rich, well-drained soil really to thrive. They are heavy feeders and do best when the fertilizer contains a high percentage of organics and plenty of nitrogen. They also need ample moisture, and those in dry soil look awful. Do not worry if they do not bloom well when they are young. As a young plant, the more the growth, the less the bloom. When they become mature, they will bloom as they should.

There are several cultivars of note, but since propagation by cuttings is unsatisfactory and grafting is difficult, they are very expensive. Gathering seed from unusually fine isolated specimens is the next best thing. There may be quite some variation in trees for sale. Choose a plant with large, glossy leaves which are set closely up and down the branches. This indicates that the tree will be dense.

The most beautiful tree I believe I have ever seen was one found by Hubert Nicholson of Commercial Nursery, Decherd, Tennessee. This enormous, isolated tree had the most beautiful rounded leaves with an underside of brown and the most perfect of flowers. He named the tree 'Charles Dickens' for the owner, not the author.

SWEET BAY
Magnolia virginiana

Mature Height: 60 feet
Growth Rate: Medium
Unique Features: 3-inch, fragrant white flowers
Best Use: Ideal for blocking hot sun over a long time period since it is evergreen to 10° F.
Fall Color: Semi-evergreen to evergreen
Problems: No serious problems

I am convinced that if this fine tree went under any other name than Magnolia, it would be more widely used. Unfortunately, there is always the very sticky comparison with the Bull Bay or Southern Magnolia. So often back in my days in the nursery, I heard, "If I'm going to get a Magnolia, I want a *real* Magnolia." Thus, a very fine tree which is used in a very different way cannot escape being the poor cousin of the Southern Magnolia.

Try to think of the Sweet Bay in a different light. The gray bark, the green leaves with white undersides, the narrow top and almost evergreen foliage, are

Fraser Magnolia

The evergreen Southern Magnolia is a great contrast with deciduous trees in the winter.

Fraser Magnolia blossom

Southern Magnolia blossom

characteristics which make the tree worthwhile as a small shade tree for confined places. The Sweet Bay will thrive in a wide range of soils, from swampy wet to normal garden. Just give it a chance and you will like it.

OTHER MAGNOLIAS

FRASER MAGNOLIA
Magnolia Fraseri

Height: 40 feet

This Magnolia identified by William Bartram in Georgia in the late 1700's is primarily noted for the 18-inch-long leaves which have two "ears" at the bottom. It is a coarse tree like the Bigleaf Magnolia described above, and is worthwhile only as an interesting plant for woodlands or the edge of lakes, ponds, or streams. The head is a little more loose and open than the Bigleaf Magnolia and will give less shade if that is to be its purpose. The flowers are creamy-white, 10 inches across, and come in the late spring.

CUCUMBER MAGNOLIA
Magnolia acuminata

Height: 100 feet

The main reason to plant a Cucumber tree is because of its very fast growth and the fact that it is less coarse than the other deciduous Magnolias mentioned. The blooms are insignificant, not noteworthy enough to be considered when deciding about planting this tree. The habit is rather stiff and narrow for many years before the branches begin to arch outward, opening up the head. For the normal planting it should be considered in the narrow-head rather than the wide-head group, for only a few of us will live to see the wide-open tree.

MAPLE
Acer sp.

There is no genus of trees which offers as much as the maples (*Acer*). In this group you will find dwarf trees and monstrous trees and almost every size in between. The maples grow in a wide range of conditions and are perhaps the best group from which to choose the tree for your landscape.

Not all maples are suited to our climatic conditions, however. Many, like the Silver Maple (*Acer saccharinum*), will grow well but develop serious problems. Some like the Norway Maple (*Acer platanoides*) are not happy with our long growing season and our heat. There are maples like the Sycamore Maple (*Acer pseudoplatanus*) which should be planted but are seldom found in nurseries.

Two of our best large-growing shade trees are in the maple genus, Red Maple (*Acer rubrum*) and Sugar Maple (*Acer saccharum*); and one of our best small-growing shade trees, Japanese Maple (*Acer palmatum*).

These maples should be avoided: Box-Elder (*Acer Negundo*); Crimson King Maple (*Acer platanoides* cv. 'Crimson King'); Norway Maple (*Acer platanoides*); and Silver Maple (*Acer saccharinum*).

Japanese Maple, larger-growing green form

Burgundy Lace Japanese Maple

Bloodgood Japanese Maple

JAPANESE MAPLE
Acer palmatum

Mature Height: 25 feet
Growth Rate: Slow
Unique Features: Lacy leaves, sometimes red
Best Use: Ideal for restricted areas or for a specimen tree
Fall Color: Red
Problems: Be sure to keep watered and fertilized. Die-back of the leaflets in the spring is usually caused by a late frost which touched the emerging tips. New foliage will replace damaged leaves.

The Japanese Maples are fantastic small-growing trees, ideal for restricted areas as well as for specimen trees where something unusual is needed. The red forms, which are very small-growing, may be easily grown in half-barrels or large tubs to adorn terraces, patios, and decks. These are some of the best of all trees for this purpose.

The green form grows much larger and faster than the red-leaf cultivars. It is largely overlooked for the interest seems to be always in the red-leaf types. This is unfortunate, because the green-leaf Japanese Maple is a superb plant which has the definite advantage of faster and larger growth and will quickly perform in situations where the red-leaf forms would take forever.

The red-leaf forms color best in rich soil and plenty of sun. Fertilize all the Japanese Maples each year with a slow-release nitrogen tree fertilizer to increase the growth rate and to keep the leaves colored well.

The red-leaf Japanese Maples are difficult to graft or root from cuttings. Thus, most are grown from seed and even the best selections from known red-leaf cultivars will have considerable variation in coloration. These are much less expensive than grafted plants but the results may not be as worthwhile. The green form is easily grown from seed, and as a result is much more reasonably priced.

Red-leaf cultivars include the following:

Bloodgood Japanese Maple
Acer palmatum cv. 'Bloodgood'

Mature Height: 15 feet
Growth Rate: Slow
Unique Features: Red foliage
Best Use: As a specimen tree for color
Fall Color: Red
Problems: No real problems

This is the best of the red-leaf cultivars for normal Japanese Maple leaf formation.

Laceleaf Japanese Maple
Acer palmatum cv. 'Dissectum'

Mature Height: 12 feet
Growth Rate: Very slow

Unique Features: Red, lacy-leafed foliage
Best Use: As a specimen tree for color
Fall Color: Red
Problems: No real problems

This is a very lacy-leafed cultivar which takes many, many years to reach its mature height. Another cultivar, 'Burgundy Lace,' is even slower in growth and seldom grows as tall as ten feet.

RED MAPLE
Acer rubrum

Mature Height: 100 feet
Growth Rate: Medium fast
Unique Features: Strong wood, deep roots, scarlet flowers in spring, and fall color
Best Use: Excellent as a large, shade tree
Fall Color: Wide variation from bright red, orange-red to yellow
Problems: No serious problems. However, there is an unusual and beautiful leaf spot in the spring which may cause concern, but does not damage the tree.

The best recommendation that I can give for the Red Maple is that when I moved into my house and found a severe sun problem, I planted two of them. They have done better than I hoped or expected. The largest one planted was a 2- to 2 1/2-inch caliper balled and burlapped tree, and the smaller one was a 1- to 1 1/2-inch caliper balled and burlapped tree. The second tree was backed over by the furnace installer's truck. It was badly skinned and knocked loose in the ground. I almost replaced it, but finally decided to pull it straight and let it grow. Here is what they have done in 16 years:

	TREE NO. 1	TREE NO. 2
Caliper When Planted	2–2 1/2 inch	1–1 1/2 inch
Height When Planted	10–12 feet	8–10 feet
Spread When Planted	3 1/2 feet	3 1/2 feet
Caliper 16 years later	16 inches	14 inches
Height 16 years later	50 feet	40 feet
Spread 16 years later	35 feet	30 feet

The Red Maple is one of the very best trees for the South. It is native, has practically no problems, is relatively fast-growing, has strong wood, and has moderately deep roots so growing grass underneath is not impossible until the tree nears maturity; it blossoms in the very early spring; and the leaves have good color in the fall. What more can you ask for?

It amazes me that a tree with all of these attributes is so often rejected for the Silver Maple, which may grow faster but is weak-wooded and shallow-rooted, is attacked by a mealybug-type insect which drips horribly on everything under-neath, and has little fall color and unspectacular blossoms. Why? Just because it is faster-growing. In my opinion the Silver Maple has no redeeming feature and should be avoided at all costs. If the builder plants one on your new property, refuse to close until he replaces it with a Red Maple or some other tree of your choice. If there is a Silver Maple on your landscape design, get a new designer. Sound harsh? I have seen dismay on the faces of so many people when the first of the Maple Phenacoccus strands begin to drip all over the grass (if any grass can grow underneath), attracting yellow jackets and ants to the area. "What can we do?" they ask. Then such disappointment when I say, "Prune it at the ground with a chain saw." This carefully-nurtured tree which finally is providing shade is either going to have to be commercially sprayed each year, at great cost, or cut down. "Why didn't you plant a Red Maple?" I always ask. The answer is the expected one: "The man said this would grow faster."

I hope that you are convinced, now, of two things: (1) Rate of growth is not the all-important consideration in choosing a shade tree, and (2) The Silver Maple is not worth the effort.

The Red Maple is a most valuable tree and *is* worth the effort. It will provide shade very quickly in its young life because of its branch and leaf density. This tree, unlike the Sugar Maple which will be discussed next, does not have a central leader all the way to the top but sets large arching branches from the main trunk. These give the tree a very wide head which will shade a large area.

Don't plant the Red Maple too close to a house or some of these arching branches will have to be removed to prevent damage to the roof. Just plant it a little farther away from the house and all will be well.

Red Maples are generally propagated from seed collected from the woods. This gives a tremendous variation in leaf size, form, and fall color. Though not a serious problem, it is nevertheless somewhat disappointing when your tree is not as large-leafed or doesn't have the fall color some of them are capable of having.

There are some cultivars of the Red Maple which are regularly bud-grafted by nurserymen and should be considered very strongly when you purchase your tree:

October Glory Red Maple
Acer rubrum cv. 'October Glory'

Mature Height: 80 feet
Growth Rate: Medium fast
Unique Features: Leaves are lustrous green and are held longer than most.
Fall Color: Crimson

Red Sunset
Acer rubrum cv. 'Red Sunset'

Mature Height: 80 feet
Growth Rate: Medium fast
Unique Features: Heavily textured summer foliage
Fall Color: Brilliant reds to yellows

Left to right, the author's two Red Maples and one
Sugar Maple were all planted at the same time.

Red Maples have a spreading shape.

A very large, old Sugar Maple

Fall color of Sugar Maple

Large Pin Oak

Chestnut Oak

SUGAR MAPLE
Acer saccharum

Mature Height: 130 feet
Growth Rate: Medium slow
Unique Features: Excellent head, strong wood, fall color
Best Use: Ideal shade tree for the middle and upper parts of the region
Fall Color: A range from yellow to orange to flame
Problems: There is a maple wilt which is not widespread. A good fertilizing program and plenty of water will keep this tree healthy if attacked by the fungus.

I have said that the Southern Magnolia is a perfect tree. Every New Englander is probably up in arms and a few may have already discarded this book as useless tripe. I should have been more protective of my reputation and put an asterisk by that statement, referring forward to the following:

Of all the *deciduous* trees, the Sugar Maple is the best! It is strong and tough. It has a beautiful rounded head made by branches growing off a central leader. Its foliage is rich green, fairly large, and densely set, making the shading factor excellent. There is no more beautiful fall color, with the possible exception of the bright yellow of the Ginkgo. The orange-to-flame fall color is the "show" for which New England and the Southern Highlands are famous.

The Sugar Maple is not a fast-growing tree, but it begins to be beautiful and provide shade while still a young tree. The beautiful oval head of a young Sugar Maple will block the sun and offer shade as quickly as almost any tree.

Beside the two Red Maples which I planted to make our living room bearable in the summer, I planted a Sugar Maple at the same time. I placed the Sugar Maple in a spot where the wider-headed Red Maple would have blocked our view. Here are the comparisons between the Sugar Maple and the larger Red Maple which I planted:

	TREE NO. 1 Red Maple	TREE NO. 3 Sugar Maple
Caliper When Planted	2–2 ¹/₂ inch	2–2 ¹/₂ inch
Height When Planted	10–12 feet	10–12 feet
Spread When Planted	3 ¹/₂ feet	2 feet
Caliper 16 years later	16 inches	12 inches
Height 16 years later	50 feet	30 feet
Spread 16 years later	35 feet	21 feet

The photograph on page 119 shows how effective these trees have been in such a short period of time.

Green Mountain Sugar Maple
Acer saccharum cv. 'Green Mountain'

Mature Height: 75 feet
Growth Rate: Medium slow

Unique Features: Can stand summer heat; foliage is large, dark green and densely-set
Best Use: Excellent oval-headed shade tree
Fall Color: Orange to scarlet
Problems: No major problems

OAK
Quercus sp.

There is no other tree with the massive beauty and strength of an oak. The word has come to mean strength and sturdiness. In the South, our vision of a massive shade tree is almost always of the oak since so many of our rural and city houses have been built under or around one or more of these stately trees.

Look at oaks as landscape plants in two different ways: (1) oaks already on the property, and (2) oaks to be purchased and planted.

Oaks which are already on a property should be cherished and guarded, no matter what the specie. The oaks in an established landscape should need no special care unless you observe some problem developing. Oaks have few problems, so this should be very seldom. Oaks on land which is being graded or developed in a manner which might change the topography or damage the roots should be carefully tended once this work has been finished.

There is a difference between the oaks which may be found on a piece of land and those which are suitable for planting in a landscape. Our native oaks, like the White Oak and Southern Red Oak, have a root system which makes transplanting difficult. The best oaks for transplanting are the Chestnut Oak, Pin Oak, Water Oak, and Willow Oak.

Since oaks are generally massive trees, give them plenty of room. Their root systems are extensive and grass is difficult to grow underneath. In the right place, there are few trees which are better.

CHESTNUT OAK
Quercus prinus

Mature Height: 100 feet
Growth Rate: Slow
Unique Features: Broad head, heavy foliage
Best Use: As a large specimen lawn tree for heavy shade
Fall Color: Yellow
Problems: This tree has large acorns which make cleanup difficult and mowing a problem; be sure not to sling an acorn and hurt someone.

This vigorous oak is not used as often as it should be. The foliage is heavy, dark, and attractive. The trunk divides at about $1/4$ of the mature height, making a wide-headed tree ideal for massive shade. Give it plenty of room. Of all the oaks it has the best foliage, in my opinion, and its density makes its shading potential excellent.

PIN OAK
Quercus palustris

Mature Height: 80 feet
Growth Rate: Medium
Unique Features: Pyramidal, formal shape, red fall foliage
Best Use: As a specimen tree planted in groups, each planted 20 feet apart, or as individual specimen trees
Fall Color: Vivid scarlet
Problems: Do not grow in alkaline soil. Chlorosis will occur and constant applications of iron will be necessary.

Many old-time Southerners commonly refer to the Willow Oak, *Quercus phellos,* as the Pin Oak because the Willow Oak has narrow "pin" leaves.

The real Pin Oak is a very unusual tree, one of the best lawn trees available. Its beauty is in its most unusual growth habit which makes a precise pyramidal head. The upper branches are upright, the middle are horizontal, and the bottom are drooping. If allowed, the bottom branches will sweep the ground. It is one of the most formal of our shade trees because of this unusual habit of growth. The leaves are typically "oak" shape, of moderate size, and regularly and deeply-lobed. They turn a vivid red in the fall.

This tree is widely used because it transplants so well, not having a tap root like many oaks, but a fibrous root system. Older trees are difficult to grow grass under, but this problem doesn't occur for many years.

The Pin Oak is overused as a street tree. I have seen them block after block like soldiers marching off to battle. This is fine for younger trees, but unfortunately when they grow older they spread out into the street and up into wires, making a butchering action necessary. Then you see who lost the war.

As a lawn tree with plenty of room, the Pin Oak is in its element.

SAWTOOTH OAK
Quercus acutissima

Mature Height: 50 feet
Growth Rate: Medium
Unique Features: Small in height, but very broad
Best Use: One of the best lower-growing trees for use as a wide-headed shade tree
Fall Color: Insignificant color
Problems: No serious problems

The Sawtooth Oak is a relatively recent introduction by the U.S. Department of Agriculture. It is not a tall-growing tree, but its spread is as great as its height, making a rather unique specimen. It is the ideal tree for locations where a tree in the 40- to 50-foot height range is needed. The leaves are shiny and toothed like a saw, set densely enough to give good shade. It is one of the fastest growing oaks.

WATER OAK
Quercus nigra

Mature Height: 80 feet
Growth Rate: Medium

Unique Features: Fine texture
Best Use: As a medium-sized specimen tree for relatively quick shade; also useful as a street tree
Fall Color: No fall color
Problems: Prolonged leaf fall and small leaf size that make removal difficult

The Water Oak is one of the faster-growing oak trees, widely used by landscapers for quick, heavy shade. I have never been fond of the Water Oak or the Willow Oak because they shed their leaves over such a long period of time that, coupled with the fine texture, leaf removal is a real chore. There are many trees of far greater beauty which are less troublesome. I list it merely because it is so widely known and used. If there are some on your property, don't cut any down for my sake, but if you are looking for a tree to plant, try again.

WILLOW OAK
Quercus phellos

Mature Height: 70 feet
Growth Rate: Medium
Unique Features: Dense head
Best Use: As a specimen shade tree or as a street tree
Fall Color: No significant fall color
Problems: No significant problems

The Willow Oak is also not one of my favorite trees. If you have one, live with it, for it will make good shade. There are so many better shade trees that planting one is not advisable, in my opinion. The same drawbacks apply to this tree as to the Water Oak. The leaves are fine, like a willow leaf, and fall over a very long period of time, making leaf-raking and pickup an annual chore of large proportion. The fine texture seems to have some appeal, however, for it is widely planted and does look attractive when the sun is hot and shade is needed.

BRADFORD PEAR
Pyrus Calleryana cv. 'Bradford'

Mature Height: 40 feet
Growth rate: Fast
Unique Features: White blooms, good foliage, excellent fall color
Best Use: Use as a small lawn specimen tree or also for quick shade over patios and decks.
Fall Foliage: Gorgeous maroon
Problems: The only serious problem is their tendency to develop competing trunks with very narrow angles, which may become weak and split with any stress. They are grafted onto the stock of the specie, which may sucker. Remove any suckers as soon as you see them.

Seldom does a new, highly-advertised tree live up to its press enthusiasm. The Bradford Pear has more than lived up to its buildup, and it has become one of the South's most widely-planted trees. It does have so much to offer: excellent spring

Pecan

Bradford Pear

A contorted limb of a Virginia Pine

White Pine

Japanese Pine

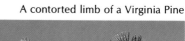

blossoms; heavy, dense, dark green summer foliage; and beautiful maroon fall color. In fact, it is a beautiful tree. The oval head of dense foliage makes some of the best shade imaginable. I planted one of these trees many years ago, and it grew into one of the most beautiful specimens I have seen. The whole back side of our house was shaded and we were ecstatic.

However, the Bradford Pear does have a serious fault, which we discovered to our horror. It has a tendency to send heavy trunks upward which compete with the main trunk. These have very narrow "V" angles which eventually grow against each other. In a huge windstorm I lost one-half of the tree. The next year I lost the other half. Now I am having the old sun problem again which this great tree had solved.

The tree is so worthwhile that you should plant it anyway, being careful to remove any trunks which may develop at a narrow angle with the main trunk. Don't go off to Egypt as we did, or some other place, for several years and return to find your tree has become weak.

I just hope that this most popular tree will not be overplanted. They seem to be everywhere these days. If you use them wisely, they will be the best trees you have.

PECAN
Carya illinoinensis

Mature Height: 150 feet
Growth Rate: Medium
Unique Features: Edible nuts
Best Use: As a shade tree that should be planted at least 40 feet from the house
Fall Color: No fall color
Problems: The wood of pecans is brittle and may break during severe ice storms. Fertilize with a product designed for pecan trees that contains zinc to prevent rosette.

When I was in the catalog nursery business, I loved my father's description of the pecan. He always headlined the copy, "Pecan, The Dual Purpose Tree." It is certainly that. It provides abundant nuts and excellent shade at the same time.

Throughout the countryside of the South, you will find huge pecans growing in the yards of many of the older country houses, providing the dual roles of an excellent nut tree and a wonderful shade tree. It is worth considering. Even though the tree takes a long time to reach maturity, it starts giving shade (and nuts) much sooner.

I will discuss pecans in more depth in the volume on vegetables and fruits, which will include nut trees. There are some things you will need to know about cross-pollination and planting procedures.

PINE
Pinus sp.

Pines grow throughout almost all of the South. Old cotton fields, ditch banks, and most idle land soon sprout some sort of pine. Betsy says, "Deliver us from all these skinny pines!" We do have a lot which are pretty pitiful as shade trees. Pines do have a purpose, though, and may be just the right thing for a given spot or a certain problem. They do grow fast and will quickly screen an area from prying eyes and noise.

Not all pines are right for all our area. Where I live, 30 miles north of Atlanta in the foothills of the Blue Ridge, the White Pine does very well. My father lives 30 miles south of Atlanta and cannot grow them. The White Pine is for the upper part of our region only. On the other hand, the Slash Pine has problems with ice and will break badly during heavy ice and snow storms, so it does best in the lower part of our region which is less likely to get these disasters.

There are many pines which are native or which have been introduced into the South and do well for us. Ten are listed as native to Georgia alone. It is difficult to choose from among so many natives and satisfactory introductions. I am closing my eyes and choosing the five most commonly grown by nurserymen and most useful as additions to the landscape.

You should know that pines are susceptible to several serious pests. The most disastrous is the Southern Pine Bark Beetle which can decimate a tree in a relatively short time. If you suspect these, call your State Forestry Commission's Urban Tree Unit and discuss the best way to handle the situation. In general, though, never cut pines during the growing season. Always tend any wounds as quickly as possible. Be careful to prevent mechanical damage to a pine tree.

EASTERN WHITE PINE
Pinus Strobus

Mature Height: 120 feet
Growth Rate: Medium
Unique Features: Soft gray-green foliage
Best Use: An excellent lawn specimen tree as well as a fine tall hedge or screen
Foliage: 5-needle pine with a soft texture
Problems: Root rot is particularly bad the farther south you go in this region; good drainage is essential. Insects, including aphids and scale, may attack, but they generally do not cause serious damage.

This is one of the superb native trees of the upper part of our region. The huge White Pines of the mountains are as stately and magnificent as any trees you will find. The White Pine of the landscape seldom reaches this great size. The older ones will eventually reach 50 to 60 feet after many years. Even so, these trees add much in contrasting color and texture to plantings.

White Pines are also easily pruned and make excellent screens. A White Pine hedge is a beautiful sight. Pruning must be done correctly if the tree is to respond with tight, thick growth. Make the cuts of the small branches in an area where there are needles growing. If you don't leave a part of the branch with a few needles, new sprouts may not come.

The Eastern White Pine does not grow well in hot, sticky clay soil. In this type of soil, they are frequently attacked by root rot fungi, which quickly kill the plant. Plant in loose, well-drained soil. If they are to be grown in a heavy, sticky clay area, amend the planting area with ground bark, perlite, and any other materials available to give good drainage. Do not overwater these plants when they are young.

The Eastern White Pine will grow 1 foot per year or more when young, but after it reaches 20 to 25 feet, its growth rate slows significantly. This makes them particularly good for tall hedges and for blocking the sun away from problem areas of the home.

JAPANESE BLACK PINE
Pinus Thunbergiana

Mature Height: 130 feet
Growth Rate: Slow
Unique Features: Grows by the sea
Best Use: Excellent plant for the seashore; good as a rock-garden tree or as a contrasting plant to other evergreens
Foliage: Dark green 4 1/2-inch-long stiff needles
Problems: No serious problems

Since the main advantage of the Japanese Black Pine is its ability to withstand salt spray, it is used extensively in seaside gardens. It also represents for us in the South an alternative to the Scotch Pine. Both are stiff, large-growing plants which withstand considerable pruning to improve upon the natural and somewhat grotesque habit of growth.

LOBLOLLY PINE
Pinus Taeda

Mature Height: 100 feet
Growth Rate: Fast
Unique Features: Fast-growing
Best Use: As tall screens or sun blocks
Foliage: 6- to 9-inch-long needles in bundles of three
Problems: Susceptible to the Southern Pine Bark Beetle; place where it will not be subjected to mechanical injury

The Loblolly Pine is to the upper part of the region what the Slash Pine is to the lower part: a very fast-growing evergreen tree with moderately-long needles. This is not the type of tree you should plant for shade, but it is the type to plant for a tall-growing quick screen or a tree which will grow quickly and effectively as a sun block. I have seen these used very advantageously as heavy plantings along the edge of the property or on large acreages to screen out noise from highways and railroads.

As screens they are too often overplanted, which is all right if they are thinned as they grow into conflict with one another. Most people will not thin them, and so the trees are jammed together, causing brownout and poor growth. Start with 12-foot spacings, taking out every other tree when they touch. Since eventually they will lose their bottom limbs, an evergreen shrub should be planted between and forward so that you cannot see under the screen.

SLASH PINE
Pinus Elliottii

Mature Height: 100 feet
Growth Rate: Fast
Unique Features: Fast-growing; graceful needles
Best Use: As a fast-growing tree to screen out noise and unsightly surroundings
Foliage: Dark green 12-inch-long needles in clusters of three
Problems: Susceptible to the Southern Pine Bark Beetle; should not be used in areas subject to ice and snow

The Slash Pine is one of our fastest-growing trees and is used extensively for reforestation and planting for pulpwood and timber. It is somewhat more beautiful than the Loblolly Pine because of its long needles. It is very susceptible to breaking when weighted down by snow and ice. Young trees which are weighted over may break or be so badly bent that they must be physically straightened or removed. In areas subject to snow and ice, substitute the Loblolly Pine.

VIRGINIA PINE
Pinus virginiana

Mature Height: 50 feet
Growth Rate: Medium
Unique Features: Interesting growth habit
Best Use: As a specimen tree in a spot where its unusual habit adds to the beauty of the landscape
Foliage: Dark green twisted needles of 2 to 3 inches
Problems: Subject to the normal pine maladies

The Virginia Pine is a great landscaping tree for just the right spot. The irregular, gnarled branches make a most unusual growth habit and a tree that is excellent for rock gardens and those unique spots where something unusual is required. It is a smaller-growing tree which takes many years to reach its mature height. Oddly enough, this irregularly-shaped tree may be severely pruned as a young plant and developed into a beautiful Christmas tree.

NEWPORT PURPLE LEAF PLUM
Prunus cerasifera cv. 'Newportii'

Mature Height: 25 feet
Growth Rate: Medium
Unique Features: Dark red summer foliage, white spring blossoms; does bear a few small plums
Best Use: As a colorful, small tree for restricted locations in the full sun
Foliage: Purple to red all season
Problems: It is susceptible to borers, and any wound should be tended and sealed with tree dressing. Also, the tree should be pruned each winter to prevent crossing limbs from developing.

The Newport Plum, like the Bradford Pear, might well be listed as a flowering tree rather than a shade tree. I would not argue with that classification. It is considered among the shade trees because the dearth of colored-foliage trees which grow well here and its small size put it into a class which is underpopulated.

The Newport Plum is the best of the purple or red-leaf plums and one of the most colorful of our summer trees. It does not grow large enough to be suitable as heavy shade but it is quite useful for cooling the area over patios or outdoor living areas. It should be grown in full sun to develop the best leaf color; in the shade, the leaves fade out and tend to be green.

One caution: Like many plums and related plants, it tends to develop many cross branches which should be removed during the dormant season. These will develop into a mass of conflicting branches which could weaken the tree and give it an irregular shape. These limbs can rub together, making a wound which is a place for borers to enter and cause severe damage. The Newport Plum should be planted in a location where mechanical damage may be prevented, because borers will enter any wounds.

❧ YELLOW or TULIP POPLAR
Liriodendron tulipifera

Mature Height: 150 feet
Growth rate: Medium
Unique Features: Heavy foliage, unusual flowers
Best Use: As a marvelous huge shade tree
Fall Color: Bright yellow if there is ample fall moisture; if dry, leaves turn brown and drop.
Problems: No serious problems

The Yellow Poplar is too common to be highly prized as a shade tree to purchase and plant here in the South. Perhaps being so common makes it unwanted. I have a great feeling for this tree since I grew up with two huge specimens framing our country home. These two trees had grown up in the battle trenches dug during the latter phase of the Civil War Battle of Jonesboro. The trenches were still visible when my father chose this location for his house and even today one of these ancient specimens survives. The other was hit by lightning many years ago and died.

This tree has a real place in our landscapes for it grows relatively fast, has excellent clean growth, makes marvelous shade, and transplants well. The flower, though interesting, comes after the leaves and is not particularly noteworthy except up close. The Yellow Poplar must be given plenty of room or it will not develop into the beautiful tree it is capable of becoming. It will take at least 60 feet to prevent crowding and give it ample room to develop to its fullest.

Be careful when purchasing or cutting wood for the fireplace. Yellow Poplar wood is not suitable because it will "spit" hot embers which have burned many a country house.

Norway Spruce

Newport Plum

Sourwood

August blossoms of Sourwood

 SOURWOOD
Oxydendron arboreum

Mature Height: 75 feet
Growth Rate: Slow
Unique Features: Summer flowers, early scarlet fall color
Best Use: As a specimen tree
Fall Color: Earliest in the area to change color; scarlet by September
Problems: No significant problems

The Sourwood is the first of our trees to turn in the fall. It may be easily spotted in the woods when you see a tree in August with red fall foliage. It is spectacular. The summer blossoms are also attractive and will mark the tree as well. Some of the best honey made comes from hives set in an area in the mountains where there is no clover and the bees have only the Sourwood flowers to provide nectar. The seed pods hang on the tree for many months and remain attractive.

The shape is noteworthy, being a formal, narrow pyramid with the lower branches weeping downward. Sourwoods are not grown by too many nurserymen since they are slow and must be root-pruned often. They may therefore be expensive but they are well worth having.

NORWAY SPRUCE
Picea abies

Mature Height: 150 feet
Growth Rate: Very slow
Unique Features: Tight, dense evergreen
Best Use: As a formal specimen tree
Foliage: Needled conifer
Problems: Does not do well in hot, dry soil and should be planted where it obtains plenty of moisture; soil should be well-drained to avoid root rot

The Norway Spruce is the best of all the spruce to grow in the South. I have never seen one even approaching 150 feet in the South, though farther north I have seen many. It is one of the most beautiful trees of Canada and the far northern U.S. Achieving its great beauty takes much more moisture than we have here in the South.

The young trees are dense and formal, but as the tree gets older, the branches become pendulous and the form is softened considerably. It is a very popular evergreen conifer and is used more, perhaps, than it should be, for the Hemlock and the White Pine are certainly superior trees in its class. I list it because there is a certain beauty about it, and there is always room for a more unusual specimen tree of its type.

 SWEET GUM
Liquidambar styraciflua

Mature Height: 120 feet
Growth Rate: Medium

Unique Features: Heavy foliage, scarlet fall color
Best Use: As a specimen tree for shade or blocking the sun
Fall Color: Beautiful scarlet
Problems: No insect or disease problems, but fruit can be messy

I grew up climbing a Sweet Gum tree. Of all the trees we had, my favorite was the huge Sweet Gum in our backyard. I could scamper to great heights with little effort and feel that I was on top of the world. What a glorious sensation it was for a boy of twelve!

Dr. John Cornman of Cornell University gathered us all into a carry-all one fall day and drove way out from Ithaca to show us a very special tree. We stopped and everyone looked in awe at a scrawny red-leafed tree which was unusually well-colored even for maple country. I was not particularly impressed, which caused a stir, but why be impressed by that scrawny Sweet Gum when my climbing tree back home was ten times bigger? What they were looking at in Upstate New York may have been a rare and uniquely beautiful specimen to them, but it was worse than a runt to me.

We are living in Sweet Gum country here in the South, and we are better for that. This is a beautiful tree with a dense pyramidal shape, excellent summer and fall foliage, and no real problems except the fruit or "Sweet Gum balls" which dry on the tree, then fall to the ground and become the nemesis of anyone walking barefoot or trying to mow the lawn.

BLACK WALNUT
Juglans nigra

Mature Height: 150 feet
Growth Rate: Slow
Unique Features: Heavy tree, large nuts
Best Use: If you have one growing, keep it as a specimen tree
Fall Color: No fall color of note
Problems: Don't let little boys battle with the fruit.

I list the Black Walnut not as a tree to buy and plant but a tree to know about if you have one growing on your property. There are many better trees to plant than this slow-growing, coarse tree with fruit which are large and very messy to deal with on the ground.

A huge specimen Black Walnut is a sight to see and should be preserved. The wood, if you ever want to cut the tree, is quite valuable for furniture. But it isn't something to go out and buy, for it will take many, many years to grow to be anything particularly good.

We had one when I was growing up, and I received many a good walloping for having pitch battles with the fruit that would leave a horrendous stain on clothing which heaven and earth couldn't get out.

One health-food friend claims a cancer cure from the flesh surrounding the nut, but so far the medical profession hasn't agreed. So just keep the tree for what it is: a huge, coarse, unusual tree which will always yield a pretty penny if you sell the wood.

❧ WEEPING WILLOW
Salix babylonica

Mature Height: 30 feet
Growth Rate: Fast
Unique Features: Unusual weeping branches
Best Use: Commonly used near water where its graceful branches sweep the surface
Fall Color: No fall color
Problems: This tree is beset by so many insects and diseases that being concerned is about all you can do. Spraying is difficult because of the tree shape.

The Weeping Willow is planted only because it has a habit of growth so unique and different from other trees. The long weeping branches sweep the ground and form a rare and exotic sight.

Unfortunately it is beset by too many problems to be planted for any reason except its unique habit of growth. Since there is no other tree like it, we put up with willow borers, willow aphids, and Japanese beetle attacks just to have this cool, pendulous, and perhaps nostalgic tree.

It is extremely fast-growing and even the young trees are attractive. Though it is beautiful, plant it knowing you have been forewarned of the possible problems.

Weeping Willow

CHOOSING TREES FOR SPECIAL SITUATIONS

It is relatively easy to choose a shade tree for the normal landscape locations on the property. The lists and descriptions which I have given you should allow you to make the choice with little effort. There are other situations which are not so easy. Here are some suggested trees to use for several of these specialized situations.

BETWEEN THE SIDEWALK AND THE STREET

Trees planted along streets will add tremendously to a city, village, or neighborhood. They afford wonderful relief from the hot sun's beating down on parked automobiles. Street trees block noise, clean the air of dust and pollutants, and reduce the temperatures in an area through evaporation.

But remember that the space between the sidewalk and the street is a classic disaster area. Trees are hit by cars, pedestrians, bicycles, and all sorts of other mechanical contrivances. It is really a war zone. Therefore the tree must be tough to survive the ordeals of a street.

The area between the sidewalk and the street or the open area in the sidewalk must be large enough for the tree to become established. A minimum 8 × 8-foot square is required, though a 12 × 12-foot square is better.

Choose street trees with the following in mind:
- Since mechanical injuries will be frequent, the tree must be resistant to borers and other problems with the bark and wood.
- The tree should have a narrow, upright habit to keep wide-spreading limbs out of the way of cars and trucks.

Street trees are a tremendous asset, but must be tough to survive.

- The tree should grow low enough to prevent interference with utility lines if present.
- Choose a tree which is resistant to automotive and other street pollutants.
- A street tree should be deep-rooted so it can spread under paved areas and find moisture.
- The wood should be strong and not brittle, for breakage is common along streets.

The following list of trees fit most of the above criteria. Before choosing a street tree, read its complete description and note, particularly, its height. Fit one of the following into the specific requirements of your location:

Ash, Green	Hemlock	Pear, Bradford
Beech, American	Linden, European	*Pine, Eastern White
Birch, River	Magnolia, Sweet Bay	Plum, Purple Leaf
Cherry Laurel	Maple, Red	Sourwood
Ginkgo	Oak, Pin	Sweetgum
Hackberry	Oak, Water	

Flowering trees are frequently suitable for street plantings, and should also be considered with this caution: Many flowering trees have insect and disease problems and are best not used. The dogwood, which at one time was a favorite for street plantings, should not be used because the frequent mechanical injuries will invite the destructive flat-head borer. The best flowering trees for street plantings will be discussed in Chapter 5, Southern Flowering Trees.

TREES FOR CONTAINERS

Terraces, decks, and open porches may need shade, yet afford no soil for planting a shade tree. Do not be deterred; some trees may be planted in large containers and will grow for years. Shade trees grown in containers will not grow as tall as they will in a natural state. Therefore, the heights listed for each type will not apply exactly. The best type of tree under these circumstances is one with arching branches. The mimosa was ideal until the mimosa blight made it risky to grow them. There are other trees which may also be used:

Ash, Marshall Seedless	Magnolia, Sweet Bay
Birch, River	**Maple, Japanese
Cherry Laurel	***Mimosa
Honeylocust, Green Glory	Pear, Bradford
Loblolly Bay	Plum, Newport

*For the upper South only.
**Use the green form, which grows faster and larger.
***The mimosa may be used as a very fast-growing tree for this type of situation with the reminder that the blight may strike as it matures. However, since tub trees must be replaced as they grow too large anyway, the mimosa may last as long as other trees, and is very appropriate for this use.

Suggestions For Growing Trees in Containers

1. Use as large a container as possible. A whiskey half-barrel is excellent.
2. Fill with a well-prepared soil mixture. Use:

   $^1/_3$ garden soil

   $^1/_3$ ground bark or peat moss

   $^1/_6$ perlite

   $^1/_6$ cow manure
3. Do not start with too large a tree. A 1-inch caliper tree is ideal.
4. Measure the ball of earth and be sure that when you plant, the top of the ball is below the edge of the container.
5. If there is room, place 4 inches of coarse gravel in the bottom for drainage. Be sure there are ample drain holes in the bottom of the container.
6. Place enough of the prepared soil on top of the gravel so that the ball is at the correct depth.
7. Set the ball in the container and position the tree properly. Remember that it is hard to move a container after it is filled with soil.
8. Pack the prepared soil around the ball until the container is half full.
9. Remove the burlap from the top of the ball and from around the stem. It is best to cut it off with a knife. Trees which are grown in containers are easier to handle, and eliminate the need for this step.
10. Pack soil around the rest of the ball until the soil level comes to the top of the ball. Do not cover the ball with soil.
11. Water thoroughly, placing the hose nozzle at the stem and slowly soaking until water comes through the drain holes.
12. Each time you water, soak the plant in this manner, until water comes through the drain holes. Water again only when the surface of the soil begins to feel dry to the touch.
13. Fertilize with a good tree and shrub fertilizer in the early spring, and thereafter about every six weeks until August. Tree fertilizer spikes are excellent.
14. Prune to make the branches grow the way you want, but *never* top the tree.

ESPALIERING TREES

The art of espalier can add a most interesting touch to walls and other structures. This unusual practice, which dates back for centuries, can be used very effectively with some trees.

The criterion for choosing a tree to espalier is that the tree should never be too large for the structure on which the espalier is to be fashioned. I have seen the great Southern Magnolia espaliered on the side of a house. About the time that the tree had attained its full potential as a beautiful espalier, its growth rate increased so drastically that pruning was constant and finally the plant became so large that the only thing you could see was the large trunk.

Dwarf trees are ideal, and dwarf fruits are widely used for this purpose. Using fruits to espalier will be covered in the volume on fruits and vegetables. Flowering trees and some taller-growing flowering shrubs are also good to espalier.

Follow these criteria when selecting a tree to espalier:
- The tree size should be manageable.
- The structure should be loose and open.
- The limbs should be limber and easy to train.

Some of the best trees to espalier are the Southern Buckeye (*Aesculus Pavia*), Loblolly Bay, Japanese Maple, and Newport Plum.

PURCHASING SHADE TREES

I have said that you must carefully choose the kind of shade tree you want, for this will be a long-term association. The same is true for actually picking out that particular tree at a nursery. When should you pick it out, and how?

PLANTING SEASON

The best time to plant shade trees is after they are dormant in the fall, through the winter, and until early spring. This gives the roots ample time to become established before the new leaves appear and before the tree's demands for water are greater. The earlier the tree is planted, the better the first year's growth should be.

CHOOSING A TREE IN A NURSERY

There are three ways you may find the tree at a nursery: bare-root, balled and burlapped, and container-grown. You will find detailed descriptions of these in Chapter 3, Planting Trees and Shrubs.

The size of a tree is measured by the caliper (diameter) of the trunk measured above the basal flair. The caliper is generally measured at 3 feet above the ground or slightly below the first branch, whichever is lower.

Generally speaking, trees which are dug bare-root should not exceed 1 inch in caliper. Balled trees may, with the aid of a machine, be as large as the machine can handle.

I prefer a balled and burlapped or container-grown tree which is about 2 inches in caliper. This size may be handled without too much difficulty, and the tree is large enough to begin making shade quickly.

Inspect the trees in the nursery carefully and choose the one which conforms as much as possible to the following:
- The trunk should be straight.
- Branches should be well-shaped and coming from the trunk in a wide angle. Avoid trees whose main branches grow from the trunk in a tight "V."

- The main shoot or leader must not be damaged or broken.
- The ball should be tight and solid, and the trunk should not wobble in the ball.
- The tree should not have heavy roots protruding through the burlap.

HANDLING YOUR NEW TREE

It is important to handle the tree very carefully after purchasing it. Never pick it up, or allow the nurseryman to pick it up, by the main trunk. Lift the ball by the cords binding the ball, or by the handles on the container. Very heavy plants may be carried more easily by rolling the ball onto, and lifting it into, a sling.

Try to place it in the hole correctly the first time. Lifting a heavy tree out of a deep hole may be damaging to the ball and to you.

PLANTING THE TREE

The rules for planting are found in Chapter 3, Planting Trees and Shrubs. Remember to use every possible technique to give the tree a chance to take hold and begin good, strong growth. You have invested a lot in your tree, so do the job right!

PRUNING YOUR NEW TREE

Shade trees should need very little pruning when they are planted. Unlike shrubs and fruits, shade trees should be left alone to develop their own shapes. The grower should have made the very early necessary structural cuts. You should merely prune any broken or damaged branches. If by chance there is a branch coming from the trunk at a very tight angle, remove the whole branch at the stem with a good clean, flush cut because it is liable to break later in a storm. Remove any weak side growth. Paint any cut surface with tree paint. *Never top a shade tree.* Pruning the main leader will damage the future shape of your tree.

STAKING THE NEW TREE

A shade tree is probably the largest plant you will ever buy. It is a plant whose root system must grow and anchor the plant into the ground. For the first year, these roots are not extensive enough to prevent the tree from wobbling in the ground in heavy wind. This back and forth movement may break the newly emerging feeder roots and slow down the plant's growth. Very early planting, well ahead of the new leaves, helps prevent this problem, but staking is the best way to insure that the tree stays firmly in the ground. Always stake trees which are over 5 feet in height. Smaller trees may be staked but the procedure is not absolutely necessary.

The side-by-side method is useful in staking small- to medium-sized trees. Don't forget to cover the wires to protect the trunk.

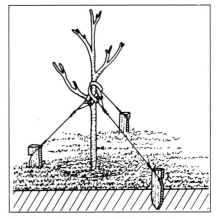

The triangular method of staking. Protect trunk from damage by covering the wires with pieces of garden hose.

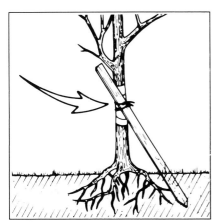

The one-stake method may be used on trees less than 3-inch caliper. Protect trunk from damage from the stake by using a heavy wrap.

KEEPING YOUR SHADE TREE GROWING

Choosing and planting your new tree is only the beginning. Your dreams of a stately, useful tree are not realized when the soil is packed around the roots of the newly set plant. There is a lot of growing to be done before the performance of the tree lives up to your hopes and expectations. It takes water and fertilizer to keep the tree growing rapidly and strongly.

WATERING

The first thing you will need to do after planting your tree is to be sure that it is well-watered. Despite the extreme care which you and your nursery-man have given, the root system has been damaged in handling. Handling the tree correctly and planting properly will minimize this damage. Despite all efforts, there will be a great need for speed in developing a new and extensive feeder root system. The earth around the new plant must not be allowed to dry out. There is a difference in the texture of the soil around the ball and the surrounding soil which you have prepared. Yours should be better, and you want the new roots to grow into your soil. The best way to encourage this growth is to keep the soil damp. Never let the ball from the nursery dry out. The saucer which I suggested making around the outer edge of the hole you dug will aid in holding water and helping it to slowly seep into the old ball as well as the new surrounding soil. It is also good to place the nozzle of the hose at the trunk of the tree and water very slowly.

Watering of older, established trees may be done by making the same kind of collar on the ground around the tree at the drip line or outer edge of the branches. Filling this saucer during long, dry periods will keep the rate of growth as fast as possible for the type of tree.

I like and frequently use a root probe. These are made for fertilizing deep and for watering. They allow the water to seep very slowly into the root zone deep in the ground. These watering and feeding devices are ideal when there is particular stress on the tree, as during prolonged droughts or after a severe winter when roots of trees, especially evergreens, may have been damaged.

FERTILIZING

Fertilizing a tree, especially when you are seeking maximum growth, is important. Apply fertilizer in February and March as the roots become active following their dormant period. This is especially true of deciduous trees, which seldom need a second application during the growing season. Evergreen trees may be fertilized twice, first in February or early March, and second in early June.

The best growth I have ever had by a shade tree was from using a combination of 50% dehydrated cow manure and 50% 10-6-4 fertilizer by weight. Now that dehydrated cow manure is almost impossible to find in large bags, the next best thing to use is one of the slow-release nitrogen tree fertilizers. If neither of these is available, use a 10-10-10 fertilizer, a root feeder, or tree spikes.

A good rule of thumb is to use, at each application, 1 pound of fertilizer per inch caliper (diameter) of the trunk measured 3 feet above the ground or just below the first branch, whichever is lower.

The feeder roots of a shade tree are at the outer extremity of the plant, under the drip line or tips of the outer branches. Put the fertilizer into holes bored 2 to 3 feet into the ground with a tree auger. Make the holes in two rows, one slightly outside the drip line and one slightly inside. Triangulate the holes. (See illustration.) Make the holes 1 foot apart for small trees and 2 feet apart for large ones.

Count the number of holes you have bored and divide the amount of fertilizer needed (caliper in inches times 1 pound) by that number. Place this amount of fertilizer in each hole. At this point, fill the holes with water to start the fertilizer acting quickly.

Root feeders and tree fertilizer spikes are also acceptable ways to get the proper nutrients to the roots.

After a tree is growing well and attaining the size you want, it does not generally need fertilizer unless there are stress conditions like drought or severe freezing. If summer drought has caused defoliation or reduced leaf size, fertilize the next year at the proper time. If the stress is caused by freezing, fertilize in February or March or as soon as the ground warms after the cold passes.

PRUNING

If there is a question in your mind about whether or not to prune a shade tree, the best decision is not to prune. *Never top a shade tree.* Leave the leader or central trunk alone. Topping a shade tree will probably alter its growth pattern and ruin its shape.

I learned that lesson the hard way. When I was about twelve, some friends and I had a fine baseball game on our front lawn. My mother had just planted two 4-foot-high magnolias. She had visions of their growing into stately trees to frame our house, which sits on a hill. Unfortunately,

Never top a shade tree; if you do, you'll ruin its shape.

When pruning, don't leave a stub, which can create a perfect home for insects and diseases.

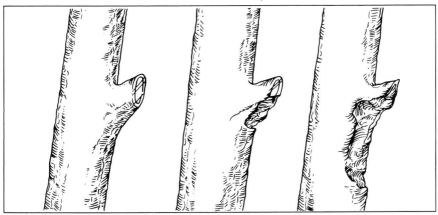

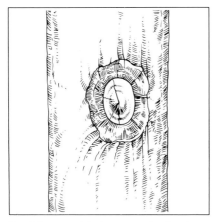

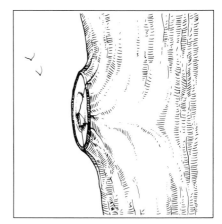

Don't leave a stub; however, don't cut so close that you damage the bark of the main trunk.

Proper cut showing collar preserved.

one of our long fly balls landed in the top of one of those trees, nipping out the terminal shoot. Fifty years later, my mother still tells everybody that the reason that magnolia is so funny-looking is because I knocked the top out playing baseball. The other one, which was in foul territory and remained unscathed, is an absolutely beautiful tree to this day.

This doesn't mean that bothersome limbs on the roof or branches in the gutter cannot be removed. They certainly can. But trees make their own shapes, and man's efforts seldom help.

If you must prune, do it in the late fall after the leaves come off the tree or during the winter when the tree is dormant. Treat any cuts larger than the thumb with a sticky tree paint to prevent rotting or the entrance of borers in some types.

The Bradford Pear is an exception to these rules and will need some rather constant surveillance. It has a tendency to send up very narrow-angled branches which can give you severe problems in the future. This happened to me. I lost a gorgeous tree in a windstorm because of a secondary shoot which developed at a very narrow angle when I was overseas. Do not prune the leader of a Bradford Pear, but always remove any narrow-angle branches before they develop into seriously weak, competing trunks. Since my disaster, I have inspected many Bradford Pears and find there are tremendous numbers in which potentially disastrous conditions are developing.

Any pruning should be done carefully. Use a curved pruning saw to remove any heavy limbs which are too large for a lopping shear to cut. Make the first few cuts on the underside of the limb to prevent tearing of the bark when the topside cut penetrates most of the limb and the limb begins to fall. The cut should be as close to the trunk or other limb as possible so that the wound will heal.

Pruning to change the growth direction of a limb must be done in young, one- or two-year-old wood. New shoots will seldom sprout from

This Bradford Pear, at the author's house, split due to a weak "V" and is now gone.

older, heavily barked wood. Removing all the leaf area of a limb will almost always result in the death of the remaining part. Removal of this dead stub will have to be done, later, so do it right the first time.

TREE PROBLEMS

The best way to cure problems is not to have them in the first place. Avoid types of trees which are prone to insects, diseases, and growth difficulties. As I said earlier, tree spraying is very expensive and usually must be done by professionals with powerful sprayers which will reach the top of huge trees. My mentor, Nelson Crist, used to say that the best way to cure the awful phenacoccus insect on Silver Maples was to prune the tree with an axe, right at the ground! He was wiser than most of his clients would give him credit for. They would always buy insecticide and powerful sprayers to kill this plague. Yet they always admitted that Nelson was really right. They should have gotten rid of the tree and started over.

Buy types of trees which, if they have problems, can overcome them on their own. When a new and strange problem does occur, contact your state's Urban Forestry Unit. These fabulous professionals can help you objectively better than anyone else.

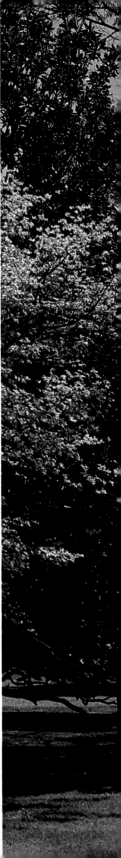

CHAPTER 5

SOUTHERN FLOWERING TREES

The bare arms burst forth with extraordinary beauty, suddenly appearing as if this tree had the sole responsibility of defining a Southern spring. Nowhere else on earth is there such a plant growing naturally as the dogwood does in the South. William Bartram wrote of the forests of dogwoods in Georgia, other authors have written their praise, and artists have painted their beauty. If ever there was a tree which deserved the title of flowering tree, it is our dogwood.

No Southern home landscape seems truly complete without this tree of such grace and beauty. The dogwood is not, however, the only spectacular flowering tree of the South. There are many more. We move now through the Southern landscape looking at trees whose flowers are their major reason for being added to the garden.

It is easy to shift our thinking from a stately maple to a flowering peach when defining whether a plant should be called a shade tree or a flowering tree. The maple is massive and its arms reach out to shelter us from the blazing sun. The flowering peach is small and there is hardly room for two to crawl under it. The flowers of the maple are barely noticeable, while the blossoms of the flowering peach are spectacular.

The hard part of the defining process comes when we look at a Bradford Pear or a Yoshino Cherry. Each is equally

Flowers of Bradford Pear

The Bradford Pear is both a flowering tree and a small shade tree.

A young double-flowering peach provides quick beauty.

at home either as a shade tree or as a flowering tree. Definitions in the garden are usually arbitrary and sometimes may be confusing, even though they are meant to clarify.

Many authors of great reputation would not separate the two groups as I have done, but I think it best, and hope it is a help and not a hindrance to you in choosing the right tree for your garden or landscape.

Shade trees, as I said before, are a capital investment. You will probably plant only one or two for the purpose of providing relief from the hot sun. Large, expensive specimens may be purchased to provide relief more quickly. Shade trees are friends who have come to stay for a long time and should be chosen just as carefully as when you choose a human friend.

Flowering trees are used to enhance the beauty of a landscape, to provide the color needed at a particular season or in a particular spot. They do not need to be so large or expensive when purchased because many of them grow rapidly and begin performing early.

Their blossoms are the important asset of these trees, and it is for their beauty and show that we plant them, not primarily for how far their limbs will reach to cool a sunny window or a hot porch. Shading potential is the secondary asset of a flowering tree, just as flowering potential is the secondary asset of a shade tree.

SELECTING FLOWERING TREES

BLOOMING DATE AND SEASON

The time of bloom is most important for those choosing a flowering tree. It seems a simple task to say that dogwoods will be in bloom on an exact day each year or that your Yoshino Cherry will be in bloom for your daughter's wedding on the twenty-first day of April. These are questions which I am constantly asked. Spring festivals and weddings must be planned months in advance, so if you can see the dogwood buds, why can't you tell when the blossoms will come?

The exact flowering time of any plant is controlled by several factors in addition to the genetics of the plant. The more important ones are temperature, day length, the number of sunny days as opposed to cloudy days, the amount of moisture in the ground, and the vigor of the tree. These factors must combine to condition the buds to open, and they control both the speed of opening and the length of time the flowers are attractive.

The best we can do is to give relative flowering dates like late winter, early spring, mid-spring, and late spring for flowering trees which blossom on wood grown the previous summer or fall. Flowering trees whose blossoms are set on growth of the current season are generally summer-flowering and often, but not always, flower over a longer period of time than the spring-flowering trees. Their bloom times may also vary considerably because of the factors mentioned above.

Fortunately in the South there is some flowering tree which may be chosen for bloom at any time during the growing season. I said that it is difficult to predict exactly when any specific flowering tree will bloom. However, the general blossoming times are known and should be considered when choosing the specimen for your landscape. The chart on page 148 gives the general time of blossom for each type of flowering tree which can be grown in the South.

One of the more consistent blooming trees, at least in my area, is the dogwood. My grandfather rather accurately predicted the blooming dates for dogwoods of the Atlanta area by authoritatively announcing, "Dogwood Sunday, this year, will be the Sunday closest to the tenth of April." Each year his prediction was the same, and year after year he was correct. My father and I have taken this prediction upon ourselves, and in all my life I can remember only three or four years when we were off the mark. With

SPRING-BLOSSOMING	SUMMER-BLOSSOMING	FALL-BLOSSOMING
Flowering Cherries	Chaste Tree	Autumn Higan Cherry
Flowering Crabapples	Crape Myrtle	
Dogwoods	Golden-Rain Tree	
Flowering Magnolias	Sourwood	
Flowering Peach		
Flowering Pear		
Redbud		
White Fringe Tree		

this consistency in mind, I am going to key all other spring flowering trees to the dogwood, so if you know the flowering date of the dogwoods in your specific area, you will have a general idea when any other spring-flowering tree will bloom.

One of the most important factors to be aware of is whether the tree blossoms before or after the leaves appear. A good contrasting example is our common dogwood, *Cornus florida,* and the Chinese Dogwood, *Cornus Kousa.* Our native tree always blossoms before the leaves appear and is a clear unmuted white, while the Chinese Dogwood always blossoms after

Cornus florida, our native dogwood, blossoms before the leaves put forth.

The *Cornus Kousa,* Chinese Dog-wood, blossoms after the leaves put forth and is not as spectacular.

A Kwanzan Cherry with its blossoms muted by its leaves

the leaves appear, and the green subdues the white, making a much less spectacular show. Some trees vary because of weather factors, and their effect changes as they vary. In the years that the Kwanzan Cherry flowers before the leaves start to emerge, we take pictures and acclaim it as "the greatest." In some years when the flowers appear with the first emergence of the leaves, we are much less enthralled.

Summer-flowering trees are more uniform, and unless there are severe heat waves, droughts, or even severe freezes of the previous winter which disturb the new growth, they will blossom pretty well on schedule year after year.

OTHER FACTORS TO CONSIDER

There are other factors besides bloom date which are important in deciding which flowering tree should be planted.

Height and Breadth

Flowering trees grow best, just like shade trees, when they are allowed to grow naturally without excessive pruning. Give them the space they need.

Rate of Growth

It is important to know how fast a flowering tree will begin to perform. Few flowering trees have the strength of an oak, but seldom will they be used where wood strength is vital. Within reason, the faster a flowering tree begins to perform, the more desirable it is.

Insect and Disease Problems

Many flowering trees are closely related to fruiting trees of the same genus. They are susceptible to the same insects and diseases which afflict the fruiting forms. However, since many of these problems are attacks on the fruits, we may ignore them because we seldom grow a flowering tree for its harvest.

Habit of Growth

Good clean growth is most important for all plants. Flowering trees are no exception. Those which grow without need for constant pruning and strengthening are most desirable. There are some flowering trees whose form is the main reason for their being used. The Weeping Cherry, for instance, might be chosen specifically for its pendulous habit of growth.

Color of Blossoms

There is nothing more displeasing than the sight of a mauve Redbud blossoming next to a bright pink Magnolia. Color is important not only for the effect of the individual plant but also for blending with other plants blossoming at the same time.

ALL ABOUT THE SOUTH'S BEST FLOWERING TREES

Spring-Flowering Trees

FLOWERING CHERRIES
Prunus sp.

The flowering cherries make up a most important part of our flowering tree list. Certainly everyone is familiar with the magnificent plantings around the Tidal Basin in Washington, D.C., which consist of the Yoshino Cherry and a smaller number of the Kwanzan Cherry. Throughout the South, these two flowering cherries are grown with great success. There are others which do quite well, including the beautiful Weeping Cherry whose graceful pendulous branches give a softness found in few other plants.

Many communities have adopted the flowering cherry as their tree for mass beautification. One such community, Mountain Brook, near Birmingham, Alabama, is one of the most beautiful in the South when the Yoshino Cherries are in bloom.

Most flowering cherries are relatively short-lived, a fact which you should consider when planting one. I have two fully-mature Kwanzan Cherries which are now over 30 years old and still doing well. However, once past the 30-year mark, most flowering cherries are living on borrowed time.

If you do not plant flowering cherries in full sun, the bloom will be sparse. Grow them in rich but well-drained soil and fertilize them well every year with a slow-release nitrogen formula for trees, or a 10-10-10 formula when trees are young and a 5-10-15 formula for older trees.

The flowering cherries are subject to a number of problems. The worst of these is the Peach Tree Borer, which quickly enters any wounds caused by lawn mowers or other mechanical devices. Other insects such as the Shothole Borer, Eastern Tent Caterpillar, Scale, Japanese Beetles, and Aphids may be a problem in some years. Discuss these with your local Urban Forestry Unit or County Extension Agent for the best controls.

The main causes of difficulties in flowering cherries are lawn mowers and nylon filament weed trimmers. These can cause severe injury to the bark and subsequent entry of a number of the above pests. Be careful, when using these machines, never to get close enough to damage the bark.

HIGAN CHERRY
Prunus subhirtella

There are two cultivars of the Higan Cherry which are useful in the garden: the Autumn Higan Cherry and the Weeping (Higan) Cherry. They both flower early, with blossoms well before the leaves, giving a delightfully airy and refreshing sight before the dogwoods.

Autumn Higan Cherry
Prunus subhirtella cv. 'Autumnalis'

Height: 25 feet
Bloom color: Pink

This is an unusual form of the Higan Cherry which blossoms in the fall and on and off during the warmer periods of winter as well as in the early spring. The flowers are semi-double and very heavily set. The tree is vase-shaped and upright. This rather unknown cherry is very worthwhile for its fall bloom.

Weeping Cherry
Prunus subhirtella cv. 'Pendula'

Height: Top-grafted type—12–15 feet; Basal-grafted type—20–25 feet
Bloom color: Pink

This is the most common of our pendulous or weeping cherries. The pink flowers come on arching branches which will brush the ground if allowed to. The blossoms appear most years in late March, and before the dogwoods.

The common way that nurserymen grow these is to graft them on a straight 6-foot trunk of Mazzard Cherry, which makes a very formal and precise plant. The "weepers" arch upward, outward, and downward from the union and thus the height is restricted to 12 to 15 feet. I prefer the more graceful basal-grafted trees which may be available in some nurseries. As the tree grows upward, you must remove the side branches to the point where you want the head to begin. Thus the graft union is made at the ground level and the tree is allowed to grow more naturally.

The top-grafted weeping cherries are susceptible to a number of problems, especially borers, in the graft union, which tends to be weak. The basal-grafted types are longer-lived and less of a problem.

JAPANESE FLOWERING CHERRY
Prunus serrulata

The Japanese Flowering Cherries are a spectacular group of our spring-flowering trees. In this group are found the finest of the double flowering cherries. They are not long-lived, but for most of us the 30 or 40 years they grow are quite enough.

Kwanzan Cherry
Prunus serrulata cv. 'Kwanzan'

Height: 25 to 30 feet
Bloom color: Rose-pink

This is one of the most popular flowering cherries, with large, double rose-pink powderpuff blossoms which generally come in late April after the dogwoods. A fast, warm spring may bring the foliage out at the same time as the flowers, lessening the spectacular effect somewhat, but in most years the flowers arrive on bare branches and the effect is magnificent. The tree grows to 20 feet or more and may be almost as wide as tall. It has excellent foliage cover and can double as a small shade tree.

A Yoshino Cherry in the street plantings of Mountain Brook, Alabama

Yoshino Cherry

Kwanzan Cherry

Kwanzan Cherry

Mt. Fuji Cherry
Prunus serrulata cv. 'Shirotae'

Height: 25 to 35 feet
Bloom color: White

Mt. Fuji Cherry is a double white form of the *Prunus serrulata* group. It is sometimes referred to as the white Kwanzan Cherry, but the flower has fewer petals than Kwanzan. It blossoms generally before the leaves appear, and at about the same time as Kwanzan, after the dogwoods.

Shogetsu Cherry
Prunus serrulata cv. 'Shogetsu'

Height: 25 feet
Bloom color: Pale pink with white center

This is the finest of the pale pink double-flowering cherries. The blossoms are very pale pink with a white center, and with about 30 petals, or as many as Kwanzan. The blossoms come later than Kwanzan. The tree is not as vigorous as Kwanzan or as tall-growing, but is certainly worth having in the garden.

TAIWAN CHERRY
Prunus campanulata

Height: 25 feet
Bloom color: Rose

This is the earliest of the flowering cherries, and it is often ruined by late freezes. When it blooms, it is spectacular for there is little else in bloom at the time. The rose-colored single flowers are in clusters.

YOSHINO CHERRY
Prunus yedoensis

Height: 35 feet
Bloom color: Pale pink to white

This is the cherry which makes up the majority of the famous Tidal Basin plantings in Washington, D.C. It is one of the easiest of the flowering cherries to grow in the South and is widely used in community plantings.

It is a rapid-growing tree which will begin to blossom at a very early age. The blossoms are pale pink to white and literally cover the tree. They usually blossom just before the dogwoods, which gives a long season of great magnificence when planted with our native tree.

It is larger than the dogwood and a better street tree if it can be protected from mechanical damage. The wide head makes it ideal for a patio tree but it is not long-lived, having an average life span of only 30 to 40 years.

Of all the flowering cherries, this is perhaps the best for general use. Year after year the Yoshino Cherry flowers with a rare beauty found in few other trees.

❦ FLOWERING CRABAPPLES
❦ *Malus sp.*

The flowering crabapples are a significant part of spring for us. These trees blossom before their leaves appear and thus give some of the most spectacular show which we have each year.

The list of flowering crabapples suitable for the South is long and I will name only those which I have observed to be worthwhile, though you may have grown other satisfactory ones.

These trees are relatively fast-growing and much less susceptible to borers than the flowering cherries. However, some of the flowering crabapples are susceptible to leaf diseases like Cedar Apple Rust, so avoid plantings if there is a common Red Cedar nearby. Observe the same rules about mowers and trimmers, for there can be attacks through the wounds that are caused by these machines.

Most flowering crabapples are rather small in height, though some may be as broad as they are tall. Seldom do they exceed 25 feet.

The spring flowers of the crabapples are the main reason we plant them, but there are other significant characteristics which add to their beauty:

- **Fruits:** Many of the flowering crabapples have fruits from which jelly may be made. These fruits may also produce an additional beauty later in the season.
- **Leaf color:** There are varieties of crabapples with attractively-colored foliage all season, providing good contrast to green shrubs and trees during the summer and fall months.
- **Attractiveness to birds:** The smaller-fruited crabapples are attractive to a number of birds, and having them in the garden will add song birds to your landscape.

The taxonomy (classification) of the crabapples is extremely difficult to describe. The majority of those which we grow are crosses producing hybrid forms of very mixed backgrounds. Since you and I are not as interested in the exact classification as we are in choosing the best tree for a location, I am not going to try to pinpoint the precise taxonomic position of most of them, but will merely address them as cultivars of the genus *Malus*.

There are a number of native crabapples of much merit. The Sweet Crabapple, *Malus coronaria*, is found on many properties in the South and if present should be carefully preserved. The sweet-scented blossoms and green crabapples are both worth the work it takes to keep the tree healthy. These are seldom found in nurseries since it is difficult to make them grow straight while they are young, and very few nurserymen will go to the trouble of propagating them.

The crabapples blossom just before the native dogwoods in most years but will vary considerably according to the season. Count on crabapple blossoms with the Kurume azaleas.

CALLAWAY CRABAPPLE
Malus × cv. 'Callaway'

Height: 25 feet
Bloom color: Pink bud, white flower

Floribunda Crabapple is broader than it is tall.

Callaway Crabapple has large, edible fruit.

Sweet Crabapple

Dolgo Crabapple

Hopa Crabapple

This crabapple was discovered at Callaway Gardens in Georgia and is one of our very best. The main attraction is the pink buds which open into a large white flower. The fruits are bright red and large (1 inch), showy on the tree, and excellent for jellies.

The tree is disease-resistant and very clean in growth; continual pruning is unnecessary. The round head of the tree gives it a most attractive shape. The leaves are green throughout the summer.

DOLGO CRABAPPLE
Malus cv. 'Dolgo'

Height: 20 feet
Bloom color: Pale pink

This is another crabapple which has worthwhile large red fruit ideal for making jelly. The flowers are white and the foliage a clean green all summer. The growth habit is clean and eventually the tree forms a rounded head.

FLORIBUNDA CRABAPPLE
Malus floribunda

Height: 20 feet
Bloom color: Pale pink

This is one of the first nursery-propagated crabapples and the parent of many of the newer varieties. It is still one of the best. Though some of the newer varieties bloom heavily every other year, the Floribunda Crabapple is showy every year. The buds are deep pink and very attractive prior to the magnificence which occurs when the pale pink petals unfurl and the tree becomes a mass of pale pink. There is little in the landscape which can rival the Floribunda Crabapple in full bloom.

The tree is not as clean a grower as Callaway, so it must be watched for cross-branches and weak crotches. Remove these when you first see them so that you may avoid future trouble.

The fruit are small and yellow, with little use except to attract enormous numbers of birds. We transplanted a large one of these from our growing nursery to the garden center location where it was one of the most pleasing sights in the landscape. One of its side benefits was the Cedar Waxwing birds that came through in the fall headed south and had a great feast on the fruit. Then as they returned in the spring, they would actually devour the petals of the flowers.

HOPA CRABAPPLE
Malus cv. 'Hopa'

Height: 25 feet
Bloom color: Rose

This is a very widely-grown crabapple of good clean growth and large rose flowers. The fruit is large red and may be used for jellies, though 'Callaway' and 'Dolgo' are superior for this purpose. The best attributes of the 'Hopa' are its heavy flowering nature and good clean growth. The main detraction is that the color of the flower has a mauve tint as the flowers finish, making them an unpleasant contrast with many other shrubs blossoming at the same time.

RADIANT CRABAPPLE
Malus cv. 'Radiant'

Height: 20 feet
Bloom color: Red

This is one of the best red-flowering crabapples. It also has reddish foliage in the spring. The red fruit are medium-sized and persist for many months, giving the tree an extra attraction into the fall.

OTHER CRABAPPLE CULTIVARS

There are other crabapple cultivars with special attractions. If you are looking for fragrant flowers, try **Spring Snow, Wild Sweet Crabapple,** or **Zumi Calocarpa**. Colored foliage is another attraction. The **Royalty Crabapple** has deep purple foliage, while the **Selkirk Crabapple** foliage is a bronze color.

DOGWOODS
Cornus sp.

Dogwood blossoms mean spring in the South and throughout much of the country. This is the best of all American flowering trees, and is widely adapted to our gardens and landscapes. In the South the name dogwood refers specifically to *Cornus florida*, the great flowering dogwood of our forests, fields, and landscapes. But that is not true everywhere. The name "dogwood" actually arose in England where a preparation made from the bark of *Cornus sanquinea* was used to treat mangy dogs.

Other dogwoods are used as landscape plants. The Chinese Dogwood, *Cornus Kousa Chinensis,* is of some value for us and will be described in detail below. The brightly-colored stems of some native shrub dogwoods give an interesting contrast through heavy layers of snow, and are used extensively in the North.

The dogwood of our forests is the prize of the landscape. These trees grow to magnificent size, some as tall as 40 feet with a trunk over 3 feet in diameter. One of the largest I have ever seen is on a small street in mid-town Atlanta. When it blossoms, the cloud of white covers the tiny yard, and TV crews and photographers have a field day.

The wood of the dogwood is extremely hard and at one time it was used extensively to make spindles for cotton mills. This practice caused the destruction of many magnificent specimens, which is a great pity because the tree is long-lived and many would still be here if it had not been for this commercial use.

The "Legend of the Dogwood" seems to have no basis in fact. The idea that the tree's wood was used to make the cross upon which Jesus was crucified is out of the question, since the plant is not known in Palestine. However, their supposed religious significance may have helped to save many dogwoods which might have fallen to the commercial axe.

FLOWERING DOGWOOD
Cornus florida

This is perhaps the most magnificent of all flowering trees of the temperate zone, and we are particularly fortunate that it is native to the South. Many dogwoods grow naturally and every effort should be made to protect and preserve these native trees.

The flower of the dogwood is unusual. The true flower is the little yellow center which opens after the showy "petals." These "petals" are really bracts or modified leaves which surround the little yellow blossom. The bracts are what make the Flowering Dogwood and the Chinese Dogwood so showy. Those dogwoods which produce no bracts do not have the appeal of those which do.

The time of bloom is also important. The blossoms of our Flowering Dogwood appear before the leaves, offering a much greater show than the Chinese Dogwood, whose leaves appear before the blossoms and mute the effect.

Each area of the South has its own Dogwood time. In my area it is always the early part of April, with little variation from year to year. Dogwood Sunday, year after year, *is* the Sunday closest to the tenth of April, just as my grandfather always predicted.

There are several specific points to remember when using dogwoods:

- Dogwoods blossom best in sunny locations.
- There is a tremendous variation in the blooming qualities of dogwoods grown from seed.
- The dogwood is very susceptible to attacks of the Flat Head Borer and should never be planted where subjected to possible mechanical injury.
- They are very shallow-rooted, and weed-killers should never be sprayed on the ground underneath.
- They do not respond well to pruning and must be allowed to grow naturally.

Many nursery trees are grown from seed, which will give a tremendous variation from plant to plant. Likewise, trees moved from natural areas may or may not have the blooming qualities you desire. It is best to purchase named cultivars of the flowering dogwood because these have known qualities and will perform as expected.

Dogwoods do have problems. The Flat Head Borer is perhaps the most life-threatening of all. This larva invades the bark through almost any mechanical injury. The best cure is prevention. Never injure the bark by using a lawn mower or string trimmer close to the trunk of a dogwood.

The dreaded Petal Blight distorts the bracts, ruins the flowers, and then spreads to the leaves and spots them. Weather conditions determine the severity of Petal Blight attacks. In "slow" seasons, when the buds open early and the bracts take many weeks to develop, there is more probability of severe Petal Blight damage than in "fast" seasons, when the buds remain tight until just before bursting into full bloom. It is possible to spray the flowers with a fungicide as the buds begin to open; spray them again when you see the first color in the bracts; and spray a third time as the petals fall (to prevent leaf spotting). However, since this is generally our rainiest season, the effectiveness of the spray may be reduced by being washed off. Most people simply ignore the problem, enjoying the blossoms in all the good years and forgetting them in the occasional blight years.

WHITE FLOWERING DOGWOODS

Cherokee Princess Dogwood
Cornus florida cv. 'Cherokee Princess'

Habit: Upright
Bloom size: Large
Fall foliage color: Bright red

This introduction by the noted plantsman Hoskins Shadow of Winchester, Tennessee, is one of the better grafted cultivars and a companion to his red 'Cherokee Chief.' The tree is noted for its clean upright growth and early-blooming characteristics.

Cloud 9 Dogwood
Cornus florida cv. 'Cloud 9'

Habit: Spreading
Bloom size: Large
Fall foliage color: Bright red

Henry Chase, Sr., of Chase Nursery near Huntsville, Alabama, found this dogwood in a group of trees grown from seed. Henry showed it to me, and I thought it was the best of all white cultivars of the Flowering Dogwood, and still do. In fact, I was with Henry the night he chose the name 'Cloud 9,' and thus feel closely kin to this fabulous tree.

'Cloud 9' is more spreading than most of the cultivars on the market and thus assumes the shape of the beautiful older native trees. The bracts are very large and almost overlap, giving an appearance of a huge mass of white. I have noticed, over the years, that 'Cloud 9' opens very quickly in the spring and seems to be less susceptible to Petal Blight. This is not a scientific fact but mere observation on my part.

This is one of the quickest to bloom after planting, and after only a few years in the ground, it will be setting over 100 blossoms per tree, a phenomenal number. It is a cultivar which consistently sets large numbers of flowers throughout its life.

Double White Dogwood
Cornus florida cv. 'Pluribracteata'

Habit: Spreading
Bloom size: Medium, 7–8 bracts
Fall foliage color: Red

This is an oddity which has no great advantage over the species. The extra bracts are a conversation piece, but the numbers of flowers set are not great, and the flowers are often formed on the underside of the branches, reducing their visibility. The Double White forms blossoms at the end of the dogwood season, so it has some advantage in extending the blooming time of the group.

PINK AND ROSE-RED FLOWERING DOGWOODS

Cherokee Chief Dogwood
Cornus florida cv. 'Cherokee Chief'

A huge White
Flowering Dogwood

The grafted cultivar 'Cloud 9' sets many blossoms, even at an early age.

The blossom of a dogwood is the inner yellow part. The showy bracts are not a part of the flower.

Cloud 9 Dogwood

Double White Dogwood

Pink Flowering Dogwood

Chinese Dogwood

Cherokee Chief Dogwood

Blossom of Chinese Dogwood

Habit: Upright, very clean
Bloom size: Large
Fall foliage color: Red

'Cherokee Chief' is by far the best of all the red flowering dogwoods. It is the discovery of Hoskins Shadow and is one of his premier achievements in a life filled with notable horticultural work. The best feature of this tree, besides the rich red color of the bracts, is its outstanding growth characteristic. The tree has a central leader and it branches uniformly, making it an ideal lawn specimen tree. It blooms at the end of the white dogwood season.

Pink Flowering Dogwood
Cornus florida cv. 'Rubra'

Habit: Upright
Bloom size: Medium
Fall foliage color: Red

The pink form of the dogwood is said to appear in the wild upon occasion, though I have never seen one. The main reason for its use is its color, which is lighter pink than such fabulous cultivars as 'Cherokee Chief.' Plant this cultivar where a light pink dogwood is a better color combination with other plants blossoming at the same time. In our area the Pink Flowering Dogwood reaches its peak as the white forms finish.

CHINESE DOGWOOD
Cornus Kousa Chinensis

The Chinese Dogwood is well-adapted to the South and beautiful specimens are often seen. The main reason for planting it is that its blossoms appear about a month after our native tree, thus extending the dogwood season. But this lateness constitutes a disadvantage for the tree, since the bracts of the blossoms appear on top of the foliage and thus the white flowering effect is greatly muted. The tree itself is not as beautiful as the native dogwood since its branches do not spread nearly as much and its head is much more compact. If the Chinese Dogwood weren't compared constantly to our native tree, it would be far more widely used, for it is a beautiful sight at a time when the crabapples, cherries, and native dogwoods have finished.

There are a few other native dogwood trees which are seldom planted but are possible to find in wooded or natural areas you might have. These do not have the blossoms of our native Flowering Dogwood, but they can be relished as natural and interesting forms of the specie. The following is the best in the small-tree group:

PAGODA DOGWOOD
Cornus alternifolia

This is often found in the wild and confused with the native Flowering Dogwood. The leaves are similar but the flowers appear later and without bracts. The flower cluster resembles a large Queen Anne's Lace and the berries are rather profuse and dark blue. The leaves are alternately set, rather than opposite like the Flowering Dogwood, so it is easily recognized by looking at the leaves on the branch. It is not worth purchasing, but if you find it already growing, you should protect it.

❧ FLOWERING MAGNOLIAS
❧ *Magnolia sp.*

This group of flowering trees has extraordinarily large and showy white to dark rose flowers, and provides some of our best early spring color. This early bloom is both a blessing and a trial. The blossoms are some of our best, but their earliness may bring blossoms at a time when freezing conditions can swoop down upon us and leave the tree with no color except brown.

The later-flowering types should be chosen for the points of greatest interest in the landscape. The earlier types can be confined to places where good bloom will be spectacular, but ruined blooms unnoticed. Plant them among other trees or tall shrubs at the edge of natural areas and enjoy the blossoms during springs which do not have extreme up-and-down temperatures.

The flowering Magnolias commonly grown for their spring blossoms originally were brought from the Orient and are therefore often referred to as "Oriental Magnolias," even though many of the currently-used cultivars were developed in this country and in England. There are several groups worth considering for our gardens:

- **Yulan Magnolia,** *Magnolia heptapeta,* which is represented by the plant referred to in the trade as *Magnolia conspicua* or *Magnolia denudata.*
- **Liliiflora Magnolia,** *Magnolia quinquepeta,* which is noted for the cultivar 'Nigra.'
- **Saucer Magnolia,** *Magnolia × soulangeana,* which has a number of cultivars found in nurseries, the one of greatest worth being 'Alexandrina.'
- **Star Magnolia,** *Magnolia stellata,* which is found as the species.

The Oriental Magnolias may be grown as large shrubs or small trees. Since my preference is to grow them in a tree form, I am treating them here with the flowering trees.

YULAN MAGNOLIA (*Magnolia denudata* or *conspicua*)
Magnolia heptapeta

Height: 35 to 40 feet
Blooms: Large, white, fragrant
Blooming time: Two weeks before dogwoods

The Yulan Magnolia, more commonly called by nurserymen *Magnolia denudata*, is one of our really spectacular Oriental Magnolias. It grows easily into a tree if the main stem is allowed to be predominant by removing all the competing shoots which originate from the base. It should be given plenty of room so that the branches may develop outward and form a large head. The flowers are very large, over 6 inches across when fully open, and have 9 petals. The Yulan Magnolia blooms late enough to miss most of our freezes, and seems to withstand light frost.

MAGNOLIA NIGRA
Magnolia quinquepeta cv. 'Nigra' (*Magnolia liliiflora*)

Height: 12 to 15 feet
Bloom: Lily-shaped, deep purple-red
Blooming time: Two to three weeks before dogwoods

The Magnolia 'Nigra' is a well-known and long-used Oriental Magnolia in the South. The deep purple-red flowers are longer and slimmer than the *Magnolia* × *soulangeana*, which is even more widely grown. This Magnolia, however, blossoms later than *M. soulangeana* and thus escapes more late freezes.

It really should not be classified as a tree, for it is more of a shrub. Prune it to a single trunk, remove the lower branches, and develop this into a delightful small tree which will readily grow over Mahonia and other deep shade plants.

The new cultivar, 'Jane,' is a more bushy plant but has the advantage of flowering after the dogwoods, which keeps it from being damaged by freezes.

ALEXANDRINA SAUCER MAGNOLIA
Magnolia × *soulangeana* cv. 'Alexandrina'

Height: 20 to 25 feet
Bloom: Light pink outside, white inside
Blooming time: Three to four weeks before dogwoods

'Alexandrina' is my choice of all the Saucer Magnolias. It makes a delightful small tree covered with large saucer-shaped flowers which are the best pink of the group. It is earlier than the 'Nigra' and has more possibility of freeze damage, but in most years it escapes unscathed.

STAR MAGNOLIA
Magnolia stellata

Height: 25 feet
Bloom: White with many petals
Blooming time: Very early, with the first warming trend

The Star Magnolia, with its 4-inch flowers of many petals, is my favorite of all the Oriental Magnolias. Its fragrance is an added blessing. It is most often grown as a shrub, but once you see it in tree form, you will discard the shrub idea and prune it into a tree.

The Star Magnolia would be a near-perfect flowering tree if it were not for its early blossom time. Year after year they pop open with an early warm spell, only to be severely damaged by the next Arctic front which sweeps our way. This early blooming tendency can be alleviated to some extent by planting it on the northwest side where it gets the coldest temperatures. Never plant in a southern exposure or near a warm wall, or you will certainly lose the bloom. This may seem a good reason to reject this plant, but once you have seen a mature specimen in full bloom, you will understand why people delight in growing it.

Star Magnolia

Yulan Magnolia blossoms

Yulan Magnolia
Alexandrina Magnolia

Alexandrina Magnolia blossoms

❧ DOUBLE FLOWERING PEACHES
Prunus Persica

The Double Flowering Peaches can be amazingly effective in the landscape. The young branches are covered with large multi-petaled flowers in such mass that they add tremendously to our spring blossom time.

They are seldom as effective as they could be because few people will take the time to head the tree properly when it is young, or care for it as it grows older. It is, after all, a form of the fruiting peach and does best when treated like one. For the most effective bloom, prune correctly at 2 to 3 feet to start lateral branches which will develop large numbers of late summer shoots to blossom the next spring. Flowering Peaches should be encouraged to grow heavily and to form large numbers of fruiting shoots. They should be properly fertilized and kept free from the destructive Peach Tree Borer. Never plant where mechanical damage is a possibility.

DOUBLE RED FLOWERING PEACH
Prunus Persica cv. 'Rubroplena'

Height: 25 feet
Bloom: Double red, 1 1/2 inches across
Blooming time: Before dogwoods and with fruiting peaches

This cultivar sounds as though it would be spectacular. Though it does have considerable merit, its darker flowers do not seem nearly as showy as the Double White Flowering Peach. The two cultivars contrast well one with another, however, and this may be the best way to use this plant. But do not crowd flowering peaches; allow them to grow free-standing as exciting specimens.

DOUBLE WHITE FLOWERING PEACH
Prunus Persica cv. 'Alboplena'

Height: 25 feet
Bloom: Double white, 1 1/2 inches across
Blooming time: Before dogwoods and with fruiting peaches

I like the Double White Flowering Peach better than any other cultivar. Properly grown, this is one of the outstanding sights of spring. Grow it as a free-standing specimen so that it has every opportunity to develop as a healthy, vigorous tree.

❧ BRADFORD PEAR
Pyrus Calleryana cv. 'Bradford'

Height: 40 feet
Bloom: Small, white, and in masses
Blooming time: About the time of dogwoods

This tree is described in detail with the shade trees because it is worthy also of that distinction. However, if you need a white spring-flowering tree of fast growth and large proportions, you should consider the Bradford Pear.

Double Red Flowering Peach blossoms

Double White Flowering Peach blossoms

Bradford Pear blossoms

There are other new cultivars of *Pyrus Calleryana* which you should also consider. These have not had the track record of Bradford Pear, so I list them with reservations.

'**Aristocrat**' is a looser-growing tree than the Bradford. Its main advantage seems to be that its heavy branches come out at better angles than the Bradford, which reduces the possibility of splitting.

'**Capitol**' forms a tighter head than the Bradford, making it better for small yards. It is also a better tree to line narrow streets.

'**Whitehouse**' has a narrow pyramidal crown, making it an ideal tree for small yards and narrow streets. It changes colors very early in the fall.

REDBUD
Cercis canadensis

Height: 30 feet
Bloom: Mauve-pink in clusters
Blooming time: Just before the dogwoods

Don't be mad when I say that I do not like this tree. Some people do, and it's a free country. The Redbud does have extensive bloom; it does blossom during the height of spring's color; and it does blossom late enough to escape freeze damage. There, in my opinion, its worthwhile features end. The blossoms are a mauve which seldom blends well with anything but a few early white dogwoods. The trees are messy, shedding multitudes of seed pods everywhere, and the fast-growing tree loses dead branches constantly. We had two in our landscape when we bought our home, and every year Betsy pleads with me to cut them down. Listing their disadvantages has convinced me that now is the time.

There is a marvelous white form of *Cercis canadensis* which is discussed below. Use it instead of the Redbud.

WHITE JUDAS TREE
Cercis canadensis alba

Height: 20 feet
Bloom: Pure white in clusters
Blooming time: Right before the dogwoods

The White Judas Tree, sometimes called the White Redbud, is a worthwhile addition to the garden. The enormous numbers of flower clusters are formed in masses on the branches, on the limbs, and even on the trunks of the plant. It is a cloud of white when in full blossom.

This tree is somewhat slower-growing than its mauve parent and seldom reaches its full height. It is really a worthwhile addition to the landscape. Unfortunately, this plant is not widely grown since it is difficult to propagate, and so when found, it tends to be expensive.

WHITE FRINGE TREE or GRANCY GRAY BEARD
Chionanthus virginicus

Height: 20 feet
Bloom: White tassles formed in clusters
Blooming time: Two to three weeks after dogwoods

Though the White Fringe Tree is most often seen as a large flowering shrub, a few of the better nurserymen like Hubert Nicholson of Decherd, Tennessee, are growing this marvelous plant in tree form. There is great merit in this practice, for few trees are in bloom when it is, and it is extraordinary.

There is some confusion about its correct name. In the South it is more often known as Grandfather's Gray Beard or sometimes Old Man's Gray Beard. In England it was often called Grand-sire's Gray Beard, a name that was colloquialized to Grancy Gray Beard, which is still common with some of our old-timers. By whatever name you choose, this is an extraordinary plant with some of the most beautiful flowers of any of our native plants. Give the White Fringe Tree as much sun as possible and fertilize it well to maximize its straight growth in tree form.

Summer-Flowering Trees

There are not many trees for summer bloom, but if you choose carefully, you can find a type of tree which will blossom during each of the summer months. There are also some shade trees which will act as interesting flowering specimens. Among these are our great Southern Magnolia, the Virginia Magnolia, Loblolly Bay, and Sourwood.

Some flowering shrubs are also suitable to be trained as small flowering trees. The Rose of Sharon (Althaea), Crape Myrtle, *Hydrangea paniculata* cv. 'Grandiflora,' and Witch Hazel are some which I have seen formed into attractive summer-flowering trees.

The following descriptions include the latter group but not the former. If these great shade trees interest you as possible flowering specimens, refer to their descriptions in Chapter 4, Shade Trees.

CHASTE TREE
Vitex Agnus–castus cv. 'Latifolia'

Height: 15 to 20 feet
Bloom: Panicles of aromatic blue blossoms
Blooming time: June through much of the summer

The Chaste Tree is often overlooked as a small flowering tree because it is not hardy in the areas of so many garden writers. Though it may be damaged severely in below-zero weather, it is quite a useful tree in the South.

Redbud

White Fringe Tree

Chaste Tree

Near East Crape Myrtle

Golden-Rain Tree

This plant is most commonly grown as a flowering shrub, being pruned severely each winter to encourage heavy growth on which large numbers of flowers are formed. However, it also has great appeal when grown in the tree form. Reduce the young plant to a single, strong shoot which becomes the trunk of the tree. Allow this trunk to develop naturally with a number of heavy side branches growing outward and upward. It is wise to prune back the younger wood in the winter every third or fourth year to encourage fresh new growth on which large numbers of blossoms will form. Leave the main structure alone when you do this pruning so that you may always keep the interesting tree shape.

The flowers of the Chaste Tree are borne over much of the summer. They are aromatic, exuding a delightful musty, herbal fragrance. The foliage is also mildly aromatic, and its bluish color gives a good contrast to the rich green of many of our other trees and shrubs. The specie has blue flowers, and so does this cultivar. There is a white form (I think its flowers are a little dirty-looking) which is not really suitable for a tree and is used more as a shrub.

❧ CRAPE MYRTLE
Lagerstroemia indica

Height: 20 feet
Bloom: Huge panicles of various colors
Blooming time: Early summer until fall

The Crape Myrtles make some of our finest flowering trees. They are strictly for the South in this form since they may lack the hardiness needed to continually grow upward and make heavy trunks when the temperatures go below 0° F. There are many cultivars of the Crape Myrtle, but only the upright-growing ones are suitable for trees. The dwarf cultivars should be used only as shrubs. The tree form is my favorite way to grow the plant, though there is certainly nothing wrong with a beautiful Crape Myrtle shrub. The light tan wood of the trunk and frequently peeling strands of bark create an interesting effect.

As you purchase the small plants in a nursery, choose those with one or more straight, strong stems which may be trained into trunks. A clump of three

CRAPE MYRTLE CULTIVARS FOR TREES

RED	WHITE
CAROLINA BEAUTY: Deep Red	COMMON WHITE: White
WILLIAM TOOVEY: Watermelon Red	NATCHEZ: Clean White
TEXAS RED: Deep Red	
HOUSTON RED: Bright Red	

PINK	PURPLE
NEAR EAST: Very Pale Pink to White	COMMON PURPLE: Royal Purple
COMMON PINK: Bright Pink	

or more trunks is the most attractive. Prune off the side branches until the tree has reached the desired head height, then allow a head to develop.

The Crape Myrtle has a very long period of bloom. The first blossoms generally come in June and the last in September, though on occasion there may be a few small blossoms at the time of frost. Good growing conditions make for good blossoms since they are set on newly-formed shoots. For best bloom, keep the plants watered and fertilized until late summer. Prune Crape Myrtles in the winter to force the new shoots in the spring and early summer which will set buds and form blossoms.

There is little difference in the growth of any of the above cultivars, and you should choose one whose color fits best into your landscape. My favorite of all the Crape Myrtles is Near East, which has the coolest and most exquisite palest-pink flowers. It is a much cleaner flower than the White Crape Myrtle, which has a tendency to look dirty as the flower truss finishes.

GOLDEN-RAIN TREE
Koelreuteria paniculata

Height: 30 feet
Bloom: Yellow in large clusters
Blooming time: June

The Golden-Rain Tree is often thought of as the Southern answer to the beautiful northern Laburnum or Golden-Chain Tree, which is one of the most beautiful of all summer-flowering trees but which will not grow well here in the South. The only similarity between these trees is that both have yellow flowers in the early summer.

The Golden-Rain Tree grows well here and should be used for the yellow flowers in June and the interesting bladder-like fruit pods which follow. These two factors make this tree interesting for much of the summer. The flowers are bright yellow, formed in large pyramidal clusters which stand upright on the branches. The leaves are compound, quite long, and very interesting. The leaves have no fall color, but the bladder-like fruit persists and remains interesting during the fall season.

The Golden-Rain Tree grows in almost any kind of soil and needs only a yearly fertilizing to keep it healthy. It naturally forms an attractive tree and needs no pruning unless some problem occurs. It is wide-spreading, growing almost as wide as it is tall. The head is more or less rounded but tends to be flat-topped. The tree seeds freely, and the little trees sprouting around it are a wonderful way to increase the number of Golden-Rain Trees in your landscape.

SOURWOOD
Oxydendron arboreum

Height: 75 feet (after many years)
Bloom: White in hanging clusters
Blooming time: Mid-summer

The Sourwood is discussed in detail with the shade trees. It is perhaps more of a flowering tree than a shade tree for most of us, since it is very slow in growth and becomes attractive because of its summer flowers many years before it produces shade. The white, slightly drooping flower clusters are most interesting and the tree continues its show for many months because of the persistent seed clusters which follow the flowers. The fall color is outstanding.

STEWARTIA
Stewartia sp.

The Stewartias are seldom-grown and little-known plants, some of which are native to the Southern United States. It is a pity that these unusual summer-flowering trees are not propagated and used in our landscapes, for they certainly provide a wonderful show in the summer. If you make the effort to find these for your landscape, you will be greatly pleased with their interesting beauty. The attractive flowers are sometimes likened to a *Camellia sasanqua*. Some of the species have unusual red bark which flakes off in plates, making an interesting pattern on the trunks and providing an added interest to the landscape.

All the Stewartias listed below should be grown in well-prepared loose, rich soil containing a great deal of humus. They all do poorly in tight, sticky clay soil and should not be grown in full sun, but given morning sun and afternoon shade. They grow best when the soil has ample moisture but is well-drained.

SILKY CAMELLIA
Stewartia Malacodendron

Height: 12 feet
Bloom: White with purple filaments, 4 inches across
Blooming time: Summer

The *Stewartia Malacodendron* is found in the lower part of the South, usually in more sandy soil. A few growers list it, and it is worthwhile for those of you in the lower part of our region. For the upper part of our region the Mountain Camellia, *Stewartia ovata*, is better.

MOUNTAIN CAMELLIA
Stewartia ovata, Forma *grandiflora*

Height: 15 feet
Bloom: White with purple filaments, 4 inches across
Blooming time: Mid-summer

This plant is listed by most authors as a shrub, but I have often seen them growing by my trout streams in the North Georgia mountains as beautiful 15-to-20-foot trees. In either form, they are spectacular and worth using in the landscape. The flowers are large and white, with purple filaments which make them a rare sight. In the North Georgia mountains they blossom around the first of July, but in the higher Smokies they are later.

JAPANESE STEWARTIA
Stewartia Pseudocamellia

Height: 50 feet after many years
Bloom: White, cupped, 2 $^1/_2$ inches across
Blooming time: Mid-summer

The Japanese Stewartia is more commonly found in nurseries than our native species. The flowers are not as showy, but the bark is more interesting, and it is more naturally a tree than the other two. It is certainly worth adding to the landscape if you can find it.

Flowering Shrubs Pruned as Trees

These general groups comprise the majority of the flowering trees which you will use but there are others, especially those which are often grown in shrub form but may be easily pruned into an attractive flowering tree. The althaea is a good example. I have a dislike for most althaeas because they are so terribly overused and have such bilious colors. However, I trained a pale pink cultivar into a tree form, and it was perfectly beautiful through most of every summer.

Other flowering shrubs which may be pruned into tree form are the Mountain Hydrangea, *Hydrangea paniculata* cv. 'Grandiflora'; the Smoke Tree, *Cotinus Coggygria*; and Witch Hazel, *Hamamelis virginiana*.

Dogwoods and other spring-flowering trees blossom on old wood.

GROWING FLOWERING TREES SUCCESSFULLY

PLANTING

It is easy to plant flowering trees since most which you might purchase from a nursery are smaller than the shade trees. See Chapter 3, Planting Trees and Shrubs, for detailed information on planting techniques.

It is generally not necessary to stake flowering trees unless the tree is over 6 to 8 feet tall. Stake these taller trees as you do shade trees.

Immediately after planting flowering trees, soak them to settle the fresh soil around the roots and thoroughly wet the root ball. Continue weekly soakings until the leaves have come out and reached their mature size. After that, soak them in periods of very dry weather.

KEEPING FLOWERING TREES GROWING AND BLOOMING

Choose flowering trees which need little maintenance, except in cases where a specific tree's assets are so great that you are willing to "go the extra mile" to keep it healthy. The ones I have described should give you the least trouble, and your main effort should be to keep the plants fertilized for growth and pruned for shape and cleanliness.

It is most important to know the relationship between the growth habit and the bloom habit of a flowering tree. The type and age of the wood on which the flower buds form determine how they should be pruned and fertilized.

Blossoms on Old Wood

Spring-flowering trees blossom on wood grown the previous summer. Any pruning which disturbs the bud formation or removes the bud wood will reduce the number of blossoms in the spring.

Generally, flowering trees should need very little pruning after the original structural development mentioned in the descriptive lists above. Do minor shaping as soon after blossoming as practical. Heavy, structural pruning must be done in the dead of winter despite the possible loss of some flowering wood. There is too much chance of borers entering the tree if you prune in the spring or summer while these insects are active.

Fertilize spring-flowering trees about the time they blossom. This forces the new wood which will form the buds for next year's bloom.

Blossoms on New Growth

Summer-flowering trees almost always blossom on the new growth which is set as the weather begins to warm. Anything which encourages this new growth will help the quantity and quality of the flowers. Pruning and fertilizing of these trees is done in the winter.

PRUNING FLOWERING TREES

As noted above, flowering trees will need some pruning to help them produce the buds or shoots which will produce enormous numbers of flowers. The time of pruning is noted above when I discussed the habit of blossoming on old or new growth. The method of pruning is not hard.

Spring-flowering trees need less pruning than summer-flowering trees. Dogwoods, for instance, should never be pruned unless there is a dead branch or some severe growth problem. The flowering counterparts of fruit trees, such as flowering cherries, crabapples, flowering peaches, and flowering pears, should be pruned only to prevent future problems. Crossing branches, stems which develop upward through the center of the plant, and wood which is diseased must be removed. The only other pruning which is needed is to keep the older growth thinned out so there is plenty of healthy new growth from the younger wood. Remember, the flowers of these trees form on wood that was grown the previous summer. Pruning is done to encourage that new growth each year. Other spring-flowering trees need little if any pruning. Remove dead, diseased, or damaged wood, and that is all that is necessary.

Summer-flowering trees need much heavier pruning. The growth which comes out each spring and summer produces the shoots on which the flowers will occur. Crape Myrtle, Chaste Tree, and the like should be pruned heavily to force the wood which will bloom. This is done by cutting back the previous season's growth severely. This will force a number of strong, new shoots on which the blossoms will appear.

PROBLEMS

In the descriptive information, I have given some drawbacks to a few of the trees which you will be growing. Note these carefully.

The most serious problem I have found over the years is mechanical damage to the bark of flowering trees. Lawn mowers, string trimmers, and automobiles which hit many of our flowering trees invite disaster. These

Borers attacking a Kwanzan Cherry

Borer damage resulted from a lawn mower hitting and loosening the bark of this dogwood.

Dogwood Petal Blight, leaf stage

2-4-D damage showing on a dogwood in a lawn area

breaks in the bark are ready-made doors for borers and diseases to enter your tree. Whenever there is mechanical damage of any kind to one of your flowering trees which is susceptible to these problems, give the wound your immediate attention. Clean the wound and remove all the loose bark, using a knife to form the wound in a round or elliptical shape. Treat the area with a solution of Lindane or some other recommended borer spray. After this dries, seal the wound with a sticky tree-wound dressing or a good wood glue. Apply additional Lindane treatments during the height of the borer season. Check with your County Extension Agent for the correct times.

Treat leaf spots, bacterial blights, and other diseases the moment you see them. Your local nurseryman or County Extension Agent will help you with the latest and best controls.

Avoid the use of some weed control chemicals under flowering trees. Since most of these trees are shallow-rooted, the 2-4-D weed killers can be extremely damaging to the roots. Before using weed killers under these trees, especially dogwoods, find out if the chemical is likely to cause harm. A good rule is to avoid the use of any chemicals under a flowering tree.

MULCHING

Flowering trees respond well when they are grown in areas free of grass or other plants which must be trimmed or cut, and away from areas where the soil is going to be worked for flowers. This eliminates the possibility of mechanical damage, harm from lawn weed killers, and disturbance of the shallow roots while working the soil.

Mulched islands of flowering trees are a practical way to eliminate many of these problems. However, never allow the mulch to pile against the trunks of the trees. This may be disastrous. Always leave an open collar around the trunks.

CHAPTER 6

SOUTHERN SHRUBS

Like steel beams in a huge building, shade trees provide the structure of the landscape, while flowering trees embellish the design and give the extra flair which each home needs. But the real building blocks of the landscape are the shrubs. Shrubs pull everything together into one unified scheme.

What is a shrub? *Hortus Third* describes it as: "A woody plant that remains relatively low and produces shoots or trunks from the base, not tree-like or with a single trunk. . . ."

Since shrubs make up a large group of plants, they should be divided into several parts for easier study. I will show you through the shrub part of the garden in several steps. We will first consider evergreens, primarily broadleaf evergreens like the hollies, which are such an important group of plant materials for the South. But we will also consider the narrowleaf evergreens suited to our climate, such as the junipers.

Azaleas, Rhododendrons, Camellias, and the other flowering evergreen shrubs could be considered just as "flowering shrubs," but I will treat them as a separate group because their evergreen nature sets them apart from the many deciduous flowering shrubs we may grow.

Then we will look at the deciduous flowering shrubs, such as Forsythia. Like flowering trees, they add spice to the basic landscape plan.

Finally, we will look at a very different type of flowering shrub, the rose, which has played such a vital role in gardens for so many centuries.

SELECTING SHRUBS FOR YOUR LANDSCAPE

How do you choose the right plant for a given spot? I wish it were as easy as it might seem. All of my horticultural life I have been dealing with the homeowner's disappointments when a "dwarf" plant grew up and covered a picture window, or when handsome plants suddenly became ugly after the first cold, or when one after another plants in a foundation died, leaving a snaggle-toothed appearance.

The landscape is intended to enhance the beauty of the home and the quality of life. Improper plantings too often do just the opposite.

Ask yourself the following questions before planting a shrub:

- What kind of shrub do I need?
- How will it fit in with other shrubs in the same area?
- What exposure does the planting spot have?
- How much sun or shade does the spot get?
- What is the condition of the soil in that spot?
- At what height do I want the shrub kept?
- How many plants do I need for that spot?
- What characteristics do I want in a shrub?

Aucuba is an ideal plant for shade.

Juniper and holly do well in sunny spots.

The purpose of a professional landscape plan is to aid you in making these decisions. A plan can save you time, money, and disappointment, and is generally well worth the cost.

The hardest situations to deal with are renovating old established landscapes and correcting poorly-planned new landscapes. Repairing is more difficult than making afresh.

My purpose, while taking you through the shrubs which may be grown in the South, is to help you look at the horticultural characteristics of the material which is found in nurseries or already growing in your current plantings. You must then choose the shrubs most suitable for your own property.

Shrubs are generally structural plants in the landscape—the building blocks, as I said before. But you may also want to grow certain shrubs simply because you like their unique characteristics. I have seen very beautiful landscapes which were devised as arboretums or gardens for specialized plants. It is just as enjoyable to be a collector of shrubs as it is to be a collector of iris, or daylilies, or any other group of plants. Rosarians are collectors or specialists in a given type of flowering shrubs just like holly collectors, azalea enthusiasts, or viburnum lovers. Many of us find collecting shrubs for the sheer enjoyment a very worthwhile gardening adventure.

FACTORS TO CONSIDER

I mentioned some questions which you should ask yourself before choosing a shrub for your landscape or garden. Keep these in mind as we move through this part of our garden study.

The following are important considerations as you begin your plantings or try to improve those which you already have. Study these before making your lists or going to a nursery. Then coordinate what you find here with those plants which are specified on your landscape plan. Know what the needs of the plant will be before you make your purchase.

Mature Height

The height a plant will grow is naturally of tremendous importance. An understanding of commonly-used terminology will help avoid many problems.

Heller's Holly is low-growing.

Some junipers literally hug the ground.

The author's 16-year-old son Chris stands under a Burford Holly planted when he was a baby. This is the way a Burford Holly grows naturally.

Dwarf Burford Holly grows pretty large also.

Dwarf does not mean low-growing in all cases. The Dwarf Burford Holly, for instance, will grow to a height of 10 feet if you do not prune it. It is too often used wrongly as a low-growing shrub in front of windows only 2 or 3 feet above the ground. The term dwarf is relative to the parent, which, in the case of the regular Burford Holly, may grow very large (to 15–20 feet). Thus, Dwarf Burford Holly refers specifically to its relationship in size to its parent, not to other plants.

Low-growing is the better term to look for when searching for plants which will not grow too large for a picture window.

A Dwarf Burford Holly which has been restricted by heavy pruning and has developed a very heavy trunk.

Prostrate means lying on the ground, and plants of this type are best used as bank covers or in place of the more usual ground covers.

Slow-growing is a term used for many plants commonly found in foundation plantings. The Globe Arborvitaes are commonly-used plants which grow very slowly, but which eventually become very large. They should be planted with this fact in mind, and may be very suitable in a spot for many years but eventually will have to be removed.

Pruning to Restrict the Size

Choose a shrub to fit the spot. Disaster always occurs when we plant shrubs which grow too large for a location. Popular shrubs like Burford Holly, Red Tip Photinia, and Pfitzer Juniper are often placed in restricted locations with the idea that they may be pruned severely when they grow out of bounds. This works at first. But then the plant begins to look butchered.

When I moved into my house there were several very large Burford Hollies which had been planted many years before under windows which were 6 feet above the ground. The first few years I worked with them, pruning severely each spring. Following each pruning, long shoots would burst forth and cover up the windows again. The main trunks had reached a diameter of 4 inches, and even stubbing back was impossible. I finally just dug them up and started over with the lower-growing Carissa Hollies, which have remained beautiful for over ten years.

A good rule of thumb is that we can restrict a plant to about 50% of its natural height by pruning it each year.

Cold Hardiness

Choose shrubs which are hardy in your micro-climatic zone. Never place marginally-hardy plants in foundation plantings or use them for screens or other important purposes where their loss would severely damage your landscape design. We have had several very bad freezes which killed many plants that had been growing successfully for many years. But if we let these abnormal cold spells govern our shrub choices completely, we would

The Banana Shrub is marginally hardy in the upper South.

find ourselves growing a very restricted list of plants. For each group of plants in the descriptive list, I will give the hardiness zone (see zone map on page 23). The zone designation will indicate the plant's general ability to survive cold in that area. Remember, though, that your own home may be in a micro-climatic zone which can be either colder or warmer than the general zone. Check with the old-timers of your area for their experiences with any given plant if you have any doubt as to whether it will survive the cold there.

Use Gardenia, Southern Tea Olive, Loquat, Banana Shrub, and other plants of similar hardiness level in areas where die-back or complete loss will not be disastrous to your plantings, since they are marginally cold-hardy. Some plants, like the *Camellia japonica,* should be carefully placed so that the cold west wind does not dry their leaves in the winter.

Soil Conditions

Many factors help plants to develop to their fullest potential. Choosing shrubs to fit particular soil conditions and amending the soil to accept a plant's specific needs are a major part of having beautiful shrubs.

The pH of the soil is a most important consideration. Most evergreens need a soil with a lower pH (a more acid soil) than many flowering shrubs, trees, herbaceous flowering plants, and vegetables do. Poor growth and yellowing (chlorosis) occur in many evergreens when they are grown in soil with a high pH (too alkaline). Though correcting with treatments of iron compounds will restore good color, it is a rather constant job. It is better to choose the right shrub for your pH or correct the alkalinity prior to planting by using sulfur. The soil may also be kept acid enough by always using an acid fertilizer.

Drainage affects plants tremendously. Tight, sticky soil which holds excessive moisture can be disastrous. Many of our shrubs simply die away in poorly-drained soil. Amend the soil before planting! It is almost impossible to correct a bad situation fully after plants are growing.

Don't plant evergreens too deep. The top of the ball should be partially exposed when the planting hole is filled.

GROWING SHRUBS SUCCESSFULLY

PLANTING

Follow carefully for shrubs the general planting principles found in Chapter 3. Be especially careful not to plant too deeply. I have seen many plantings of evergreens completely ruined by too-deep planting. Azaleas, Rhododendrons, Hollies, Camellias, and all the other broadleaf evergreens face imminent death when their stems are covered with soil. Be careful!

Bed planting is really the only way to succeed with foundation plantings and groupings of shrubs. Follow the general rules for bed planting found in Chapter 3.

MULCHING

Mulching is necessary to protect shallow-rooted plants during the hot and dry times of the summer and also during the times in the winter when the ground is cold and perhaps frozen. Good mulching practices also make a neater, cleaner landscape free from weeds and unwanted plants.

Improperly done, however, mulching may be damaging to plants. Never pile pine straw or other mulches against the stems of shrubs. Always leave an open collar around the stem.

FERTILIZING

Shrubs definitely need yearly applications of fertilizer to continue growing properly, since there is seldom enough fertility in our soils to support continuous healthy growth.

The timing of your fertilizing is also important. Make the main application in the early spring just before the new growth starts. Non-flowering evergreens may respond to another *light* application in late June. However, if the shrubs blossom in the spring, apply the fertilizer *after* the blossoms have finished.

Fertilizing too late in the season may disturb the setting of buds for the following year. A good rule is never to fertilize spring-flowering shrubs after June or the burst of growth may prevent good bud formation.

INSECT AND DISEASE CONTROL

Shrubs are susceptible to attacks from all sorts of insects and diseases. It is best to choose plants for large groupings, like foundation plantings, which have as few problems as possible.

Sometimes new cultivars start out with few problems, only to have an insect or disease condition develop later on. The Red Tip Photinia was introduced as a wonderful, colorful plant for general landscape use. Nothing seemed to bother it badly until the Photinia Leaf Spot disease suddenly became widespread. Now this wonderful plant is a real problem, for it needs frequent sprayings to keep it growing healthily.

PRUNING

There are strict rules of pruning which we must respect. Shrubs should not be constantly pruned nor pruned at certain times of the year. Do major pruning of non-flowering evergreens just before the new growth begins, usually in March. You can lightly tip the new growth in early June to shape your plants and to help them fill in loose and bare areas. Never prune evergreens after early July because the new growth which will follow may be damaged by the first freezes of the fall.

Prune flowering shrubs, both evergreen and deciduous, according to the way their bloom buds are set. A good rule of thumb is to prune all flowering shrubs which blossom before June first after they have finished blooming. These plants will blossom on wood which was grown the previous summer, and if you prune them before they blossom you remove the wood on which they flower. Never do anything like pruning or fertilizing which changes the growth pattern of these plants after early July. Azaleas,

CORRECT　　　　**"OK"**　　　　**WRONG**

The correct way to prune allows sunlight to reach from top to bottom. The wrong way allows shading of the lower portion and causes die-out.

Roses are pruned in early March.

Camellias, and many other flowering shrubs begin setting buds in July, and a spurt of growth caused by pruning or fertilizing may prevent a large number of flower buds from setting.

Prune summer-flowering shrubs, those that generally blossom on the new growth, in the dead of winter if the plants are deciduous or in early March if they are evergreen.

Exceptions to this rule are important. Most of our modern roses, so-called everbloomers, will blossom before the first of June, but they also blossom on new growth. Prune them in late February or early March. The proper time and method of pruning roses will be covered in the section on roses as flowering shrubs.

Rhododendrons and some Azaleas will blossom *after* the first of June, but since their blossoms are set on wood which was grown the previous summer, you still must prune them *after* they blossom.

CHOOSING THE RIGHT SHRUBS FOR YOUR GARDEN AND LANDSCAPE

I see many fascinating shrubs as I travel over much of this globe. My constant thought, and Betsy's, is, "I want one of those for our garden." So few that we see can be grown here in our area. We have deep cold snaps that eliminate many of the exotic shrubs I have seen, and we have very hot summers that eliminate many others. Years of experience has defined for me those which do well here. We must confine our foundation plantings and large groupings to plants which have the least number of problems or the least chance of dying in the cold. We can devote other garden areas to experimental, exotic, and new types of plants which we might like to try.

GROUPS OF SHRUBS

I wrote in the beginning of this chapter that a study of shrubs would be easier if we looked at them in groups. For clarity I have divided shrubs into the following groups: first, the Evergreens, including Broadleaf Evergreens and Coniferous Evergreens; next, Azaleas, Camellias, Rhododendrons, and Other Flowering Evergreens; then the Deciduous Flowering Shrubs; and, finally, Roses.

The **Broadleaf Evergreens**, such as the Burford Holly, are the South's greatest shrubs. We are extraordinarily fortunate to have such a wide list of these plants which we can grow successfully. They are the basic building blocks of our home landscape. There are suitable broadleaf evergreens for foundation plantings, background shrubs, borders, and screens. In fact, every one of our needs could be filled by one of our broadleaf evergreens.

The **Coniferous Evergreens**, such as the Shore Juniper, are the needle plants which are such an integral part of the landscape in colder climates. We use them for texture contrast and in areas where their special characteristics are better suited to the location than the more popular broadleaf evergreens.

I prefer to list **Azaleas, Camellias, Rhododendrons, and Other Flowering Evergreens** separately from the deciduous flowering shrubs because they are distinctive and may be used quite suitably also as broadleaf evergreens. The *Camellia sasanquas* in particular make excellent foundation plants with the added feature of wonderful blossoms. Azaleas make wonderful evergreen groups, with the added advantage of magnificent flowers. Azaleas, Camellias, and Rhododendrons are the big three in this group, but there are others worth having also. Among them are Mountain Laurel and Pieris. Consider all of them when choosing your basic materials list.

The **Deciduous Flowering Shrubs** are some of the gems of the garden and landscape. In the old days they were used far more than now, when we have so many Azaleas and Camellias from which to choose. There is still nothing more beautiful than Forsythia, Spirea, and Viburnum in bloom in the spring. There are also deciduous flowering shrubs which blossom in the summer garden when few, if any, flowering evergreens are colorful. Study these different plants and choose ones for your garden which will add the color which no other group of plants will give.

Growing **Roses** is a specialized area which requires specialized techniques. I am very partial to roses. I think there is nothing so beautiful as a bed of gorgeous hybrid teas in full flower. Unfortunately, roses are vastly oversold, with new ones flooding onto the market each year. How many times have you read about the Rose of the Century, only to find several years later that it is no longer being produced? New roses are not always better roses, and disappointing results have led to the decline of roses in popularity as a garden plant in the South.

Roses in our part of the country have many disease problems. Too few of the newer varieties have been bred for our conditions, but there are many older ones which we can use with great success. I will give you some pointers about growing better roses as well as choosing varieties which have fewer problems.

Now let's look at some of the specific plants which I have found extremely well-adapted to our region.

ALL ABOUT THE SOUTH'S BEST EVERGREEN SHRUBS

Broadleaf Evergreens

❦ GLOSSY ABELIA
Abelia × grandiflora

Zone: 6
Natural Height: 8 to 10 feet
Best Use: Background shrub or hedge
Habit: Loose with upright shoots; may be pruned severely
Light: Full sun to part shade
Points of Interest: Small white flowers in the summer
Problems: May be semi-evergreen in extreme cold

The Glossy Abelia is not used as widely as it was many years ago. It is still a worthwhile shrub but is more attractive when allowed to develop into a free-form shrub rather than tightly pruned into a formal foundation shrub or hedge. The small white flowers are attractive.

Cultivars of interest include the following:

DWARF ABELIA
Abelia × grandiflora cv. 'Sherwoodii'

This small-growing Abelia is ideal for low foundation plantings, for growing on banks, or for borders. The foliage and flowers are smaller than the Glossy Abelia.

PINK ABELIA
Abelia × grandiflora cv. 'Edward Goucher'

The Edward Goucher Abelia is interesting for its more colorful flowers and for the showy calyxes which follow the blooms, providing interest for several months. Since the plant is neither as heavy nor as tall-growing as Glossy Abelia, you can use it in more restricted places where you need a larger shrub than 'Sherwoodii.'

❦ AUCUBA
Aucuba japonica

Zone: 8
Natural Height: 8 to 10 feet
Best Use: Heavy shrubs for dense shade
Habit: Upright, naturally stalky
Light: Light to dense shade

Points of Interest: Shiny green foliage and red fruit on the female plants
Problems: Grows poorly in dry or poorly-drained soil; subject to a severe fungus when in poor condition; cannot stand direct sun

The green Aucuba is used much less frequently than the variegated form. It does have a place in dense shade and well-drained soil. The female plants have a bright red fruit which adds to its attractiveness. All Aucubas tend to become leggy unless kept properly pruned with the top more narrow than the bottom.

Though the heavy foliage may seem a bit coarse, it is acceptable since there are so few shrubs which will grow in as deep shade as it will. Also, the plant seems to withstand city pollution well.

Cultivars of interest include the following:

GOLD-DUST AUCUBA
Aucuba japonica cv. 'Variegata'

The Gold-Dust Aucuba is the most popular member of the family, widely used for deep shade in many of our landscapes. The green leaves speckled with gold give some of the best variegation of any of our shrubs. It has the same requirements as its parent. It is smaller-growing, reaching only six to eight feet, and may be kept pruned to four feet without much difficulty. There are female forms which produce red berries.

GOLD-LEAF AUCUBA
Aucuba japonica cv. 'Picturata'

This variegated cultivar has a large yellow blotch in the center of the leaf.

There are other leaf forms as well as low-growing types which may be found upon occasion in nurseries. In my experience they all do equally well and should be chosen according to the variegation or height which best suits your plan.

WINTERGREEN BARBERRY
Berberis Julianae

Zone: 6
Natural Height: 7 feet
Best Use: Barrier plantings
Habit: Upright
Light: Full sun to light shade
Points of Interest: A very spiney, sticky shrub with yellow flowers
Problems: May be dangerous where small children play

Although there are many barberries found in nurseries, this is the only evergreen one commonly produced. It has excellent, almost holly-like foliage which remains attractive all the year. It is, however, an extremely spiny plant, being armed with tough, long needle-like stickers which can easily harm a child falling into it. They should be used as barrier plants where animals and even humans are to be kept out, but not where small children are playing.

❦ COMMON BOXWOOD
❦ *Buxus sempervirens*

Zone: 6
Natural Height: 6–8 feet (after *many* years)
Best Use: Foundation plant
Habit: Formal and tight
Light: Sun to part sun
Points of Interest: Tight, thick appearance
Problems: Boxwood decline caused by poor soil; Box Leaf Miner which riddles
   foliage

The gardens of the old South were built to a great extent around the wonderful boxwood. No other plant has all its characteristics of being a near-perfect foundation, small background, or border plant. Other plants are chosen in its place for a number of reasons, and some are even called by its name, like Boxwood Holly or Boxleaf Euonymus.

Its use, however, has declined over the years because it does have problems and must be grown well to be attractive. When understood and grown properly, it can be one of the most beautiful plants of the garden.

Boxwoods need special attention from the day they are planted on throughout their life. To ignore a boxwood is to invite its decline and subsequent "ratty" appearance. Here are some rules which will allow you to have beautiful boxwoods with a minimum of trouble:

1. Plant boxwood in well-prepared beds into which ground bark, perlite, peat moss, and well-prepared soil are mixed.
2. *Plant boxwood shallowly.* Never cover the top of the ball of earth around the roots; *always* leave the stems free.
3. Mulch the plants outside the extent of the branches, never allowing mulch to cover the base of stems.
4. Fertilize in early March with an acid fertilizer.
5. Watch for the appearance of the adult Box Leaf Miner, which resembles a gnat or fruit fly. Spray immediately with Orthene or Cygon. Repeat every ten days until three sprayings have been made.
6. Trim the fresh new growth lightly to keep plants full.
7. Keep plants soaked in extreme drought.
8. Keep ice or snow off the plants to prevent bending and breaking.

Two things cause severe boxwood decline: first, worn-out soil, which becomes tight and sticky; second, soil or mulch which builds up over the base of the stems, causing stem-rooting and the deterioration of the lower roots.

Healthy boxwood can make your landscape and garden extraordinarily beautiful. Don't discard them as a possible plant for your landscape because of their need for a little extra care.

A number of cultivars of the common boxwood are worthy of note. 'Myosotidifolia' has very small leaves and is excellent for edging plant beds or walks. 'Suffruticosa' is the plant I have always known as English Boxwood. The plant in the trade under this name is very slow-growing, has a less-pruned appearance and, though expensive, has a beauty which exceeds all foundation plants I have ever seen.

Common
Boxwood

Gold-Dust Aucuba

Japanese Boxwood trained as a topiary.

Cherry Laurel

Glossy Abelia

❦ JAPANESE BOXWOOD
Buxus microphylla japonica

Zone: 6
Natural Height: 6 feet
Best Use: Foundation plant, formal borders
Habit: Rounded to upright, very thick
Light: Full sun to part shade
Points of Interest: Very tight formal appearance
Problems: Winter bronzing

The Japanese Boxwood grow better in poor soil than the true boxwood. Their vigor and heat-resistance make them a better plant for those who cannot take the time to work with our common boxwood. They are more formal in appearance and take more pruning to keep the rounded shape. They also grow somewhat faster.

The best cultivar seems to be *Buxus microphylla* 'National,' a recent introduction by the National Arboretum in Washington. This cultivar is more upright, somewhat narrower, and has better winter color than the Japanese Boxwood.

❦ CHERRY LAUREL
Prunus caroliniana

Zone: 7
Natural Height: 12 feet as a shrub
Best Use: Screens, corner plants, background shrubs
Habit: Upright, but may be pruned to more rounded shape
Light: Full sun to part shade
Points of Interest: Hardy, tough, fast-growing plant
Problems: Borers

The Carolina Cherry Laurel was discussed in the chapter on trees. However, this attractive plant may be kept in a shrub form and has been widely used for many years in the South, especially for screening.

I prefer this plant over the Red Tip Photinia because it is not attacked by the terrible leaf spot disease which causes so much headache to those with Photinia hedges. Many landscapers have stayed away from this Cherry Laurel because it may be attacked by the same borer which infests all cherries and because it does need yearly pruning to be tight and thick. However, when grown as a tall hedge, background shrub, or screen, it makes a perfectly wonderful planting and is seldom bothered by the borer. It withstood the severe freezes of 1984 and 1985 in Atlanta and there are tree forms which did not have any defoliation.

Since Carolina Cherry Laurel needs space to grow, this parent form should never be planted in a restricted space. Plant them at least 4 feet apart and keep the main trunk pruned back to prevent a tree from forming. One of the most beautiful plantings I have ever seen was in the yard of friends in Griffin, Georgia. This gardener had grown the Cherry Laurel hedge for many years and made a practice of pruning it to near the ground every third or fourth year to keep the growth fresh and bushy. The first year after pruning it would resume its height of about 8 feet.

There is a cultivar listed as **Compact Carolina Cherry Laurel** which I have never grown but which, from the information I can gather, should be easier to manage than the parent.

CLEYERA
Cleyera japonica (Ternstroema gymnanthera)

Zone: 7
Natural Height: 12 to 15 feet
Best Use: Corner plantings and background shrubs
Habit: Upright
Light: Sun to part shade
Points of Interest: Reddish color in the winter; rich green, glossy summer foliage
Problems: None of consequence

The Cleyera is closely kin to the Camellia, and one of our very best shrubs. It is tight and thick, with foliage about the size of a Camellia but of more substance. This is one of the most handsome shrubs of the Southern garden and should be used in place of the more disease-prone Red Tip Photinia to give the color contrast desired in the spring. The Cleyera is not a fast-growing shrub but is handsome even as a smaller shrub. It needs little pruning except to tighten growth upon occasion.

There has been considerable confusion over the proper botanical name of this plant. Nurserymen have consistently referred to it as Cleyera until recently when some botanists have placed it under *Ternstroema gymnanthera*. I hope that *Cleyera japonica* is correct, for it is certainly easier to remember and pronounce.

COTONEASTER
Cotoneaster sp.

There are a number of Cotoneasters which have a place in our gardens. These are not well-known plants for us but certainly have a place because of their good foliage and red berries. There are a number which are prostrate and excellent for banks and other areas where a shrubby ground cover is needed. I prefer them over the more widely-used junipers, which always seem to be a bit ratty.

FRANCHET COTONEASTER
Cotoneaster Franchetii

Zone: 7
Natural Height: 10 feet
Best Use: Background shrub
Habit: Upright with arching branches
Light: Sun to part shade
Points of Interest: Red berries
Problems: None of consequence

This Cotoneaster is the best of the upright-growing evergreen species for the South. The habit is softer and the plant is easier to shape than most of the other evergreen types. It is an ideal large background shrub and is colorful with its red berries.

BEARBERRY COTONEASTER
Cotoneaster Dammeri

Zone: 6
Natural Height: 2 feet
Best Use: Evergreen ground cover
Habit: Prostrate
Light: Full sun to light shade
Points of Interest: White flowers, bright red berries
Problems: None of serious consequence

This is a wonderful ground-cover shrub with more to offer than the widely-used prostrate junipers. It has attractive white blossoms in the spring and bright red berries following the flowers in the summer and fall. It makes a wonderful sunny bank cover.

The cultivar **'Coral Beauty'** has coral instead of red berries.

ELAEAGNUS (SOUTHERN RUSSIAN OLIVE or SILVERBERRY)
Elaeagnus pungens cv. 'Fruitlandii'

Zone: 7
Natural Height: 15 feet
Best Use: Massive background shrub or hedge
Habit: Upright to rounded; may have arching branches and may even climb
Light: Full sun to light shade
Points of Interest: Rich green leaves with white and brown scales underneath; fragrant flowers and brown fruit
Problems: Very vigorous and will climb into trees if allowed; seeds freely, causing it to come up all around

Prosper Jules Alphonse Berckmans (1830–1910) was one of the foremost Southern horticulturists. He founded and ran, for many years, the famous Fruitland Nursery near Augusta, Georgia. The site of this nursery is part of the famous Augusta National Golf Course, and many of you golf enthusiasts have seen his plants as you follow the world's best golfers around this magnificent course—that is, if you were not too enthralled by the golf action.

There are many plants still in the trade which carry either the Fruitland or the Berckmans name. This plant, *Elaeagnus pungens* cv. 'Fruitlandii,' was named and introduced by P.J.A. Berckmans and is still widely grown in the South.

This is a shrub to be used wisely and only in the right spot. It must have plenty of room! In a single burst of growth, the long arching branches may grow 6 or 8

feet. We have one that Betsy spends her life pruning to keep in bounds. This plant, which was already in place when we arrived, does its job screening an unsightly area, but it does take its toll in effort because the space is too small for the plant's size. On the other hand, I needed a property screen and boundary plant in another spot, in a natural area. I planted an Elaeagnus and have never touched it in all these years. Of course, it has grown into a massive barrier but that is what I wanted, so I couldn't have chosen better.

There is a hybrid Elaeagnus, *Elaeagnus* × *Ebbingei,* also commonly known as Ebbings' Silverberry, which is more compact than 'Fruitlandii' and doesn't have the fast and massive growth. I have never grown this new form, but I understand that it is superior in most uses to the 'Fruitlandii.'

An important note: The Elaeagnus or Russian Olive widely used in colder climates is a much different plant from the above. It is deciduous and has little, if any, use in our landscapes. I see them crop up, every now and then, on landscape plans and in advertisements. In my opinion it is best to avoid them.

EUONYMUS
Euonymus sp.

Let us examine the Euonymus as a group before taking up the individual species and cultivars. This is a large group which ranges in size from medium-size shrubs to dwarf prostrate and climbing plants. There are a number of variegated and colorful leaf forms and some with other rare characteristics.

Most of the Euonymus, however, are *very* susceptible to Euonymus Scale, which can ruin your plantings unless you control it carefully. This pest certainly reduces the desire to plant a Euonymus, for who really wants that kind of bother? There are times, however, when the variegated or colorful leaves or the climbing habit produces exactly the desired effect in a particular spot and its use is required. The control of the scale is almost complete with the use of a systemic insecticide along with the fertilizer as it is applied each spring.

FORTUNEI EUONYMUS GROUP
Euonymus Fortunei

This group of Euonymus is interesting because of its habit of making a 6-foot-high shrub which is easily maintained at a height of 3 to 5 feet by regular spring pruning. In addition, however, the plant has runners which, if left unpruned, may climb as high as 20 feet. This combination of a bushy shrub with back runners is ideal for a foundation plant against a wall.

There are also some prostrate and semi-prostrate forms of this specie which are used as ground covers. The best of these is *Euonymus Fortunei radicans,* which has deep purple-red fall and winter color.

There are a number of widely-grown cultivars of *Euonymus Fortunei.* All of them are susceptible to scale, though not as severely as the *Euonymus japonica* group, which I will discuss farther on.

Colorata Euonymus
Euonymus Fortunei cv. 'Colorata'

Zone: 4
Natural Height: 3 feet
Best Use: Bank and ground cover shrub
Habit: Semi-prostrate to prostrate
Light: Full sun to part shade
Points of Interest: Low-growing and spreading; deep purple winter color
Problems: Euonymus Scale may be a problem

Emerald Gaity Euonymus
Euonymus Fortunei cv. 'Emerald Gaity'

Zone: 5
Natural Height: 5 feet with back runners to twenty feet
Best Use: Foundation plant against a wall
Habit: Round and bushy with trailing runners which climb
Light: Full sun to light shade
Points of Interest: Green foliage with a white margin
Problems: Euonymus scale may be a problem

Sarcoxie Euonymus
Euonymus Fortunei cv. 'Sarcoxie'

Zone: 5
Natural Height: 6 to 8 feet
Best Use: Foundation plant against walls
Habit: Bushy with back runners
Light: Full sun to light shade
Points of Interest: Glossy deep green foliage
Problems: Euonymus Scale may be a problem

JAPANESE EUONYMUS
Euonymus japonica

The Japanese Euonymus is a widely-grown plant commonly found in nurseries. There are many interesting variegated forms. I have found that they are too susceptible to Euonymus Scale to be used except on rare occasions. The cultivar *Euonymus japonica* 'Minima' is sometimes referred to as boxleaf Euonymus and sold for planters and edges. It is a beautiful plant but it may be devastated by scale unless you give it constant treatments with systemic insecticides. In a unique spot it may be worth the effort.

SOUTHERN EUONYMUS
Euonymus kiautschovica (formerly *Euonymus patens*)

This Euonymus is generally referred to as *Euonymus patens* and has been grown in the South for many years. It seems to be the most resistant to Euonymus Scale.

Elaeagnus

Cleyera

Boxleaf Euonymus

Southern Euonymus

Emerald Gaity Euonymus in the Spring

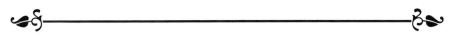

There are plantings in my father's garden which have survived for almost 50 years without cold or scale damage.

Upon occasion, *Euonymus kiautschovica* will be semi-evergreen, especially when temperatures range below 0° F. This rare occurrence should not detract from its use since it is a fine evergreen with attractive seeds in the fall which adds a great deal to foundation and background plantings. The best of the cultivars is 'Manhattan.'

Manhattan Euonymus
Euonymus kiautschovica cv. 'Manhattan'

Zone: 5 (fully evergreen in zone 7)
Natural Height: 10 feet
Best Use: Foundation and background plantings
Habit: Dense and upright
Light: Full sun to part shade
Points of Interest: Dense, strong growth and fall orange fruit
Problems: Should be kept trimmed to remain dense

The cultivar 'Manhattan' is the best of the Southern Euonymus, with better color and more dense growth than the specie. It is relatively fast-growing, an advantage when you are seeking quick backgrounds or foundation covers.

GARDENIA or CAPE JASMINE
Gardenia jasminoides

The South would not be the South without the Gardenia. This rich evergreen shrub is covered with delightful waxy white flowers with such intense fragrance that the garden is filled with perfumed air when they bloom.

Unfortunately the Gardenia is not dependably hardy through much of the South. Zero weather will kill the plant back severely, and long periods of frozen ground will cause the leaves to "burn" and the plant to be unsightly with a covering of brown leaves. Never use a Gardenia as a foundation planting in areas where the temperature will reach 10° F. They will certainly be unattractive.

My suggestion is to keep these facts in mind but plant the Gardenia anyway whenever the right location is available. Gardenias are best used in places which get morning sun and are protected from the hot winter southern sun. Never plant them in the afternoon sun or in a western exposure where they are in the path of the cold west winds which devastate us in the winter. A good location would be a walled or shrub-enclosed garden with plenty of protection from the hot mid-day and afternoon sun in winter. The warm wall of an enclosed garden is ideal.

The cultivars are confusing. I grew up in the time when there were considered to be two forms of this plant, *Gardenia fortunei* and *Gardenia grandiflora*. My observation (and general nursery opinion) was that the *G. fortunei* blossomed on both old and new wood, while the *G. grandiflora* blossomed on old wood only. The blossoms of *G. fortunei* were smaller, had petals which did not overlap but were separate, and were set from May through July; the blossoms of *G. grandiflora* were larger, had overlapping petals, and were set primarily in May and June. Now, however, there seems to be lack of agreement on these facts.

The *Gardenia fortunei*, now listed as *Gardenia jasminoides* var. *Fortuniana*, is not described with the above qualities. The *G. jasminoides* cv. 'Mystery' seems to be the closest to what I knew as *G. grandiflora*. Perhaps we have lost the old "Everblooming Gardenia" which my father used to sell with great relish. One well-known nursery lists a *Gardenia jasminoides* cv. 'Veitchii' which is ever-blooming. The 'Veitchii' of my early days was an entirely different plant, blooming only in May and June.

I apologize for leaving you confused! I am, too.

Gardenias have some other problems besides the possibility of cold damage. The worst is White Fly, which is most often noticed by the sooty fungus which results, leaving a black film on the top sides of the leaves. Killing the White Fly and washing the leaves with a strong stream of water will remove the unsightly sooty film.

Gardenias are acid-loving plants which must be grown in peaty soil that has good moisture-holding capacity but also drains well. They do poorly in wet, soggy soil. Always fertilize with an Azalea-Camellia fertilizer which will give the acidity needed to help prevent chlorosis.

Many gardeners in the upper South who have been unsuccessful growing these plants outdoors now grow them in large tubs which are placed in greenhouses or solariums for the winter. The Gardenia is well worth the effort.

In nurseries today you will find the cultivars listed below, including the prostrate form which I call "Creeping Gardenia."

AUGUST BEAUTY GARDENIA
Gardenia jasminoides cv. 'August Beauty'

Zone: 8
Natural Height: 5 feet
Best Use: Specimen shrub in a protected place
Habit: Bushy and rounded
Light: Morning sun with light afternoon shade
Points of Interest: Waxy white flowers over a long period
Problems: Susceptible to cold damage and White Fly

The leaves of 'August Beauty' are smaller and narrower than the specie; therefore the plant never looks as dense.

MYSTERY GARDENIA
Gardenia jasminoides cv. 'Mystery'

Zone: 8
Natural Height: 8 feet
Best Use: Specimen shrub in a protected place
Habit: Bushy and compact
Light: Morning sun with light afternoon shade
Points of Interest: Large, waxy white flowers in May and June; large, glossy green leaves
Problems: Susceptible to cold damage and White Fly

'Mystery' is an excellent cultivar with large, glossy green leaves and large waxy flowers.

CREEPING GARDENIA
Gardenia jasminoides cv. 'Radicans'

Zone:　8
Natural Height:　2 feet, but also spreading
Best Use:　Pots or planters in very protected places and in greenhouses and
　　solariums
Habit:　Low and spreading
Light:　Light shade to full sun
Points of Interest:　Glossy foliage with small waxy white flowers of excellent
　　fragrance
Problems:　Cold damage and White Fly

HOLLY
Ilex sp.

Hollies are one of our most important groups of plant material. The broadleaf ever-green hollies comprise a large portion of all our landscaping material. There are very low-growing forms of holly, forms which grow into trees, and every size be-tween. There are hollies with small leaves like Boxwood and those with large leaves like Gardenias. Somewhere in this vast group of plants is probably one or more which you will want to use.

Hollies are acid-loving plants and should be grown in rich, high-humus soil which drains well. Holly decline, especially prevalent in the boxleaf hollies, is often caused by tight, sticky soil, which invites attacks of root rot disease. Put foundation plantings in beds which have been well-prepared with additions of peat moss and bark to improve the structure. Plant on the shallow side with the top of the ball of earth exposed and no soil or mulch around the stems.

A Leaf Miner is a problem on some of the American Hollies and should be controlled with a good systemic insecticide. Otherwise hollies are relatively free of insect and disease problems, though scale may occur on Chinese Hollies which are planted in a poor location and are not growing well. Healthy holly plants seem to overcome almost all their problems on their own.

Hollies are dioecious: that is, there are both male and female plants. Unless specified, the cultivars are female plants with a capacity to set berries. There is some concern whether each planting of hollies should have a male plant amongst it. But since hollies are bee-pollinated, and since bees have a working radius of one mile from the hive, I have seldom seen plants which were not naturally getting pollen from male plants in the woods. If setting berries is a problem, you may add a male cultivar or have the berries set parthogenetically with a spray of an artificial growth regulator. A light mist of these materials will "set" the berries, which then will have visual beauty but will not be viable.

Not all holly berries are desirable. The fruit of the black-berried types generally detracts from the beauty of the shrub; therefore many people prefer sterile or male cultivars of these over the fertile female types. Black-berried plants also often set their fruit very heavily, resulting in a yellowing or lightening of the foliage color when the fruit are mature. This is particularly true of some of the Japanese Hollies.

I will treat the hollies here in groups: first, American Hollies, *Ilex opaca*; second, Chinese Hollies, *Ilex cornuta*; third, Japanese Hollies, *Ilex crenata*; fourth, Yaupon Hollies, *Ilex vomitoria*; and fifth, hybrid hollies, which constitute a large number of our newer cultivars.

AMERICAN HOLLY
Ilex opaca

Zone: 6
Natural Height: 40 to 50 feet
Best Use: As large specimens or as background or screen plants
Habit: Upright and pyramidal
Light: Moderate shade to full sun
Points of Interest: Heavy foliage and bright red berries
Problems: Holly Leaf Miner

The American Holly is more of a tree than a shrub and has been included with the other trees. A huge American Holly tree is a beautiful sight. However, it takes many, many years for it to reach its maximum height of 30 to 50 feet. Thus it may be used as a background shrub quite well. It is frequently used in screens or hedges, or as a large specimen plant.

The American Holly is a stiff, heavy, pyramidally-shaped plant. Its main attraction is its evergreen nature and its large numbers of bright red berries in the fall and winter.

Make background or screen plantings with the long-range size of the plants in mind. They are most attractive when allowed to form without too much interference from each other or other plants so that the pyramidal shape is preserved. Plant them at least 10 feet apart.

The cultivar 'Greenleaf' is not as stiff as some of the older cultivated forms like 'Croonenburg.' It is somewhat faster-growing, and responds well to shearing.

The cultivar 'Mascula' is a male tree for planting where pollination is a problem.

CHINESE HOLLY
Ilex cornuta

Zone: 6
Natural Height: 15 feet or more
Best Use: Large specimen or background shrub
Habit: Compact and rounded
Light: Sun to part shade
Points of Interest: Very spiny foliage and large red berries
Problems: Scale on occasion but few other problems

The parent Chinese Holly is widely used like its cultivars. Its dark green foliage has heavy spines and five points and is a perfect background for the large red berries. It is tighter and more rounded than the Burford Holly but much more "sticky" in appearance. It is best used in large spaces and is beautiful as a specimen plant. Never place it in a restricted area because heavy pruning ruins its shape.

Leaf Miner is a problem on
many hollies.

Carissa Holly

Chinese Hollies are
extremely spiny.

Dwarf Chinese Holly

A large Chinese Holly
trained into tree form
by the author

203

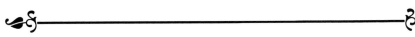

The Chinese Holly cultivars are some of our best evergreens. Most of the cultivars grow large and should be planted with the proper spacing in mind. Choose the smaller-growing cultivars for restricted areas and low foundation plantings. Most berry well, and their bright red berries against the dark, glossy green foliage in fall and winter are a sight to behold.

They seem to be alternate bearers; that is, they berry heavily one year and lightly the next. This may be alleviated to a certain extent by removing the old berries before they blossom in the spring. The Cedar Waxwing birds will often do this for you as they return from farther South each spring. I have seen them strip a huge Burford Holly in a couple of days. Rather than interrupt their feast, you should invite them to stay since this removal will help set next year's crop.

Chinese Hollies have few problems and are ideally suited to the South. If scale does show up on the backs of the leaves, a systemic insecticide spray will easily control it. Keep your plants well-fertilized with an acid fertilizer to keep them growing well and to prevent chlorosis.

It is possible to prune them severely but you should avoid the need by using the correct size cultivar for the location. Do heavy pruning in the early spring and trim for shape after the new growth hardens up. Berries are set on wood grown the previous season, so severe pruning or removal of last summer's growth will reduce or even eliminate your berry crop.

There are many cultivars found in nurseries. The following are the ones I have found adapt well to most home plantings here in the South. They are listed in order of natural size.

LOW-GROWING CHINESE HOLLIES
(3 to 6 feet)

Carissa Holly
Ilex cornuta cv. 'Carissa'

Zone: 7
Natural Height: 5 feet, but easily kept to 3 feet
Best Use: Low foundation plantings and heavy borders
Habit: Compact and rounded
Light: Full sun to part shade
Points of Interest: Compact form, glossy green foliage
Problems: Few, if any

Carissa Holly is the most compact of the Chinese Hollies. It has only one spine at the end of the leaf and is less sticky-looking than the Dwarf Chinese Holly. It is easily kept in bounds and is suitable for plantings in front of low windows.

Dwarf Chinese Holly
Ilex cornuta cv. 'Rotunda'

Zone: 6
Natural Height: 6 feet but may be kept easily at 4 feet
Best Use: Low foundation plantings
Habit: Compact and rounded

Light: Full sun to part shade
Points of Interest: Low growth and spiny leaves; good rich green color when kept fertilized
Problems: Few, if any

This older compact form of Chinese Holly is widely used for low foundation plants. I greatly prefer the Carissa Holly, which is similar in habit but less spiny.

MEDIUM-GROWING CHINESE HOLLIES
(6 to 10 feet)

Dwarf Burford Holly
Ilex cornuta cv. 'Burfordii Nana'

Zone: 7
Natural Height: 10 feet
Best Use: Background shrubs or medium-height foundation plantings
Habit: Rounded to upright; easily pruned
Light: Full sun to moderate shade
Points of Interest: Red berries; glossy green leaves with a single terminal spine
Problems: Few, if any

The Dwarf Burford Holly is a much more usable shrub in most home landscapes than the parent, Burford Holly, which grows so large. Its only possible detraction is that its berry set is not as heavy as its parent's. It is certainly one of our most worthwhile upright plants.

Needle Point Holly
Ilex cornuta cv. 'Needle Point'

Zone: 7
Natural Height: 10 feet
Best Use: In corner plantings, as background shrubs, and as specimens
Habit: Upright
Light: Sun to part shade
Points of Interest: Narrow, glossy green foliage with a single spine
Problems: Few, if any

Needle Point Holly is a most attractive upright shrub with a tighter, more upright habit than Dwarf Burford Holly.

LARGE-GROWING CHINESE HOLLIES
(Over 10 feet)

Burford Holly
Ilex cornuta cv. 'Burfordii'

Zone: 7
Natural Height: 15 feet or more
Best Use: Large background shrubs or screens
Habit: Very heavy and upright; when unpruned, it tends to be pendulous

Light: Sun to moderate shade
Points of Interest: Glossy, single-spined foliage and large red berries
Problems: Scale on occasion but little else

The Burford Holly was found in Westview Cemetery in Atlanta and has become one of the most used plants in our landscape. One must remember its size listing or see pictures of the parent to appreciate how large this plant will grow. Too often it is placed in restricted areas and must be butchered each year to be kept in bounds. Plant the Burford Holly where it has plenty of room. Otherwise use one of the other cultivars of Chinese Holly which has a single spine and good berries.

JAPANESE HOLLY or BOXLEAF HOLLY
Ilex crenata

These small-leaf, dark-berried hollies make some of our finest foundation plantings. There are a tremendous number of cultivars available for almost any desired height.

These hollies generally have dense, compact forms, small boxwood-like foliage, and relatively few of the problems which plague the true boxwood. They are used mainly as foundation plants for all needed heights as well as border plants, as tub plants, and in planters.

They are mainly globe-shaped or rounded and their habit is tight and dense. Unfortunately, not enough thought and study is given to the mature heights which the cultivars attain. The very popular *Ilex crenata* 'Rotundifolia,' for instance, is often used under windows only three or four feet above the ground. The plant may naturally grow to as much as 10 feet and the resulting necessary constant pruning ruins its growth and beauty. The use of *Ilex crenata* 'Helleri' or *Ilex crenata* 'Green Luster' would give the same boxwood effect without the need for butchering the plant to keep it from covering the windows.

The dark berries are more of a detriment than an asset. The fertile female cultivars have a tendency to set berries heavily, causing a lightening of the foliage color during berry time. *Ilex crenata* 'Convexa' is particularly prone to this, in some instances becoming quite yellow after a heavy berry-set.

The Japanese Hollies have few insect or disease problems but do have some very serious growth problems when not planted and maintained properly. Follow these rules when planting and growing these hollies:

1. Always plant in beds which have been well-prepared; never "spot plant" these hollies.
2. Plant shallowly, with the top of the ball of earth slightly above the surface of the surrounding soil.
3. Keep well-mulched but *never* allow the mulch or other plant trash to pack around the lower stems.
4. Do not overplant an area. Space plants properly when you plant. Overcrowding may be disastrous.
5. Fertilize each spring with a complete evergreen fertilizer with a slow-release nitrogen. Keep plants growing well.
6. Revitalize older plantings by adding organic materials to the soil and working it in the front and back of the shrub line.

7. Choose the right-sized cultivar for the spot. Annual butchering will make the plants unsightly and cause a general decline in their vigor.
8. Do not let the plants become top-heavy. Prune so the top is more narrow than the bottom.

Treat your Japanese Hollies correctly and they will last for many years.

There are a tremendous number of fine cultivars. The following are ones which I have used or dealt with for many years and recommend highly. There may be others which you find in your local plant outlet. If you decide on their use, be sure to check all the major characteristics first.

LOW-GROWING JAPANESE HOLLIES

Heller's Holly
Ilex crenata cv. 'Helleri'

Zone: 5 to 6
Natural Height: 3 feet
Best Use: Very low foundation or border plant; may also be grown as a mass shrub for ground or bank covers
Habit: Low, compact, and mounded
Light: Full sun to moderate shade
Points of Interest: Dense compact mound form
Problems: Die-out may occur if mulch, soil, or plant trash accumulates around stems

The Heller's Holly is perhaps our most often used low-growing mound plant. It stays compact and dense with little pruning or shaping. I have seen some reach a height of 4 feet in good locations, but they generally mound at about 3 feet. Some listings refer to the height as 18 inches, but beware: Under good conditions this figure is definitely low. They also spread to a greater degree than they grow in height. Plant them at least 3 feet apart so that the individual plants may be seen rather than growing them into a mass of unidentifiable plants.

Green Luster Holly
Ilex crenata cv. 'Green Luster'

Zone: 5 to 6
Natural Height: 4 feet
Best Use: Low foundation plantings
Habit: Dense and low-growing
Light: Sun to moderate shade
Points of Interest: Compact habit and dark green foliage
Problems: Few, if any

This Japanese Holly is a little larger than *Ilex crenata* 'Helleri' but is mainly noteworthy for its deeper green and larger flat leaves. It holds its color in the winter better than 'Helleri,' which has a tendency to lose its darker color in cold weather.

A similar but slightly taller cultivar, *I. c.* 'Hoogendorn,' is reportedly excellent as a 4-foot foundation plant, though I have not grown it myself.

MEDIUM-SIZED JAPANESE HOLLIES

Compacta Holly
Ilex crenata cv. 'Compacta'

Zone: 6
Natural Height: 6 feet
Best Use: Foundation plantings, low background shrubs
Habit: Rounded and compact
Light: Full sun to moderate shade
Points of Interest: Dense, compact, rounded form and dark green foliage
Problems: None

This is one of the best of all the small-leaf hollies. It is far superior to *I. c.* 'Rotundifolia,' *I. c.* 'Hetzi,' and *I. c.* 'Convexa,' which is also known as *I. c.* 'Bullata.'

Compacta Holly needs little pruning and has excellent form and very rich, dark, lustrous green foliage.

TALL-GROWING JAPANESE HOLLIES

Rotundifolia Holly
Ilex crenata cv. 'Rotundifolia'

Zone: 5 or 6
Natural Height: 8 to 10 feet
Best Use: Background or medium hedges
Habit: Upright to oval
Light: Full sun to moderate shade
Points of Interest: Dark green foliage; taller growth
Problems: Tends to die out when crowded or overpruned

Rotundifolia Holly is a much-used, perhaps over-used, Japanese Holly. It is often placed in too restricted a location, where extreme butchering becomes necessary. But it is a fine plant when pruned lightly and used where it can grow to its natural height.

The Japanese Hollies listed above are all in the rounded to oval forms. There are others which have special forms: the 'Cherokee' cultivar of *Ilex crenata* is column form; and the 'Highlander' and 'Petite Point' cultivars are pyramid form.

YAUPON HOLLY or CASSINE HOLLY.
Ilex vomitoria

The Yaupon Hollies are native to the South and provide another group of fine small-leaf hollies. Unlike the Japanese Hollies, however, the berries are red though not all cultivars set berries heavily. Though they are not always completely evergreen in extreme cold, these few times are not enough to discourage the use of these fine plants.

Dwarf Burford Holly

Regular Burford Holly

Heller's Holly

Compacta Holly

Weeping Yaupon Holly

209

Dwarf Yaupon Holly
Ilex vomitoria cv. 'Nana'

Zone: 7
Natural Height: 5 feet (easily pruned to 3 feet)
Best Use: Low foundation plants
Habit: Dense, compact, and mound-shaped
Light: Sun to moderate shade
Points of Interest: Dense evergreen habit, low growth
Problems: May drop its leaves at about 0° F.

The Dwarf Yaupon Holly is similar in appearance to Heller's Holly and is sometimes confused with the latter plant. Although the habit is much the same, the Dwarf Yaupon tends to be slightly taller and spreads more. It will spread twice as far as its height. Plant them at least 4 feet apart so that the mound shape can be seen when the plants are older. The Yaupon Hollies have gray stems while the Japanese Hollies have tan ones (this is a good way to distinguish between the two).

There is a similar cultivar, **'Schilling's Dwarf,'** which is often seen in nurseries. It is more open and upright, showing more of the woody part of the plant, and I think it is less attractive.

Weeping Yaupon Holly
Ilex vomitoria cv. 'Pendula'

Zone: 7
Natural Height: 12 feet (at least that's the tallest I've seen)
Best Use: Specimen plants
Habit: Upright with stiffly drooping branches
Light: Full sun to moderate shade
Points of Interest: Arching, pendulous habit; red berries
Problems: Few, if any

The Weeping Yaupon Holly is a rather strange, stiff plant which, out of the proper place, has little value. Properly placed, however, its effect can be outstanding. Use it wisely and you will have a lovely plant.

MISCELLANEOUS HYBRID HOLLIES
Ilex × cultivars

There are many excellent hollies which are natural or planned hybrids. These make up a large part of our tall background and screening plants, but they also are excellent specimens for focal points and points of interest in the landscape. The following are some of the best for the South:

Foster's Holly
Ilex × *attenuata* cv. 'Fosteri'

Zone: 6
Natural Height: 12 to 15 feet
Best Use: Specimen shrub or small tree

Habit: Upright and pyramidal
Light: Sun to moderate shade
Points of Interest: Deep green, shiny foliage and bright red berries
Problems: Few, if any

Foster's Holly is an extraordinary pyramid-shaped shrub. The leaves are smaller than the American Holly and much darker and glossy. The berries are profusely-set and brightest red. Foster's Holly will produce a full plant from "tip to toe" or it may be pruned to make a true shade tree.

Nellie R. Stevens Holly
Ilex × cv. 'Nellie R. Stevens'

Zone: 6
Natural Height: 15 feet or more
Best Use: Specimen plant, background shrub, or screen
Habit: Upright and pyramidal
Light: Full sun to moderate shade
Points of Interest: Beautiful foliage and red berries
Problems: Few, if any

This is one of my favorite tall evergreen plants. It is reputed to be a cross between the Chinese Holly and the beautiful English Holly. Like the parent Chinese Holly, it does very well in the South, although the other parent, the English Holly, does poorly.

The foliage is a deep, rich, glossy green and the heavily-set berries are bright red. The leaf color is lighter than that of Foster's Holly but the leaf is larger. The plant is somewhat more dense.

Beware when you purchase this plant. Many nursery growers seem to misunderstand its true growth character and butcher it badly when it is young, trying to make an oval or round bushy plant for foundation plantings. This pruning completely ruins the future shape and you should avoid these plants. Choose Nellie R. Stevens Hollies which have a strong central trunk and are beginning to show their pyramid shape.

Savannah Holly
Ilex × *attenuata* cv. 'Savannah'

Zone: 7
Natural Height: 20 feet
Best Use: Heavy background shrub or small tree; excellent for tall screens
Habit: Upright with a moderately pyramidal form
Light: Full sun to rather heavy shade (if fertilized)
Points of Interest: Rapid growth, good foliage, and red berries
Problems: Should be kept fertilized to keep its dark green color

The Savannah Holly is perhaps our best broadleaf evergreen for fast, tall screens. It grows very rapidly and takes less pruning to keep its tight habit than do the similar hybrids, East Palatka Holly and Howard's Holly. Its only real problem is that its foliage is not as dark green in poor conditions as some of the others used for the same purpose. A little fertilizer will, however, overcome this problem and the resulting tighter, thicker form will make the fertilizing effort worthwhile.

Foster's Holly as a topiary

The correct way to grow Foster's Holly

Foster's Holly improperly used as a round bush

Nellie R. Stevens Holly grown in its
natural way

Foster's Holly trying to restore its
correct shape

Nellie R. Stevens Holly improperly made
into a hedge

The berry set is very heavy, and Savannah Hollies are extraordinarily beautiful in winter. They seem to bear heavily every year. Another outstanding characteristic is their ability to grow nicely in more shade than many other hollies. When you use Savannah Hollies in wooded areas where trees compete for nutrients, fertilize them well each year or the plants will tend to be more open and have less than the desired amount of foliage.

❦ LAUREL or ENGLISH LAUREL
Prunus Laurocerasus

These laurels are much different from our native Cherry Laurel and, fortunately for us, they are being grown and used more and more. They are strictly for the mid and upper South, growing poorly in the heat of the Coastal Plain.

The best group is the strapleaf type, of which there are two, 'Otto Luyken' and 'Schipkaensis,' which have wide usage through our region. Another, 'Zabeliana,' does well in the mountains and farther north, but is not as suited to the mid-South in general.

OTTO LUYKEN LAUREL
Prunus laurocerasus cv. 'Otto Luyken'

Zone: 7
Natural Height: 6 feet
Best Use: As a medium-sized foundation plant and for low hedges
Habit: Dense, moderately upright, and thick; slightly vase-shaped when young
Light: Sun to moderate shade
Points of Interest: Deep green foliage, clean healthy growth
Problems: Shot Hole Fungus on occasion

My wife Betsy loves this plant, and I do, too. It has every quality which a foundation plant should have: it grows well and survives cold, poor soil, general abuse, and years of life without pruning; and it does not have the disease problems which plague Red Tip Photinia and the insect problems which plague the ligustrums and privets.

Otto Luyken Laurel is the best of the English Laurels because it is more compact and cleaner-growing than Schipkaensis Laurel and better suited to our heat than Zabeliana Laurel.

Its natural height may be 6 feet but it can be kept to 4 feet with little effort. The Shot Hole Fungus which riddles Schipkaensis will attack on occasion but never to the extent where serious spraying is required.

❦ LIGUSTRUM or PRIVET
Ligustrum sp.

A Privet is a Privet, whether large-leafed or small.
Unless the last plant on earth, I'll not use it at all.

The Ligustrums or privets are much overused "cheapo" plants which should be avoided. They have no features which I have ever discovered that would justify choosing them over many other excellent broadleaf evergreens.

The variegated privet, *Ligustrum sinense* 'Variegata,' is suddenly extremely popular and much planted by builders. Remember, it is *not* evergreen.

❧ LEATHERLEAF MAHONIA
Mahonia Bealei

Zone: 7
Natural Height: 7 feet
Best Use: Deep shade as a specimen plant
Habit: Upright, multi-stemmed, and somewhat stalky
Light: Light to deep shade (never in the sun)
Points of Interest: Heavy, holly-like foliage; very early yellow flowers in clusters, followed by hanging clusters of blue berries in the spring
Problems: Does very poorly in tight soil and too much sun

This Mahonia is widely-grown as one of our more beautiful and unusual deep shade plants. Its habit as well as its foliage is stiff, and it must be used in the right place in order to be attractive. It has a tendency to become stalky and leggy, but this is not unattractive if the plant is allowed to continue its growth and naturally arch over to form a rather unusual large, bulky plant which produces numbers of very early yellow flowers followed by huge clusters of blue berries.

Pruning should be restricted to the removal of weak or unsightly stalks. Cutting back a stem is not advisable because new shoots will seldom appear.

❧ HEAVENLY BAMBOO or COMMON NANDINA
Nandina domestica

Zone: 7
Natural Height: 8 feet
Best Use: Foundation corner plantings and shade specimen plants
Habit: Upright with many heavy stems
Light: Part sun to shade
Points of Interest: Fine foliage, clusters of red berries, red fall and winter leaf color
Problems: May get stalky and top-heavy, but pruning is easy

In the 1920's and 1930's this plant was so popular and overused (like Abelia) that many people have since rejected it as being "too common." Overuse does not diminish its many excellent qualities, not the least of which is its ability to survive and be attractive in heavy shade.

The problem which many face with Nandina is that they fail to keep it growing well with annual applications of a shrub formula fertilizer and seldom prune it properly. Nandinas should be pruned each spring by removing about one-third of

Berries of Savannah Holly

Savannah Holly

Leatherleaf Mahonia

Otto Luyken Laurel

Common Nandina

Berries on a Common Nandina

the tallest and oldest stalks. These *must* be cut off at the base of the plant. This forces younger growth all the time and prevents the plant from becoming top-heavy and leggy.

There are some dwarf forms which have a place in Japanese and other miniature gardens as well as in really restrictive areas. The dwarf cultivars are: **'Harbour Dwarf,' 'Gulf Stream,'** and **'Nana Purpurea.'** Frankly, however, none of them has the wonderful foliage texture and growth habit which makes the parent so spectacular.

PYRACANTHA or FIRETHORN
Pyracantha sp.

Zone: 7 for the red-berried cultivars, 6 for the orange-berried cultivars
Natural Height: 10 feet or more
Best Use: Espaliers, heavy background plants, and free-standing specimens
Habit: Upright and open
Light: Full sun to light shade
Points of Interest: Huge clusters of berries
Problems: Wild growth and Lacebugs

Pyracantha was overused in the past, especially as a wall espalier, and is not as popular now as it used to be. When properly planted, it can be a magnificent espalier if the gardener will work at keeping it properly pruned and trained. It will not perform as you like with a once-a-year effort.

However, the Pyracantha has other uses which make it well worthwhile, for there are few plants with such huge numbers of red berries in the fall. Use the Pyracantha as a free-standing specimen shrub, or as a hedge. It can even be pruned into a beautiful small tree.

A little-known fact is that the berries make a fabulous jelly found, as far as I know, only on the South Carolina coast.

Though pruning is essential to have a tidy plant, overpruning will remove the wood on which the berries are formed. The flowers are set on wood of the previous season, which is sometimes difficult to discern, so it is best to prune at the time of flowering. This way you may leave on the plant as many flowers as you want to become fruit. You may trim the long shoots until mid-June without disturbing the following year's berries, but leave some of this wood on the plant when trimming. In other words, do not remove all the spring growth, but merely cut it back, leaving some to harden up and form flower buds.

The devastating Lacebug is quite easily controlled by the use of one of the systemic insecticides as a spray when these pests first appear.

There are many very good cultivars. Since the general characteristics are the same as the specie, I will merely list them as follows: Red-berried Pyracantha cultivars include *Pyracantha Koidzumii* cv. **'Victory,'** *Pyracantha* × cv. **'Wonderberry,'** and *Pyracantha Fortuneana* cv. **'Graberi.'** Cultivars with orange-red berries include *Pyracantha coccinea* cv. **'Kasan'** and *Pyracantha* × cv. **'Mojave.'** A cultivar with orange berries is *Pyracantha coccinea* cv. **'Lalandei.'**

There are a number of less-important Pyracanthas (the variegated, dwarf, and mound types) which might fit a spot in your garden but which are not generally used since there are better plants which give the same effect.

RED TIP PHOTINIA
Photinia × Fraseri

The Red Tip Photinia is as much overused as the Ligustrums were in the 1930's and 1940's. In fact, it rapidly replaced these plants as "the plant to use." However, I think you should avoid it like the plague because it has its own plague: a disastrous leaf spot. This unfortunate problem makes the Red Tip an expensive plant to have, because constant spraying is an absolute necessity. Why bother with a plant which requires such continuous attention? There are too many other plants which will fill the bill to use one which takes so much effort. Leave this one alone!

TEA OLIVE
Osmanthus sp.

The Tea Olive or Sweet Olive, as it is called in the deep South, is an absolutely fantastic plant in the areas where it may be grown. The Southern Tea Olive, *Osmanthus fragrans*, is actually rather tender in most of the South. The Hardy Tea Olive, *Osmanthus × Fortunei*, does well throughout the South except in the higher altitudes; the Holly Leaf Tea Olive, *Osmanthus heterophyllus*, does quite well as far north as Washington, D.C.

Some of the Tea Olives resemble hollies, but they are quickly identifiable by their foliage pattern, which is opposite instead of alternate like the hollies. The really spectacular feature of this group of plants is the wonderful fragrance of the flowers. A garden is filled with loveliness when the Tea Olives blossom.

HARDY TEA OLIVE
Osmanthus × Fortunei

Zone: 8
Natural Height: 15 feet
Best Use: Tall hedges, screens, background shrubs, and specimens
Habit: Upright and broadly oval
Light: Sun to part shade
Points of Interest: Heavy dense shrub, excellent foliage, and fragrant flowers
Problems: Susceptible to die-back at 0° F.

This Tea Olive is more dependably hardy than *Osmanthus fragrans*, but unfortunately its flowers do not have the extreme fragrance, though they are pleasant enough. Since it is large-growing, use it with its size in mind.

SOUTHERN TEA OLIVE OR SWEET OLIVE
Osmanthus fragrans

Zone: 8
Natural Height: 15 feet
Best Use: Specimen shrub
Habit: Upright and oval
Light: Sun to moderate shade
Points of Interest: Very fragrant flowers
Problems: Hardiness at below 10° F.

Although the true Southern Tea Olive is not dependably hardy in most of the mid-South, it is such an extraordinary shrub that you should use it if you can find a warm, protected place. It seldom attains its natural height in our gardens because cold will nip back the growth as it gets out of the protected area. But it is surely worth a try! The fragrance is too outstanding to miss. The orange-flowered form, *Osmanthus fragrans* Forma *aurantiacus,* has fall flowers which seem to be the most fragrant of all.

HOLLY LEAF TEA OLIVE
Osmanthus heterophyllus

Zone: 7
Natural Height: 15 feet
Best Use: Screens, hedges, and specimen plants
Habit: Upright
Light: Sun to moderate shade
Points of Interest: Excellent foliage and fragrant flowers
Problems: Keep growing healthily with spring fertilizings

The Holly Leaf Tea Olive is the best for the upper part of our region where it is more dependably hardy than *Osmanthus × Fortunei.* The smaller, holly-like leaves are densely set and the upright shrub is ideal for backgrounds and hedges. The fragrance is not as intense as the other two described above, but it is well worth using in areas where cold would limit use of the others. 'Gulf Tide' is a cultivar which I have grown and found to be a more dense plant.

 YUCCA
Yucca sp.

These very stiff and unusual plants are native to the South. In their place I suppose they are all right, but they just aren't my kinds of plants. They do have beautiful heads of white flowers and do grow in very bad soil, but they just aren't very pretty. They can also be dangerous to children playing, and more than once a child has received a rather serious injury by falling into them. They should never be planted around pools or other areas where children play.

SPANISH BAYONET
Yucca aloifolia

Zone: 7
Natural Height: 25 feet (after many, many years)
Best Use: Specimen plant
Habit: Strange
Light: Sun
Points of Interest: Unusual growth, white flowers
Problems: Can be dangerous when fallen into

This is the stiffer and taller of the two Yuccas. It seldom reaches its mature height in our area and normally is seen at about 8 feet.

ADAM'S NEEDLE
Yucca filamentosa

Zone: 6
Natural Height: 15 feet
Best Use: Specimen plant
Habit: Strange
Light: Full sun
Points of Interest: Large flower cluster, stiff growth
Problems: May be dangerous

The Adam's Needle is only slightly less stiff than the Spanish Bayonet. It is distinguishable by the threads which peel off the outer edge of the leaves. It is, like the other, a dry-land plant which may be used where few other plants will grow. However, it is also over-used and placed too often where there are better and less dangerous plants.

Marginally Hardy Broadleaf Evergreens for Protected Spots

Because of their preeminence, I have already listed the Gardenia or Cape Jasmine and the Tea Olive in spite of the fact that they are not dependably hardy in all parts of the South. The following plants also have such good qualities that they should be considered in special protected spots like walled gardens. Remember, our coldest winds are from the northwest, and if you can block them, together with the hot southern sun, you can often allow marginally hardy plants to survive.

Banana Shrub
Michelia Figo

Often listed, incorrectly, as Magnolia fuscata. It grows as a large rounded shrub with unusual creamy yellow, banana-shaped flowers with a smell of banana.

Loquat
Eriobotrya japonica

Listed as hardy in Zone 7 but few of these survive in the open in the mid-South. However, if you choose the spot carefully, so that you shield the plant from the cold west wind and you avoid the hot sun drying the leaves when the ground is frozen, the plant does beautifully.

Strawberry or Pineapple Guava
Feijoa Sellowiana

An interesting and beautiful shrub with gray-green foliage and beautiful flowers which are white with purple insides and red stamens. It must be given extreme protection.

Coniferous Evergreens (Needle Plants)

The many excellent broadleaf evergreens discussed above make up the bulk of our plantings in the South. Farther north they are not grown nearly as successfully; many cannot be grown at all. Newcomers to our region may know the next group of plants we shall discuss, the coniferous evergreens, since they make up the bulk of plantings in Zones 3, 4, and 5. The coniferous evergreens are to the colder areas what the broadleaf evergreens are to the South: the major landscaping material.

Not too many years ago, the Irish Juniper and the Golden Arborvitae were as common in our Southern landscapes as Burford Holly and Cleyera are today. One of my first jobs working as a boy in our nursery was pulling the bags of the Bagworm off five acres of Golden Arborvitae. There were many of this type of plant grown in our nursery in the 1940's: Chamaecyperus, Arborvitae, Juniper, and Cedar, to name a few. They were soon to be replaced, however, by the more indigenous broadleaf evergreens and the many wonderful broadleaf evergreens from the Orient, especially Japan. Enthusiasm for the conifers waned and not many were used until the low-growing junipers began to be produced in huge quantities a few years ago.

As we Americans seem to overdo everything, we have overused many great broadleaf evergreens, resulting in the boredom with which many are received in our landscapes today. Now interest is going back to the conifers with huge, mass plantings of prostrate junipers on banks all over the South. When looking at these masses of junipers, one yearns for a bank of prostrate Cotoneaster. Diversity and contrast make interesting design.

Since the coniferous evergreens have an entirely different texture, they do provide an interesting contrast when used with the broadleaf evergreens. The major groups of coniferous evergreens most usable in our landscapes are Arborvitae; Hemlock; Juniper; and Yew, including true yews, Southern Yew, and Plum Yew. I will also discuss a few other coniferous evergreens that may be classed as shrubs.

❧ ARBORVITAE
Thuja sp. and Platycladus sp.

After spending so many hot days picking Bagworm houses off our arborvitaes, I didn't have much appreciation for this plant until I saw in Ireland the gorgeous golden arborvitaes which had grown into trees. On one clear day, the golden tips against a blue sky was one of the most beautiful sights I have ever seen. It certainly gave me a new insight into this plant so often used in the days of my youth.

The arborvitaes are distinguishable by their flattened, single-planed branchlets which are lined horizontally (*Thuja*) or vertically (*Platycladus*) to form a compact plant which is usually round or pyramid-shaped. Their growth habit makes them impossible to prune drastically, so it is very important to choose the right size plant for the spot. Once they are overgrown, the only answer is removal, for pruning back will ruin the plant.

Bagworms on arborvitaes are a severe problem if left untended; hiding in their bags, these worms will quickly ruin an arborvitae. A systemic spray or soil application will control this pest, but don't wait too late to apply the material. Arborvitaes are not very good at replacing totally denuded areas with new growth at that point.

Attacks of spider mites may also be severe. Investigate any discoloration immediately and start a spray program using Kelthane. Any problem which causes defoliation can be disastrous to these plants. Once an area has been denuded, resprouting is difficult, if not impossible.

There are two general groups of arborvitaes used in the South: (1) the American arborvitae, *Thuja occidentalis*, which is generally tall-growing (though low-growing globe cultivars are available); and (2) the Oriental arborvitae, *Platycladus orientalis*, which may be lower-growing if you choose the right cultivar.

All the arborvitaes listed are hardy in Zone 5.

LOWER-GROWING ARBORVITAE
(*Under 6 feet*)

GLOBE ARBORVITAE
Thuja occidentalis cv. 'Globosa'

Globe Arborvitae grows as wide as it is tall and makes a dense, rounded, compact plant with deep, rich green color.

BERCKMANS' GOLDEN ARBORVITAE
Platycladus orientalis cv. 'Berckmannii'
(*Platycladus orientalis* cv. 'Aurea Nana')

This is my "Bagworm plant" and one with which I have many good as well as bad memories. The golden tips give a wonderful contrast to the dark green of surrounding shrubs. It has a compact, globe habit of growth but will grow to 6 feet with much time.

Banana Shrub

Canadian Hemlock

Red Tip Photinia

Adam's Needle

Berkmans' Golden Arborvitae will
grow large.

TALLER-GROWING ARBORVITAE
(Over 12 feet)

DARK GREEN AMERICAN ARBORVITAE
Thuja occidentalis cv. 'Nigra'

This is said to be the best of all the upright, tall American arborvitaes. Its winter color remains rich, dark green. It is upright, slightly pyramidally shaped, and excellent for hedges. This one may be sheared for shaping.

TECHNY ARBORVITAE
Thuja occidentalis cv. 'Techny'

Techny is an excellent upright arborvitae for tall hedges or screens. It is very hardy and will withstand the cold of the Southern uplands.

❧ HEMLOCK
Tsuga canadensis

The Hemlock was discussed in detail in Chapter 4, Shade Trees. However, it should be mentioned also with shrubs since it makes an excellent screening plant or tall hedge. It stands pruning well and will remain as a healthy vigorous, tall hedge for many years. (See Canadian Hemlock under Shade Trees.)

❧ JUNIPER
Juniperus sp.

Please don't be upset if I tell you that I really do not like junipers. I have tried and tried, and have been lectured constantly on their good qualities by my good friend and radio-television partner, Kathy Henderson. I still don't really feel that they are the kind of plant which I want around.

If people didn't have different opinions, how would poor farm land ever be sold? So I am listing several junipers for you to take a look at.

Junipers are not problem-free by any means. Poor soil and growing conditions cause huge brown areas and die-out to develop. Spider mites are always a threat. Any time sudden discoloration occurs, check the plants and treat them with Kelthane immediately. They are also susceptible to the bagworms mentioned with the arborvitaes.

Keep junipers growing well with good soil preparation in the beginning (work the soil on those banks before planting) and continued fertilizing each year with a good shrub fertilizer.

Because the classification and taxonomy of this genus is extremely difficult, I will list the junipers here according to use, rather than in botanical groups. I am told that even the great L. H. Bailey had trouble devising good keys to the identification of the junipers.

PROSTRATE JUNIPERS

Blue Rug Juniper
Juniperus horizontalis cv. 'Wiltonii'

This might possibly be an exception to my rule of not liking junipers. Blue Rug clings to the ground, and its branches with their bluish cast make an unusual and interesting plant.

Bar Harbor Juniper
Juniperus horizontalis cv. 'Bar Harbor'

This is a prostrate form which has bluish-silver foliage in the growing season and a plum color in winter.

Prince of Wales Juniper
Juniperus horizontalis cv. 'Prince of Wales'

This is one of the better bank-cover junipers because it takes hot sun and retains a rich green color.

Procumbens Juniper
Juniperus chinensis cv. 'Procumbens'

This is a prostrate juniper which spreads well, and is good for banks and other areas where conditions are not good. There is also a variegated form.

MOUNDING JUNIPERS

These are often classed as ground covers, but I really feel that they are mound shrubs rather than creepy-crawlies.

Shore Juniper
Juniperus conferta

Though listed by some as prostrate, in my experience this juniper should be thought of as more of a mound. It has silver-green foliage.

Blue Pacific Juniper
Juniperus conferta cv. 'Blue Pacific'

This has the same growth habit as Shore Juniper, but is a bit more compact and mounding. The color is retained during hot periods and it will take more sun and poorer conditions.

TALLER-SPREADING JUNIPERS

The best example of this group is the Pfitzer Juniper, which has retained its popularity because of its unusual "bat wing" growth habit.

Spiny Greek Juniper

Yew

Blue Pacific Juniper

Pfitzer Juniper

Prince of Wales Juniper

Screen of White Pine

Pfitzer Juniper
Juniperus chinensis cv. 'Pfitzerana'

I have seen old Pfitzers which reached five feet in height and eight feet in width. They are good for their location but don't plant near your steps; when they are older and really spread, they will be all over the place and pruning gives them a butchered look. The color is gray-green.

Newer, better types within the *Juniperus chinensis* group include **Compact Pfitzer**, which is lower-growing and has a little lighter color; and **Nick's Compact**, which is much less "bat wing" and easier to keep as a compact plant.

VASE-SHAPED JUNIPERS

There are a number of these junipers which grow upward like a vase rather than spreading like the Pfitzer types.

Blue Vase Juniper
Juniperus chinensis cv. 'Blaauw'

This is a very dense grower in the vase group with a bluish color.

Sea Green Juniper
Juniperus chinensis cv. 'Sea Green'

This vase-shaped juniper grows to over 5 feet with a spread to 8 feet, and is noted for its rich green color.

UPRIGHT JUNIPERS

These are the column-shaped and tall, oval-growing junipers. Included with this group should be the Red Cedars which were described under Shade Trees. Upright junipers are for corner plantings, specimens, and background shrubs.

Spartan Juniper
Juniperus chinensis cv. 'Spartan'

This is a tall-growing, pyramidally-formed juniper with rich green color.

Spiny Greek Juniper
Juniperus. excelsa cv. 'Stricta'

This is an older, well-known Greek Juniper which grows rapidly and should be used with caution in restricted areas. Don't let the dense form fool you; it does grow rather large.

❦ YEW
Cephalotaxus sp., Podocarpus sp., and *Taxus sp.*

These are my favorite coniferous evergreens. The needle size and shape, the rich color, and the habit of growth makes them ideal.

The true *Taxus* is the most used foundation plant in the North. It is a pity that our long growing season and heat make very few of them suitable for us. However, the Plum Yew, *Cephalotaxus*, makes a good substitute.

The Southern Yew, *Podocarpus*, must be used with caution because it can be tender in many of our winters. Protected from cold, it is gorgeous.

PLUM YEW
Cephalotaxus Harringtonia var. *drupacea*

The Plum Yew is looser, under most circumstances, than the true Yew, *Taxus*. However, it will give the same effect when tightly trimmed. This variety, *drupacea*, has a more arching habit and is excellent for very shaded areas.

SOUTHERN YEW
Podocarpus macrophyllus

The cold winters of 1983 and 1984 killed so many *Podocarpus* in the South that many have not been replanted. I hope that the effect of these winter cold aberrations will soon wear off and this fine plant will creep northward into our area once again. It is a magnificent plant which should always be set out with weather in mind. Plant *Podocarpus* in a place protected from the cold northwestern wind and hot southern sun.

The variety *Maki* has the most densely-set needles and upright growth habit. This makes it a better substitute for the true *Taxus*.

YEW
Taxus × *media*

Many of the *Taxus* are grown as ornamental landscape plants. Since they make up such a large percentage of plants used farther north, there are hundreds of cultivars from which to choose. Unfortunately, most are not happy in the South. The *Taxus* × *media* group seems to be the most adaptable. In colder, sun-protected locations, these will do fairly well. Do not use them as basic foundation material, but rather as specimen plants for contrast. This way the removal of one unhappy plant will not ruin years of work. In just the right spot, the true Yew can add a great deal to your plantings.

Other Coniferous Evergreens

LEYLAND CYPRESS
× *Cupressocyparis Leylandii*

This is an excellent hybrid between False Cypress, *Chamaecyparis*, and the true Cypress, *Cupressus*, which is one of our finest upright hedging or screening plants. It grows rapidly, stays dense and thick, is easily pruned, and resists most insects and diseases.

I think the natural growth habit is much more beautiful than the more commonly-used sheared form. The dark green color gives an excellent background and the needle texture offers good contrast to broadleaf evergreen shrubs used in front of or among these plants. The softness of the foliage texture is far superior to Virginia Cedar, and if allowed to remain natural, it is among our most handsome plants.

Watch your spacing when you purchase and plant smaller plants. They do grow large and should be spaced at least 6 feet and preferably 8 feet apart. Even though they will look skimpy when first planted, you will bless me for this advice in only a few years.

There is a cultivar, 'Naylor's Blue,' with very blue-gray foliage which makes an even greater contrast with our broadleaf evergreens. However, I much prefer the rich green of the specie except in most unusual situations.

FALSE CYPRESS
Chamaecyparis sp.

The False Cypress has been almost abandoned as landscape material for the South. Though it was once widely used, the years have taken their toll with disastrous freezes and insect attacks. There is a hard-to-find specie, the **Lawson Cypress** (*Chamaecyparis Lawsoniana*), which has survived for many years in some gardens, though many were damaged severely in 1984 and 1985.

The beauty of this plant is its rich green color, far superior to the Leyland Cypress, and the interesting needles. It is one of the important timber trees of the West, growing to 100 feet. However, in our area don't ever expect to see that height; 30 feet is a monster for a single lifetime. It is very slow-growing! Use it as a large specimen or screening shrub rather than as a tree.

There are many ornamental forms. When purchasing this plant, it is best to choose one of the many named cultivars rather than the specie.

WHITE PINE
Pinus Strobus

This plant was described in detail in Chapter 4, Shade Trees, because that is its rightful class. However, it responds to shearing very well and will remain a full shrub-like screening plant when properly handled. Plant them at least 8 feet apart and start pruning when the plants are young. The best time to prune pines is in the spring, and the best way is by pruning the "candles" or growth tips before the new needles are formed. This will keep the new growth bushy and thick.

Broadleaf and Coniferous Evergreens for Special Situations

The plants which I have described above make up the best of the general landscaping shrubs for Southern homes and gardens. They are the easiest to grow and are the ones that should be used in all except very special situations.

There are several other shrubs which have some unusual attributes but have very limited use in our landscapes because of their special growth requirements. I have seen these growing well in the South but only when planted in the absolutely ideal location or when the conditions for growth have been altered significantly so that they may thrive.

With some, like Pampas Grass, the problem is not conditions for growth but rather the proper landscaping use. Pampas Grass needs precisely the right spot; improperly used it can be an eyesore.

You may run across the plants listed below and perhaps others which may sound phenomenal. Be careful! Before planting, be sure that you understand the special requirements of these plants. Without knowledge and understanding, you may end up with a completely inappropriate plant in your landscape.

DAPHNE
Daphne odora

A trip to England or even Oregon makes you want a Daphne. I love this plant but have never been successful with it. Others have. They are to be envied!

The only Daphne with any possible chance in the South is this one, *Daphne odora*. The extraordinarily fragrant white to purplish flowers come during the first warming spell of the spring in huge clusters, lying on the terminal leaves.

Daphne must be treated with kid gloves by preparing the bed with plenty of humus to hold moisture, which it needs, but also plenty of perlite to let the excess moisture move through and away.

The cultivar, **'Aureo-Marginata,'** is said to be hardier than the specie and has deep crimson buds opening to white flowers. The leaves have an edge of yellow.

PAMPAS GRASS
Cortaderia Selloana

There is a huge clump of Pampas Grass not far from me, and its beauty prompts me to list this plant with shrubs instead of perennials. Perhaps it should be in neither since it is a grass, but its specimen use makes me put it here. In the right spot, Pampas Grass is an outstanding specimen plant. Out of the center of its huge clump of grass-like foliage arise a number of stalks producing the beautiful silky heads that are the reason for planting it. Since there are male and female plants, insist on having the female because you will be disappointed with the less attractive male flowers.

The man down the road cuts his clump severely each year, being careful not to injure the fleshy crown. In mild winters some green will remain in the clump, but in severe winters all the foliage will turn brown. Fertilize each spring with a lawn fertilizer.

❦ SANTOLINA
Santolina sp.

The Santolina are plants for very dry conditions, both in the soil and in the air. They cannot survive in heavy, damp soil or in muggy, humid spots. However, they will thrive in planters or pots on hot terraces. They are seldom satisfactory planted in the ground.

Plant Santolina in well-prepared soil with liberal amounts of sand or perlite to increase drainage. Soil mixtures with ground bark are preferred over those with peat moss since bark retains less moisture. Using gravel in the bottom of the pots or planters is also helpful. Plant where there is plenty of air movement.

There are two species available: *Santolina Chamaecyparissus*, which is gray, and *Santolina virens*, which is green.

❦ SERISSA
Serissa foetida

I am indebted to the late Jim Patterson of Putney, Georgia, a well-known nursery-man, for introducing this plant to me. It is a delightful semi-evergreen to full evergreen shrub (depending on how cold it gets) with large numbers of small white flowers covering the plant in the spring.

Serissa will grow only to about 2 or 3 feet, making a small upright plant which is excellent in part shade in a rock garden. It is not for every rockery, but it is a nice plant for those who want something different.

Serissa

Azaleas in the spring garden

AZALEAS, CAMELLIAS, RHODODENDRONS, AND OTHER EVERGREEN FLOWERING SHRUBS

On our walk through a well-landscaped home garden, we have seen the shade trees, which are needed to give structure, and the flowering trees, which provide embellishments. We have seen how the broadleaf and coniferous evergreens have been added to the structure to give form to the landscape. Now we come to the jewels of the garden which make the landscape of the South unique.

Perhaps our ideal is the waves of color seen along the paths of the South's great public gardens like Middleton, Magnolia, Bellingrath, and Callaway. But more likely each of us has seen a small garden, like most of ours, a garden with a "bracelet" or "necklace" containing a ruby or diamond, a garden with a touch of gold. The flowering shrubs are these jewels. We dress the garden with Azaleas, Camellias, and Rhododendrons, and with the deciduous flowering shrubs, which include Forsythia, Hydrangea, Viburnum, and many others.

Of all these jewels and embellishments, the group which is evergreen *and* blooms profusely is the one so uniquely Southern. Our jewels, as a group, are better here than perhaps anywhere else, and we should make the most of them.

Hino-Crimson

AZALEAS FOR THE SOUTH

Azaleas have been a part of the Southern garden almost from our Colonial beginnings. The great gardens of Charleston are made beautiful by these wonderful plants. Throughout our history and even today, they form one of the most important parts of our spectacular spring show.

The study of Azaleas is a course unto itself; this must be only an attempt to introduce them to you. Fred Galle in his marvelous book, *Azaleas*, Timber Press, 1985, has defined them so that you can understand the relationship of one group to another and from whence each has come. Others have spelled out, in detail, the design aspects of their use. I shall give you some of my own experiences with this marvelous group of plants.

The classification of Azaleas is complex. They are a sub-species of the genus *Rhododendron* and may be found in that section of many publications. They have been hybridized for such a long period of time that the botanical names are greatly confused. I deviate from the usual manner of listing both the common and the botanical name by giving only the common name in this case; otherwise we might be terribly confused, because the common name may not always be the correct one in scientific publications. The name I use will be the common name found in nurseries where you will be purchasing your plants.

The size description may also be confusing, as many of you have already found out when you planted the "dwarf" Hinodegiri and had it cover your picture window.

Azaleas are easily transplanted and may be planted all year except in the hottest months. This gives a decided advantage when trying to match colors. There are many strains of some of the old familiar varieties, each having a slightly different color. Therefore, it is most important to match the colors before purchasing plants for intermingling among established groups.

CHOOSING AZALEAS FOR THE SOUTHERN GARDEN

In general you will find several groups in nurseries:

Gumpo Azaleas are very dwarf mound-shaped plants which are not unlike a Helleri Holly. They bloom in May and are considered a Satsuki Azalea, which means fifth month. They are consistently hardy for us.

Kurume Azaleas are generally compact-growing and small-leaved with small to medium flowers, some "hose and hose" or one tube of petals inside another. The flowers are generally in clusters. They are consistently hardy throughout our area.

Indian Azaleas have medium-size leaves on moderately tall-growing plants. The flowers are large and borne individually or several in clusters. There may be a hardiness problem with the Indian Azaleas in much of our area.

Glen Dale Azaleas include a wide range of hybrids which have the compact nature of the Kurumes. In most cases, the flowers are larger. The Glen Dale Azaleas have colors unavailable in many other well-known types. They are consistently hardy for us.

You will undoubtedly run into many other evergreen groups such as Gable Hybrids, Ghent Hybrids, Kaempferi Hybrids, Knap Hill Hybrids, and others which may provide colors and bloom characteristics which are just right for you. Don't be afraid to use them. Be careful, however, to consider their mature size so that you will not place them incorrectly.

There are also a number of deciduous hybrid azaleas which have been grown in the South with moderate success. The Exbury Hybrids and Mollis Hybrids are chief among these. Use them with caution because our hot summers and cold winters are not altogether to their liking.

The native Azaleas which are so noticeable in the South's woods and forests can be a wonderful addition to the more natural areas in your landscape. They are mainly deciduous and are seldom used in the more formal areas of the landscape. This is a pity, for these are spectacular when in flower and will add a great deal of color to evergreen-backed shrub beds and borders.

Wild Honeysuckle (*Azalea periclymenoides*)

The following native Azaleas are the most commonly seen in the wild and in gardens:

- Wild Honeysuckle, *Rhododendron periclymenoides* (*R. nudiflorum*)— Pink
- Flame Azalea, *Rhododendron calendulaceum* —Flame-red
- Florida Flame Azalea, *Rhododendron austrinum* —Yellow to orange. This is found farther south than the others.

Unfortunately, these are not a standard item for most nursery growers, so you will not find a large selection of these in nurseries. However, they are a wonderful addition to garden plantings when obtainable.

There are thousands of named varieties of Azaleas, and it is impossible to give a list which would be anywhere near complete. The chart lists ones with which I have had good experience, and which, in most instances, can be easily found in local nurseries.

Flame Azalea

Florida Flame Azalea

Hinodegiri

Okinanishiki

Palestrina

Pink Pearl

Snow

Southern Charm

OUR MOST IMPORTANT AZALEAS

	SIZE	CLASS	COLOR	BLOOM TIME
BUCCANEER	Medium/Tall	Glen Dale	Orange-Red	Midseason
CHRISTMAS CHEER	Medium	Kurume	Red	Midseason
COPPERMAN	Medium	Glen Dale	Orange-Red	Late
COPPERMAN	Medium	Glen Dale	Orange-Red	Midseason/Late
CORAL BELL	Medium	Kurume	Clear Pink	Midseason
CORALIE	Medium/Tall	Glen Dale	Salmon-Red	Midseason
DELAWARE VALLEY WHITE	Medium/Compact	Indian	White	Early/Midseason
FASHION	Medium	Glen Dale	Orange	Midseason/Late
FASHION	Medium	Glen Dale	Orange-Red	Midseason/Late
FESTIVE	Medium/Tall	Glen Dale	White/Pink Stripe	Early
FORMOSA	Tall	Indian	Purple	Midseason
GEORGE L. TABER	Tall	Indian	Orchid/Pink	Midseason/Late
GLACIER	Medium	Glen Dale	White	Midseason
GLACIER	Medium	Glen Dale	White	Midseason/Late
GUMPO	Low/Mound	Satsuki	White	Late
GUMPO VARIEGATED	Low/Mound	Satsuki	White/Pink	Late
HEXE	Low	Kaempferi	Brick Red	Midseason

NAME	SIZE	CLASS	COLOR	BLOOM TIME
HINO CRIMSON	Low/Medium	Kurume	Red	Midseason
HINODEGIRI	Medium	Kurume	Watermelon Red	Midseason
KINTAIYO	Medium	Kurume	White/Edged Orange	Midseason
MACRANTHA	Medium	Satsuki	Pink	Late
MASSASOIT	Low/Medium	Kurume	Dark Red	Midseason
MOTHERS DAY	Low/Medium	Kurume	Clear Red	Midseason
OKINANISHIKI	Low	Macrantha	Orange-Red	Late
PALESTRINA	Medium	Kaempferi	White/Green Blotch	Midseason
PINK GUMPO	Low/Mound	Satsuki	Light Pink	Late
PINK PEARL	Medium/Tall	Kurume	Double Pink	Early/Midseason
PRIDE OF MOBILE	Medium/Tall	Indian	Watermelon Pink	Midseason
SNOW	Low/Medium	Kurume	White H & H	Midseason
SOUTHERN CHARM	Medium/Tall	Indian	Deep Pink	Early
STEWARTSONIANUM	Medium	Gable Hybrid	Orange-Red	Midseason
TREASURE	Medium	Glen Dale	White/Pink Blotch	Midseason/Late
TREASURE	Medium	Glen Dale	White	Midseason
WAKAEBISU	Low/Medium	Macrantha	Salmon Pink	Late

Delaware Valley White

Formosa

George L. Taber

Copperman

Coral Bells

Hexe

Glacier

GROWING AZALEAS SUCCESSFULLY

It is most important to understand the culture of Azaleas. They are plants which prefer some shade and do very poorly in hot sun. If they do not have good soil conditions, they will do badly and become a blight rather than a jewel in your landscape. Follow these rules:

1. Prepare a deep bed for planting Azaleas. Spot planting will result in poor growth over the years. Mix in liberal amounts of humus and per-lite for drainage. Azaleas require moisture but must not have "wet feet" or be grown in tight, sticky soil.
2. Plant Azaleas shallowly. Leave the top of the ball of earth an inch above the surrounding soil. Never cover the top of the ball with soil.
3. Container-grown Azaleas should have their roots pulled away from the ball so that they will penetrate the new soil rather than remain grow-ing in the old ball.
4. Mulch Azaleas each year but *never* allow the mulch to bunch up against the stems. Leave a saucer around the stems. Crown rooting occurs when damp mulch accumulates against the lower stems. This is one of the major causes of Azalea decline.
5. Prune Azaleas in the spring immediately after they blossom. The new buds will start forming in early July, so do no pruning, not even trim-ming, after early June.
6. Watch for insects. Lacebugs may be disastrous. Check the foliage for any discoloration. If leaves change color or become mottled, look for brown spots on the undersides of the leaves. If you see these spots, look for a small lacy-winged insect which will be feeding. Start spray-ing immediately with Malathion or other recommended insecticides.
7. Azaleas are plants of acid soils. High pH (above 6.2) will cause chloro-sis or yellowing between the veins. Always use an acid fertilizer to prevent this condition. Spray with an iron compound to correct chloro-sis, and correct the pH with aluminum sulfate.

Chlorosis on Azaleas

Azalea Leaf Gall

8. The swollen, rather horrible-looking leaves which may appear in the late spring are the result of an infection of Azalea Leaf Gall. Pick these leaves off and burn them to prevent further infection. Spraying helps very little.
9. Azaleas in a decline can be rejuvenated by the following actions:
   a. Clean the bed thoroughly. Remove all the mulch and plant trash from the area.
   b. Inspect the center of the plants to determine if soil has washed in and covered the stems. If it has, pull the excess soil away and uncover the stems. Do this when it is cool and when there is plenty of rain.
   c. Work the bed outside the root zone and add peat moss, ground bark, and cottonseed meal.
   d. Prune the plants back in the early spring even though you will lose the bloom.
   e. Fertilize with an Azalea fertilizer just as the new growth starts.
10. Never lime areas near Azaleas. This alkaline material can damage your plants severely.

AZALEAS IN THE LANDSCAPE

Azaleas have a wide range of uses in the landscape. Remember, though, that they should not be planted in full sun and that they do best when protected against the cold winter winds from the northwest. Otherwise use them in foundation plantings, as background shrubs, as border plants, and naturalized in wooded areas. Wherever you use them, use the same planting techniques. Always plant in deep well-prepared beds, or the results will be disappointing, if not tomorrow, then a few years from now.

They are excellent in groups of colors rather than planted alone. With Azaleas, the more the merrier. Try some of the new colors and different flower forms, and never forget the Satsuki or fifth-month Azaleas which are so great to have when all the others are gone.

Camellia japonica, our most beautiful shrub

CAMELLIAS FOR THE SOUTH

The Camellia has everything: fantastic shape, form, foliage, and flowers. This group of plants is certainly the prize of the Southern garden.

These are plants of the Orient which have been brought to us first through Europe, where they arrived from the Orient in sailing ships in the 16th century. Wherever they have been taken, they have been prized as some of the most beautiful plants of the garden.

The genus contains a number of different species including the commercial tea plant, *Camellia sinensis,* from whose young leaves are made the world's most universal drink and the largest source of caffeine. This is the same plant which has been generally known as *Thea sinensis* (or *T. Bohea*) until the taxonomists placed it correctly in the genus Camellia.

There are two commonly-grown Camellia species in the South, mainly in Zones 7 and 8. The first, *Camellia japonica,* is one of the prize garden plants of the world with its relatively large, glossy green leaves and large, perfect blossoms which are found in several forms and many colors, often with various types of variegation. The blooms come in the fall, winter, or early spring depending upon the variety. The *Camellia japonica* is mainly relegated to Zone 8.

The second, *Camellia sasanqua,* has smaller leaves, grows more profusely, and has smaller flowers. The blossoms appear in the fall and, in rare instances, in the winter. The *Camellia sasanqua* may be grown in much of Zone 7, being somewhat hardier than *Camellia japonica.*

The *Camellia japonica* is mainly a garden specimen plant, prized for its unique beauty as a shrub and for its flowers. The habit of growth is upright

Common Tea Plant, *Camellia sinensis*

Camellia sasangua gives a mass of fall blooms.

to oval. It can be used in all sorts of landscape situations from foundation plants to hedges and screens.

The *Camellia sasanqua* is used as a large foundation plant, background shrub, hedge, or specimen plant. It is also suited to the art of espalier and is easy to train in this form on walls.

These are by no means the only Camellias grown in gardens. The *Camellia reticulata* is widely-grown in California but is not consistently hardy in the South, being relegated mainly to Zone 9. The common tea plant, *Camellia sinensis*, is also an attractive garden plant. It is not consistently hardy for most of us, but my father has had one growing for many years at his home near Lovejoy, south of Atlanta. Both *C. sinensis* and *C. reticulata*, like the group of marginally hardy shrubs mentioned before, can be fun to try in protected places. The object of such a venture is to have something out of the ordinary to add spice to the walled garden.

CAMELLIA HARDINESS

The severe freezes of Thanksgiving 1950 and Christmas 1983 caused severe damage to both our Camellia species. Such aberrations in our weather should not deter us from growing these magnificent plants. However, severe, early freezes like these do point out some significant lessons about handling marginally-hardy plants which continue growing late in the season.

My friend Karl Johnson of Bloomingdale, Georgia, theorized that these plants, being native to regions of a latitude much farther north, were genetically attuned to slowing growth as the days became shorter. Since they are native to a region where the days are shorter much earlier than ours, their growth continues much later here. Being in more active growth at this later time makes them more susceptible to early freezes here in the South. Perhaps this is true. Certainly it reinforces the need to do everything possible to prevent fall growth.

Neither of the Camellia species should ever be fertilized after early July nor planted in extremely cold exposures, especially where they will be subjected to the cold northwesterly winds. There seems to be some innate difference in the hardiness of *Camellia japonica*. Herme, Jarvis Red, Lady Clare, Kumasaka, and Adolph Audusson are a few Camellias which seem to have greater hardiness. The *Camellia sasanquas* are generally much hardier than the run-of-the-mill *C. japonicas*, and it takes a real "rip-snorter" freeze, like Christmas 1983, to damage them.

Cold Damage to Camellia Blossoms

There are *Camellia japonicas* which blossom in the fall, others in the winter, and others in the spring. In most of the South it is best to rely mainly on those which blossom in the fall (early varieties) and those which blossom in the spring (late varieties). These generally escape bud or flower damage. Among winter-blossoming varieties (mid-season), you should restrict yourself to those singles and semi-doubles which will open quickly during periods of winter warmth. The most damaging conditions occur when the weather is warm for several days and the buds begin to show color, and then a sudden hard freeze ruins them as they are breaking open. The singles and semi-doubles will open quickly enough to avoid this problem, whereas the fully double varieties will certainly have bud damage. A good combination is to have double varieties for the fall and spring, and single and semi-double varieties for the winter.

Treating Camellia buds with gibberellic acid hastens their development and may be used to get winter varieties to blossom earlier than normal, before hard freezes might ruin the flowers. "Gibbing" may also increase the size of the flower whose bud has been treated.

The *Camellia sasanquas* have fewer blossom problems due to cold since they bloom mainly in the fall. The winter varieties also seem to fare better than the larger-flowered *C. japonicas* since they open more quickly. I have noted, over the years, some problem with the ever-popular *C. sasanqua*, Mino-no-yuki, which has double white blossoms in December of most years. These flowers are often hurt by those early freezes.

Avoid the fully double mid-season cultivars like this Prof. Sargent.

CAMELLIA JAPONICA CULTIVARS FOR THE SOUTH

There are a thousand or so named cultivars of the *Camellia japonica*. Seldom these days will you find over a dozen or so at any general nursery; most of the rest are propagated by Camellia enthusiasts themselves. The following is a list of cultivars which I am familiar with and which should do well throughout our area.

NAME	FORM	COLOR	BLOOM SEASON
*ADOLPHE AUDUSSON	Large Formal, Semi-Double	Deep Red	Midseason
*ALTHAEAFLORA	Semi-Double	Rose-Red	Late
BETTY SHEFFIELD SUPREME	Peony Form	White Edged Rose	Midseason
C. M. WILSON	Anemone	Pink	Early/Midseason
*DAIKAGURA	Peony	Rose and White	Very Early
ELEGANS (CHANDLER)	Large Anemone	Pink with White Petaloids	Early/Midseason
*FLAME	Semi-Double	Flame Red	Late
*GUILIO NUCCIO	Semi-Double	Rose-Pink	Midseason
HERME	Large Semi-Double	Light Pink, White Edge	Midseason
*HIGH HAT	Peony	Light Pink	Early
*KUMASAKA	Peony Form	Rose-Red	Late
*LADY CLARE	Semi-Double	Deep Pink to Red	Early/Midseason
*MAGNOLIAEFLORA	Semi-Double, Formal	Light Pink	Early/Midseason
MATHOTIANA	Formal Double	Red	Midseason/Late
MATHOTIANA VARIEGATED	Formal Double	Red-Marbled White	Midseason/Late
MORNING GLOW	Double	White	Midseason/Late
PINK PERFECTION	Formal Double	Pink	Early/Midseason
POPE PIUS	Formal Double	Cherry Red	Midseason
*REV. JOHN G. DRAYTON	Loose Peony	Deep Pink	Midseason/Late
SAWADA'S DREAM	Formal Double	White Tinged Pink	Midseason
**SEPTEMBER MORN	Semi-Double	White to Pale Pink	Very Early
*WHITE EMPRESS	Semi-Double	White	Early/Midseason

*Buds are apparently very hardy and will survive the coldest weather without damage.
**Blossoms before cold weather so cold damage to buds is no problem.
Note: Pink Perfection has the habit of setting several buds in a cluster. Disbudding all but the central bud will help bring about early opening and will reduce bud damage due to cold.

Pink Perfection

Magnoliaeflora

Lady Clare

Pope Pius

White Empress

The Pick of The List

The following are some of the best Camellia japonica cultivars for the whole season:

FALL-BLOOMING

C. M. Wilson
Daikagura
Magnoliaeflora
September Morn

EARLY WINTER AND WINTER

Adolphe Audusson
Guilio Nuccio
Lady Clare
White Empress

LATE WINTER AND SPRING

Flame
Kumasaka
Rev. John G. Drayton

CAMELLIA JAPONICAS FOR SPECIAL PROTECTED PLACES

Betty Sheffield Supreme
Mathotiana
Mathotiana Variegated
Pope Pius
Sawada's Dream

CAMELLIA SASANQUA CULTIVARS FOR THE SOUTH

The general nursery list of *Camellia sasanquas* is far shorter than that of the *C. japonicas*. I have grown many of these in my life, and the following should do well for you.

NAME	FORM	COLOR	BLOOM SEASON
AUTUMN MOON	Semi-Double	White	Fall
CLEOPATRA	Semi-Double	Rose	Fall
GULF BREEZE	Single	Light Pink	Fall
HANA-JIMAN	Semi-Double	White with Pink Edge	Fall
MAIDEN'S BLUSH	Semi-Double	Light Pink	Early Fall
MINE-NO-YUKI	Semi-Double Peony	White	Late Fall
SETSUGEKKA	Semi-Double	White with Pink Petal Tip	Early Fall
SHISHI-GASHIRA	Semi-Double to Double	Red	Late Fall
SHOWA-NO-SAKAE	Semi-Double	Rose-Pink with White Marble	Fall
SPARKLING BURGUNDY	Peony	Red	Fall to Early Winter

Cleopatra

Mine-no-yuki

Setsugekka

CAMELLIA SASANQUAS FOR SPECIAL PURPOSES

ESPALIERS	HEDGING	LOW FOUNDATIONS
Mine-No-Yuki	Cleopatra	Shishi-Gashira
Setsugekka	Maiden's Blush	Showa-No-Sakae

Choose a loose-form plant to espalier.

GROWING CAMELLIAS IN THE SOUTH

The choice of varieties is of extreme importance, as we have seen above. Perhaps these choices are first and foremost, but they are not exclusive. Location and planting techniques are also most important.

It is generally thought that Camellias should be grown in part shade, but I have seen fine specimens doing well in full sun when the soil conditions were right. The key, as with Azaleas, is to choose the right soil conditions first, or make the soil right with the use of amendments so that the roots will penetrate deeply where they are better protected from cold damage, and where they can find moisture during hot dry periods of the summer and cold, freezing conditions in the winter.

It is best to choose the ideal conditions of part shade and loose, high-humus, well-drained soil which has a slightly acid condition (a pH of about 6.0). Protection from the cold northwesterly winter winds and the hot southern winter sun will also aid in keeping plants growing year after year.

Plant Camellias in well-prepared areas or beds which have been tilled deeply. Peat moss and ground bark should be added, and if the soil is poorly-drained or tight and sticky, it is also helpful to add drainage material, like perlite.

Plant Camellias any time that the weather is cool and there is ample moisture. The fact that most Camellias are now grown in containers has extended the planting season considerably, since the root system is not damaged when they are moved. My preference for planting time is in November and December, and in the spring from the first warming trend until Easter.

Never plant Camellias too deeply. Plant with the top of the ball of earth exposed, and do not place soil on top of the ball or allow it to wash in around the plant.

Little pruning is needed on *Camellia japonicas,* which have a fine dense habit of growth. If pruning must be done, it should be after March 1st or after the last blossoms, whichever is later. Avoid trimming *Camellia japonicas* because it produces poor new growth. If pruning is necessary, cut out branches, even small ones, back to a joint.

Camellia sasanquas should be pruned in early March. Pruning may be done easily for they are not exacting in their requirements. A light trimming after the new growth will help to keep them shapely. Since the buds are set in the mid-summer, never prune either after mid-June.

Fertilizing should be done each year, about the time recommended for pruning, in both cases. Always use an acid fertilizer and one specifically formulated for Azaleas, Camellias and Rhododendrons is best.

Mulching helps bring the plants through hot, dry periods of the summer and through cold periods in the winter. It is also good for the control of weeds which might make the area unsightly. However, never allow the mulch to pile up against the stems or trunks of the plants. Keep an open saucer-like area around the center of the plant.

Both types of Camellias may suffer from decline and become weak.

This may be caused by poor initial soil preparation, planting too deep, or depletion of the soil over the years. I have found that corrective measures can bring back the life of soil which has been depleted. The following steps are helpful in restoring a plant's vigor:

1. Rake the mulch back, well away from the plant.
2. Inspect the main stems or trunk to see if soil or old mulch has built up against them. This will cause crown-rooting and a dying-off of the lower root system. When there is plenty of moisture in the ground, pull the soil or rotted mulch away from the stems.
3. Make a series of 2-inch holes in a row in front and in back of a group of plants or around a specimen. Make the holes about 18 inches apart. Fill these holes with cottonseed meal.
4. Re-mulch with fresh mulch (I prefer pine-straw) but leave an open saucer around the main trunk or stems.

SOLVING CAMELLIA PROBLEMS

Camellias are not attacked by many pests. The Camellia or Tea Scale is perhaps the worst. A good systemic insecticide application as a spray or as a soil treatment will control this pest easily.

There is a physiological disease which may be inadvertently diagnosed as a scale. This is a corking on the leaves which cannot be rubbed off like scale can be. This condition is generally the result of poor moisture-retention in the soil during periods of very dry weather and too much moisture during wet periods. The same treatment as described above for Camellia decline should help to correct this condition.

The main disease which affects Camellias through the South is Leaf Gall. Though this is more prevalent on *C. sasanqua* than on *C. japonica*, it may be seen on both. The condition is more unsightly than it is harmful since relatively few leaves on any given plant are infected. But the sight of this cancerous-looking growth sends many new gardeners into a state of panic. Spraying is relatively ineffective; the damage is already done when the condition is seen. Also, it seems to be much worse under conditions of high humidity and early warmth in the spring. Removal and burning of the infected leaves is the best way to treat this disease.

In a few areas, the dreaded Camellia Blossom Blight may be a problem. If the blossoms are malformed with brown spotting and ultimate browning, you should be careful to remove all of them from the plant and the ground underneath. This will interrupt the cycle since next year's infection will come from the ground stage of the disease.

Though it is important to protect the more tender varieties in winter, a good cultural program and the choice of hardier varieties is more important than covering with a blanket. The best advice is to choose hardy varieties and varieties which will open quickly in the winter (see above), and keep them well-mulched. A sheet over open flowers on a frosty night should prevent damage, but at the freezing stage, nothing will help except perhaps an electric blanket or a portable greenhouse.

A beautiful hybrid Rhododendron at Floweracres, the author's childhood home

RHODODENDRONS FOR THE SOUTH

I have in my landscape some perfectly beautiful native Rhododendrons, and my father has an exquisite hybrid with extraordinary red flowers. Rhododendrons are spectacular and they can be grown through much of the South even though they are not considered to be one of our easiest-to-grow shrubs. The secret is to give them natural conditions as best you can, and use the varieties which have been grown successfully in our area.

CHOOSING RHODODENDRONS
FOR THE SOUTHERN GARDEN

There are two general groups of Rhododendrons which you will see. The first is those native Rhododendrons which are found throughout much of the upper hill country and mountains of the Southeast. These are the Rhododendrons which are large, leathery-leaved, and evergreen. This group, for purposes here, does not include the deciduous native Rhododendrons which are referred to as native Azaleas.

The second group includes mainly the hybrid Rhododendrons which have been developed all over the world. Be careful in purchasing hybrid Rhododendrons. You must be aware that many will not grow in the South satisfactorily. This group contains many of the spectacularly-colored and huge-flowering Rhododendrons which have impressed us all when seen in other areas.

The hardiness factor is most important when choosing new plants which you might not be familiar with. Though there has been substantial criticism of the hardiness rating system, it is still the best we have and is an excellent indication of any given Rhododendron's ability to stand cold. For most of our area, choose those which have a hardiness rating of H-1 and H-2 for general plantings and H-3 for special protected spots.

Some of the newer Rhododendron publications fail to list the older hardiness rating system but give survivable minimum temperatures. This has advantages but still has drawbacks, for the duration of the deep freeze will affect the depth of cold a Rhododendron can take. If possible, find the hardiness rating (H-1, etc.) and use Rhododendrons with ratings suggested above.

Native Evergreen Rhododendrons

I have found our native Rhododendrons to be some of the best for the South. There was a bed full of them already growing well when I bought my country place. Perhaps your first Rhododendron experience should be with some of these tough natives.

Rhododendron catawbiense is best grown in the mountains of our area. The lilac to lilac-rose flowers come in the late spring. In gardens of the higher elevations, this specie is spectacular. Plant it where it can grow to its large 10-foot size without crowding. The leaves are about 6 inches long.

Rhododendron maximum is another large-growing Rhododendron with leaves reaching 10 inches in length. It blossoms in the early summer with flowers of rose to light pink.

Rhododendron minus has magenta to light magenta blooms in early summer. The leaves are smaller, reaching about 5 inches in length. *R. minus* grows naturally in lower elevations than *R. catawbiense* and *R. maximum*.

Hybrid Evergreen Rhododendrons

Among the hybrids are found the most beautiful of all the Rhododendrons. The colors range the spectrum, and there are found plant sizes and habits to fit almost every garden need.

Unfortunately, most do poorly in the Southern garden. Trials and visits to extensive plantings like Callaway Gardens and Biltmore Estates will show you many which do well in the range from the piedmont (Callaway) to the mountains (Biltmore). There are also extensive private plantings in all the larger population centers like Asheville, Atlanta, Birmingham, Charlotte, Chattanooga, Knoxville, and Nashville. The wise gardener will visit such plantings and note the varieties which do well in places akin to their own location. The following is a list of some Rhododendrons which I have observed performing reasonably well in the Atlanta area:

Vulcan

Nova Zembla

NAME	*HEIGHT RANGE
WHITE	
Boule de Neige	Medium
Madame Mason	Medium
Sappho	Tall
PINK	
Cynthia	Tall
English Roseum	Medium
Mrs. Furnival	Medium
**Roseum Elegans	Tall
Scintillation	Medium
RED	
America	Medium
Nova Zembla	Medium
Trilby	Medium
Vulcan	Medium
BLUE-PURPLE	
Blue Peter	Medium
Caractacus	Medium
Purple Splendour	Medium

*Medium—4 to 6 feet; Tall—Over 6 feet
**Considered one of the best of all hybrids

Blue Peter

GROWING RHODODENDRONS IN THE SOUTH

The greatest enemies of the Rhododendron are poor soil conditions and heat. We have our share of both, so we must alter the environment to satisfy their needs. Take a walk along a stream bank in the mountains and see the magnificent Rhododendrons growing so well. Look at the way they are growing, almost on top of the ground, in soil which is filled with decomposing natural forest humus. You will notice that Rhododendrons have very shallow roots which spread widely.

This gives an idea of how to grow them in the garden. Rhododendrons must be planted in beds rather than spot planted. They require humus and acid conditions with a pH between 4.5 and 6.0. They should be protected from the cold west wind and hot winter sun. Avoid locations which are especially sunny in the winter. If you follow these steps, Rhododendrons should be happy in your garden:

1. Choose a location with moderate shade. Plantings under high pines or tall hardwood trees are good but avoid full winter sun and cold western exposure. Check the nature of the soil.
2. a. Heavy clay soil: Dig out a bed at least two feet deep. Place coarse gravel in the bottom to a depth of 4 inches.
   b. Clay soil which drains well: Work the bed deeply to at least 18 inches.
3. Make a good planting mixture with about $1/4$ peat moss, $1/4$ finely-ground bark, $1/4$ good soil, and $1/4$ perlite. Mix these ingredients on the side if following Step 2a or into the bed if following Step 2b.
4. Refill the bed, if using Step 2a, with the mixed soil.
5. In both Step 2a and 2b, the surface level of the bed should be above the surrounding soil. The bed should be crowned: that is, the center should be higher than the edges. Now make a V-shaped trench around the edge of the bed.
6. Plant each Rhododendron with the root ball half in the prepared soil in the bed. Pull loose soil upward to make a mound around each root ball, but leave a saucer-shaped depression on top of the root ball to hold water. (You may need to mix extra soil to do this.)
7. Always use an acid fertilizer on Rhododendrons.
8. If the pH is above 6.0, add aluminum sulfate to lower the pH.

Rhododendrons are mainly specialty plants and their care should not be taken lightly. These special planting procedures are important to start them growing properly and get them well-established. Then they must be pampered to keep them growing well for many years. Continue to meet their basic requirement of well-drained soil which holds enough moisture to satisfy their needs, and prevent soil and mulch from building up around the plants. Remember the way you planted them—very shallowly—and keep them that way.

Fertilize immediately after blossoming with a complete acid fertilizer (Rhododendron or Azalea-Camellia Special). A maintenance amount is sufficient. *Do not over-fertilize.* A small handful for every 3 feet of height is usually ample, but it is wise to follow the recommendations on the fertilizer bag. Use less than recommended, not more, if in doubt.

Rhododendrons need little pruning. Snapping off spent flower clusters generally provides all the pruning they need. Prune heavy branches in the early spring to remove old straggly growth. Remember, however, that in all pruning operations before the blossoms appear, you may be removing the potential flowers. Since the buds will be very large by this time, be careful when pruning early.

Rhododendrons will tell you when they need water. The leaves will first begin to droop during the hotter part of the day. If they fail to resume turgidity in the evening, soak the bed thoroughly. Do not water again until they droop again.

Most problems are related to growth and poor soil conditions. You can avoid them by following the planting suggestions above and keeping the bed from losing its humus and becoming heavy and sticky. Chlorosis—yellowing of the leaves between the veins—is caused by too-high pH and should be corrected by using acid fertilizers. Plants which have been consistently fertilized with an acid fertilizer and still show chlorosis should be treated with an iron solution and the soil treated with aluminum sulfate.

Lace Bugs will attack Rhododendrons just as they do Azaleas. Watch for the change of color of the leaves and when you see it, inspect the undersides for the brown spots of residue. Spray with Malathion or another recommended insecticide.

Spider Mites also will attack Rhododendrons. If there is any mottling of the leaves, inspect for evidence of these pests. Spray with Kelthane for control.

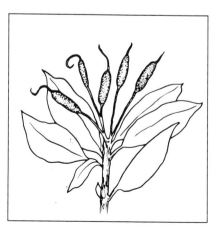

Remove seed pods to
insure next year's flowers.

OTHER EVERGREEN FLOWERING SHRUBS

As I said earlier, Azaleas, Camellias, and Rhododendrons are the big three among the evergreen flowering shrubs. But the following are two others that are definitely worth considering and should not be left out.

MOUNTAIN LAUREL
Kalmia latifolia

The Mountain Laurel is one of my favorites for a specimen plant or background shrub in shady areas. I have several growing on my place and they always blossom magnificently and require little care except yearly fertilizing. Mountain Laurel should be planted in semi-shade to shade, in rich, peaty soil which drains well. Plant the same as Azaleas.

The mature height of the Mountain Laurel is usually less than 10 feet, but after many years in excellent conditions, it may reach 15 to 20 feet. Clusters of bell-shaped flowers appear in late spring. Fertilize after blooms, using an acid fertilizer. Pruning should also be done after bloom. The Mountain Laurel has no problems worth worrying about, though the leaves are poisonous to livestock.

JAPANESE ANDROMEDA
Pieris japonica

Some call this the Lily of the Valley Shrub because of the long panicles of lily-of-the-valley-shaped flowers which come forth in mid-spring. These flowers follow very attractive buds which are noticeable all winter.

The Japanese Andromeda is a slow-growing, upright, and graceful shrub with the panicles of buds and then flowers arching outward and downward.

The Andromeda likes shade and is ideal for shady spots where you have had trouble getting a shrub to grow. However, it cannot stand tight, sticky soil, so add plenty of peat moss and bark for humus and drainage just as you would for azaleas.

Mountain Laurel

255

Flowering shrubs add so much to the home landscape.

DECIDUOUS FLOWERING SHRUBS

Many of us grew up with names like "Golden Bells," "Bridal Wreath," "Cydonia," "Grancy Gray Beard," "Mock Orange," and "Pearl Bush." These were our mothers' favorite shrubs and were an integral part of the loveliness which was provided for us as we grew up. No matter how poor a Southern family was, "Momma" seemed to find enough "butter and egg money" to order off for a shrub each year or so. I shall always cherish the sight of a rustic farm house, perhaps with paint peeling, but with one of these favorites adorning the yard.

We've become a lot more sophisticated about proper landscape design and its balance, texture, blending colors, and form, but no garden means much to me if it doesn't have one or two of my old favorites tucked somewhere.

I suppose that is why I love small English home gardens so very much. They exemplify the heart and soul of the gardener who lives there. Their flowering shrubs are like the closest of friends, a part of their lives.

There are flowering shrubs for almost every situation and, here in the South, we can use most of them. There are winter-blooming cultivars, spring-blooming, summer-blooming, and even fall-blooming. If you plan your garden properly, there is hardly a time when some flowering friend won't be sharing its beauty with you.

There are sunny-spot friends and shady-spot friends and probably a lot in between. If you can't find what you want in the local nurseries, write for some mail-order catalogs, for they specialize in flowering shrubs more than almost any other type of plant. I'll bet you'll find what you want in one of them. They may be necessarily small, for they will be bare-root, but don't let that worry you. They grow fast and don't take too long to become a real jewel in your garden.

On the following pages you will find a list of those with which I have had experience and which I know will do well for you. If I sound opinionated about some of them, chalk me off as one who knows what he likes.

The general rules are the same for flowering shrubs as for all the plants which we have seen so far:

1. Choose the right size plant for the spot you have.
2. Choose the plant for the soil conditions and the exposure which the spot has.
3. If the soil is not suitable, make it right *before* you plant.
4. Plant correctly (see Chapter 3, Planting Trees and Shrubs).
5. Prune and fertilize at the correct time of the year.
6. Control insects and diseases before the plant is extensively damaged.
7. In dry periods, water by soaking, not by sprinkling.
8. Keep well-mulched but *never* let the mulch lie against the stems of the plant.

Flowering shrubs are grown for the blossoms which they produce each year. Once your plant is growing, the hardest thing to understand is when to prune and when to fertilize so as not to disturb the blossom buds.

Some flowering shrub blossoms are formed on branches which were grown the previous summer. As in the case of Forsythia 'Spring Glory,' these may be seen quite easily in the late fall and winter. We call this "blossoming on old wood." Others produce their blossoms on short shoots

Spring Glory Forsythia

which come from wood of the previous summer, as in the case of Weigela 'Vaniceki.' Then there are the flowering shrubs, like Chaste Tree and Crape Myrtle, which set their flower buds on shoots which have been grown in the same season or, as we say, "on new wood."

The way a flowering shrub sets its bloom buds determines when it is to be pruned and when it is to be fertilized. If you don't follow this most important rule, you will not have the beauty you desire.

There is an old rule of thumb which states,"If the plant blossoms (in the South) before June 1, it should be pruned and fertilized *after* it finishes blossoming. If the plant blossoms after June 1, it should be pruned when it is dormant and fertilized as the weather warms in the spring." This is a good *general* rule but there are exceptions, like late-flowering Azaleas and Rhododendrons. In the descriptive material which follows, learn when to prune and fertilize each of your shrubs.

Flowering shrubs are extremely tolerant of most environmental conditions except cold and heat. My list of those which are best for the South are known to do all right here. There may be others which you will see listed or hear about. Don't be afraid to try a new plant if it is listed as hardy here or farther north. Plants widely used in the northern areas of the country, with which many of you newcomers are familiar, may not be able to stand our heat and long growing conditions very well. You may have to plant them in the best exposure and change their soil conditions to grow them here at all. Don't be afraid to plant one or two of your old favorites. You will never know what will happen until you try!

'Nivalis' Japanese Flowering Quince

ALL ABOUT THE SOUTH'S DECIDUOUS FLOWERING SHRUBS

❦ FLOWERING ALMOND
Prunus glandulosa

Size: Height 5 feet
Exposure: Full sun
Type of Blossom: 1/2-inch double flowers
Color: White or pink
Blossom Time: Spring
Blooming Habit: From buds on previous summer's growth
When to Prune: Winter, but little pruning is needed
When to Fertilize: After blossoms
Other Features: Low growing
Problems: Borers and diseases of plums, though not severe
Cultivars: 'Alboplena,' double white; 'Sinensis,' double pink

The dwarf flowering almond is a perfect spring flowering shrub for use as a specimen plant. The compact, low-growing shrub is most attractive covered by the small double flowers. Severe pruning is seldom necessary but if shaping is needed, prune in the winter while the plant is dormant, even though you will remove some bloom buds. Cover all large cuts with tree paint.

❦ ALTHAEA, ROSE OF SHARON
Hibiscus syriacus

Size: Shrub form, 10 to 12 feet high, 6 feet wide
Exposure: Full sun to light shade
Type of Blossom: Single or double flowers
Color: White, red, deep pink, pale pink, lavender-blue
Blossom Time: Summer
Blooming Habit: New growth
When to Prune: Winter
When to Fertilize: Early spring
Other Features: May be used as a small tree
Problems: Aphids
Cultivars: 'Ardens,' double lavender; 'Jeanne d'Arc,' double white; 'Lucy,' double rose-red; 'Paeoniflora,' double pale pink; 'Blue Bird,' large single blue; 'Diana,' large single white; 'Hamabo,' large single white with red

Many people turn up their noses at Althaeas, believing them to be too common and the colors too magenta and lavender. Many found in nurseries grown from seed or of poor quality stock do have insipid colors. But that should not condemn a plant which grows under poor conditions and blossoms much of the summer; there are many excellent cultivars which have beautiful clear colors.

I prefer the singles over the doubles because they are more spectacular with their larger blooms, with the exception of 'Paeoniflora,' which has one of the loveliest flowers of any summer shrub. The large, double, pale-pink flowers are constantly set from June to late August. It is one of the coolest shrubs around, and has been a delight on my place for many years.

Althaeas take some working with. They grow rapidly and will become very woody after only a few years. This tough old wood fails to put out the numbers of fresh shoots on which large numbers of blossoms can be set. When this happens, you should do heavy pruning for regeneration.

Prune some each winter and fertilize heavily in the spring to force the fresh new shoots on which many blossoms will be set. Removal of the green seed pods will encourage more blossoms to set.

Though aphids may be a problem, any good insecticide will control them. If a sooty-fungus should appear, control the aphid infestation and then the fungus will disappear.

✨ BEAUTY BUSH
Kolkwitzia amabalis

Size: Height 8 to 10 feet, spread 6 feet
Exposure: Sun to light shade
Type of Blossom: Clusters of 1/2-inch-long pink flowers
Color: Pink with yellow throat
Blossom Time: Late spring
Blooming Habit: Buds are set on previous season's growth
When to Prune: After blossoming
When to Fertilize: After blossoming
Other Features: The plant may get leggy and too dense, requiring severe pruning after bloom
Problems: None to worry about
Cultivars: A single specie

✨ BUTTERFLY BUSH
Buddleia Davidii

Size: Prune to keep between 5 and 6 feet; spreads to 4 or 5 feet
Exposure: Sun
Type of Blossom: Large spikes
Color: Pink, red, white, blue, and purple
Blossom Time: Summer
Blooming Habit: Flowers are formed at the end of new shoots
When to Prune: Late winter or early spring
When to Fertilize: As weather warms
Other Features: Flowers are fragrant and attract butterflies
Problems: None to worry about

The Butterfly Bush is easy to grow in any good garden soil where there is plenty of sun. I prefer cutting them back severely to force new shoots from the base and keep the plant lower. Prune out the older shoots and then prune back the younger ones which are left. Rich soil keeps the colors true.

CHASTE TREE
Vitex Agnus-castus

Size: 8 to 10 feet (trained as a shrub)
Exposure: Sun to light shade
Type of Blossom: Summer
Color: Lavender-blue, white
Blossom Time: Summer
Blooming Habit: New shoots
When to Prune: Winter
When to Fertilize: Early spring
Other Features: Aromatic flowers and foliage
Problems: Needs severe pruning every 3 or 4 years
Cultivars: 'Alba,' white; the specie is light lavender to blue

This plant has already been described as a small tree. It may be used as either. To use as a shrub, prune it severely every few years. It is one of our better summer-flowering shrubs.

CLERODENDRUM or GLORY-BOWER
Clerodendrum trichotomum

Size: 10 feet
Exposure: Sun to part shade
Type of Blossom: Clusters
Color: White with red calyx; stamens protrude
Blossom Time: Summer
Blooming Habit: On new growth
When to Prune: Winter, sparingly
When to Fertilize: Early spring
Other Features: The fruit is blue, showing above the red persistent calyx, which gives a most unusual show until after leaves fall
Problems: None of note

This is a unique, hard-to-find shrub which is well worth searching for. Its rare flowers are showy and fragrant in the summer; but the fruit is just as showy in the late summer and into the fall until cold weather.

CRAPE MYRTLE
Lagerstroemia indica

Size: Standard size cultivars (bush form) 10 feet; dwarf cultivars (bush form) 6 feet

Exposure: Full sun to afternoon shade
Type of Blossom: Globe to pyramid-shaped, terminal panicles
Color: Lavender, purple, pink, red, white
Blossom Time: Early summer until fall
Blooming Habit: Flowers form at the terminal of a new shoot
When to Prune: Winter
When to Fertilize: Early spring
Other Features: May be trained as a 20-foot tree
Problems: Sooty fungus on the leaves indicates serious aphid infestations; if you kill the aphids, the sooty fungus will disappear. White or powdery mildew may appear in the late summer. Control serious attacks with a recommended fungicide.
Cultivars: See Crape Myrtles under Flowering Trees. Dwarf cultivars are available in all the Crape Myrtle colors.

Occasionally you will see the name Crape Myrtle spelled "Crepe Myrtle." Dismiss the error as being from someone who has not grown up with the plant. *Hortus Third* lists it as Crape Myrtle, which shows that we were right all the time. The Crape Myrtle is a Southern plant and we should know how to spell it as well as how to use it.

Nowadays there are magnificent cultivars with beautiful colors. The reds are clearer, having less lavender, the whites are purer, and the pinks are less "hot." There are excellent "dwarfs" or, more accurately, lower-growing cultivars. I would say that the Crape Myrtle has arrived as a fantastic landscape plant.

Of all the Crape Myrtles, my favorite is the cultivar 'Near East,' which is a near-white with a cast of pale pink. Crape Myrtles blossom when it is hot and the reds make me even hotter, but 'Near East' cools the whole landscape.

Shrub-form Crape Myrtles must be cut back severely every few years. In the dead of winter, cut the heavy branches to two or three feet from the ground. Thin out all weak, spindly shoots at ground level. The plant will reform and produce a beautiful vase-shaped to rounded plant from the old stubs.

DEUTZIA PRIDE OF ROCHESTER
Deutzia scabra cv. 'Plena'

Size: 8 to 10 feet
Exposure: Sun to light shade
Type of Blossom: Panicles
Color: White with tinge of pink
Blossom Time: Mid to late Spring
Blooming Habit: Buds form on old wood
When to Prune: After bloom
When to Fertilize: After bloom
Other Features: Fast-growing
Problems: Should be rejuvenated every few years by cutting back severely
Cultivars: Many other cultivars are listed for *D. scabra* and other species and hybrids. Stick to this one; it's the best.

The Deutzia is a well-used flowering shrub which unfortunately has a rough and coarse appearance. The bloom makes its use worthwhile. Plant it in the background where it is not too noticeable except when it is in bloom.

❦ FORSYTHIA or GOLDEN BELLS
Forsythia × intermedia

Size: 8 to 10 feet
Exposure: Sun to moderate shade
Type of Blossom: Clusters of up to 5 or 6
Color: Yellow
Blossom Time: Early spring
Blooming Habit: Buds form on previous summer's growth
When to Prune: Immediately after bloom
When to Fertilize: After bloom
Other Features: Arching branches give graceful appearance; one of our earliest flowers
Problems: None of consequence
Cultivars: 'Beatrix Farrand,' more upright, with largest blossoms; 'Lynwood Gold,' deeper yellow color; 'Spring Glory,' large bright yellow blossoms set very heavily

The Forsythias are some of our best flowering shrubs. They have many uses, from specimen plants to background shrubs or hedges. I much prefer the natural form with the arching branches appearing as tubes of yellow in the spring. Hedging, which is widely done, seems to me to ruin the wonder of this plant, but if you insist, be sure to do your pruning immediately after the blossoms have fallen and do not continue to clip all summer or you will reduce the blossoms to a few flecks of gold over the plant each spring.

❦ BUSH HONEYSUCKLES
Lonicera sp.

The bush honeysuckles are noteworthy for their interesting blossoms. The Winter Honeysuckle, *Lonicera fragrantissima*, is not only very early-flowering but also extremely fragrant. The Tatarian Honeysuckle blossoms in May. Both of these have red fruit which follows the flowers and remains showy through much of the summer.

WINTER HONEYSUCKLE
Lonicera fragrantissima

Size: 5 to 6 feet high, 4 to 5 feet wide
Exposure: Sun to light shade
Type of Blossom: Small "honeysuckles"
Color: Creamy-white
Blossom Time: Winter to early spring
Blooming Habit: Last year's growth

Althaea Paeoniflora

Spring Glory Forsythia

Blue-Pink Hydrangea

Deutzia Pride of Rochester

Annabelle Hydrangea

Oakleaf Hydrangea in the late spring (above), in the summer (lower left), and in the fall (below)

When to Prune: After bloom
When to Fertilize: After bloom
Other Features: Flowers are very fragrant
Problems: Remove older wood every two or three years to keep compact and bushy

Winter Honeysuckle is a shrub to be used more often than it is. There are too few shrubs which will blossom with a few days of warm weather in the winter, as this one does. The Winter Honeysuckle makes the winter garden an inviting place to be and gives a hint of spring to come.

About every third year, prune out the oldest stems and rejuvenate the plant to keep fresh new wood coming out and to keep the compact shape.

TATARIAN HONEYSUCKLE
Lonicera tatarica

Size: 8 to 10 feet high, 6 feet wide
Exposure: Sun to light shade
Type of Blossom: Small "honeysuckles"
Color: White, rose, or deep rose-red
Blossom Time: Late spring
Blooming Habit: Flowers form on last year's growth
When to Prune: After bloom
When to Fertilize: After bloom
Other Features: The flowers are fragrant
Problems: May become old and stemmy; correct that by removing the very old stems to force young growth
Cultivars: 'Alba,' pure white flowers; 'Sibirica' ('Rubra'), rose-red flowers

The Tatarian Honeysuckle can become a coarse-looking shrub if not rejuvenated every few years. Properly handled, it will give an interesting flower in the late spring with a sweet fragrance which permeates the garden.

HYDRANGEA
Hydrangea sp.

There are a number of excellent Hydrangeas for the Southern garden; some blossom in the late spring (Oakleaf Hydrangea) and some blossom much of the summer (Nikko Blue). The range of color among the different species is white, blue, and pink.

These are relatively easy-to-grow plants which withstand cold well. The French Garden Hydrangea, *Hydrangea macrophylla,* is the least hardy; choose cultivars of it for their ability to survive our coldest temperatures.

ANNABELLE HYDRANGEA
Hydrangea arborescens cv. 'Annabelle'

Size: 6 feet or more
Exposure: Full sun to light shade

Type of Blossom: Large globe to oval clusters set at the end of arching branches
Color: White
Blossom Time: Mid-summer
Blooming Habit: Current season's growth
When to Prune: Winter
When to Fertilize: Spring
Other Features: Dried flower heads persist and remain interesting until winter
Problems: None to worry about

The 'Annabelle' cultivar of *Hydrangea arborescens* is the best I have found. It is superior to the more common *H. arborescens* cv. 'Grandiflora' in having more compact growth and larger blossom heads.

BLUE-PINK OR FRENCH GARDEN HYDRANGEA
Hydrangea macrophylla

Size: 6 feet
Exposure: Full sun to part shade
Type of blossom: Large globe to oval heads on short terminal shoots
Color: Blue to pink
Blossom Time: Summer
Blooming Habit: New shoots from younger "old wood"
When to Prune: Winter
When to Fertilize: Early spring, after hard freezes
Other Features: Acid soil keeps flowers blue, alkaline soil turns them pink
Problems: Severe cold may damage the younger wood from which the flowering
      branchlets arise
Cultivars: 'Nikko,' very hardy deep blue; pink cultivars, pale pink to dark rose

The Blue-Pink Hydrangeas are popular because they will grow in quite a bit of shade and still produce large numbers of colorful summer flowers. 'Nikko' seems to be the hardiest of all. You should be very careful about buying florist forcing Hydrangeas for the garden. These strains do not seem to be nearly as hardy as the cultivars propagated and sold as garden types.

The Blue-Pink Hydrangeas should be constantly renewed by removing the older, heavier wood at the ground. The best blossoms are formed on healthy shoots grown off younger one-, two-, or three-year-old stalks. Thus, they are pruned very much like a floribunda rose, by cutting out the weaker and older shoots at the ground and by cutting back the remaining strong, young stems about one-fourth.

Fertilize blue cultivars with an acid fertilizer like Camellia-Azalea Fertilizer; lime pink cultivars each year and fertilize them with a garden fertilizer.

OAKLEAF HYDRANGEA
Hydrangea quercifolia

Size: 6 feet high and 8 feet across
Exposure: Full sun to shade
Type of Blossom: Long pyramidal clusters
Color: White, turning pink as the flower matures

Blossom Time: Early summer
Blooming Habit: New shoots off young "old wood"
When to Prune: Winter
When to Fertilize: Spring
Other Features: The dried flowers persist until fall; the spreading habit will cover
banks well; the fall color is an attractive red
Problems: None to worry about
Cultivars: Several more compact cultivars are listed, though I have not tried them

The Oakleaf Hydrangea is one of my favorite flowering shrubs. It seems to thrive on neglect and is perfect for shady, wooded areas where few plants bloom satisfactorily. The heavy foliage makes it an excellent background plant, especially where a shady area needs to be blocked. Since its soil requirements are not too demanding, it is also good for banks which are almost impossible to deal with otherwise.

PEEGEE or MOUNTAIN HYDRANGEA
Hydrangea paniculata cv. 'Grandiflora'

Size: 12 feet or more
Exposure: Sun to light shade
Type of Blossom: Large pyramidal cluster
Color: White with pink
Blossom Time: Summer
Blooming Habit: New shoots from younger "old wood"
When to Prune: Winter
When to Fertilize: Early spring
Other Features: Best in a tree form
Problems: None to worry about

The Peegee Hydrangea is ideal for the higher elevations of the South, being especially adapted to the cooler nights and misty conditions of the mountains. The tree form is outstanding and there are quite a few in the Atlanta area which provide an outstanding specimen plant for these gardens.

HYPERICUM, ST. JOHN'S WORT or GOLD FLOWER
Hypericum sp.

The Hypericums are some of our best low-growing summer-flowering shrubs. There are species which grow very low to the ground and are some of our best deciduous ground cover plants. We know this as Gold Flower, though the old English name, St. John's Wort, is still used by the purist. Nowadays the name Hypericum may be heard as often as the common names.

There are many Hypericums in cultivation. The very popular *Hypericum calycinum* is widely cited as an excellent ground cover since it is the most flat-growing specie, but there is a leaf spot which often denudes the plant during our hot, muggy summers. The hard-to-find *Hypericum* × *Moseranum* will also spread over the ground and I have never seen it lose its foliage like *H. calycinum*. *H.* × *Moseranum* also has more blossoms.

Of all the Hypericums for the South, *Hypericum* cv. 'Hidcote' seems to be the best. If used as a bank cover, it should be cut back severely each winter to make it spread.

HIDCOTE GOLD FLOWER
Hypericum cv. 'Hidcote'

Size: 3 feet, spreading to 5 or 6
Exposure: Full sun for best blossoming
Type of Blossom: 2-inch cupped flower with stamens showing prominently
Color: Bright yellow
Blossom Time: Summer
Blooming Habit: Flowers form on new shoots
When to Prune: Winter
When to Fertilize: Spring
Other Features: Drooping stems will root at joints which touch the ground
Problems: None to worry about

I like Hypericum Hidcote the best of all the Gold Flowers. It is a little tall, perhaps, for a flat ground cover but if you keep it cut back in the winter, it will perform magnificently on banks and in other hot dry areas.

SUNGOLD GOLD FLOWER
Hypericum patulum cv. 'Sungold'

Size: 2 to 3 feet high, 3 to 4 feet wide
Exposure: Full sun
Type of Blossom: 2-inch flower with distinct petals and prominent stamens
Color: Bright yellow
Blossom Time: Summer
Blooming Habit: Flowers form on new shoots
When to Prune: Winter
When to Fertilize: Spring
Other Features: Low mounding plant
Problems: None to worry about

'Sungold' is more compact than 'Hidcote,' but the blossoms are neither as cup-shaped nor as showy.

 JASMINE
Jasminum sp.

There are many jasmines or jessamines which are not in the genus *Jasminum*, some of which will be covered later. There are two in this genus of great importance in the Southern garden: *Jasminum nudiflorum* and *Jasminum floridum*. January Jasmine, *J.*

nudiflorum, is my favorite because the yellow tubular flowers are some of the earliest spring flowers in the garden. Florida Jasmine is a useful late spring-flowering shrub.

FLORIDA JASMINE
Jasminum floridum

Size: 4 to 5 feet with a 4-foot spread
Exposure: Sun to light shade
Type of Blossom: Small, tubular
Color: Yellow
Blossom Time: Mid to late spring
Blooming Habit: On old, arching branches
When to Prune: After bloom
When to Fertilize: After bloom
Other Features: Branches are green, giving an evergreen appearance
Problems: Needs to be kept fertilized each year

The Florida Jasmine is an interesting compact-centered shrub with arching branches which are filled with small, bright yellow flowers in the mid to late spring. A good yellow-flowering shrub to follow Forsythia.

JANUARY JASMINE
Jasminum nudiflorum

Size: 4 to 5 feet
Exposure: Sun to part shade
Type of Blossom: Small, tubular
Color: Yellow
Blossom Time: Winter, very early spring
Blooming Habit: Last year's arching branches
When to Prune: After bloom
When to Fertilize: Early spring, after bloom
Other Features: Green stems make it seem to be an evergreen
Problems: Needs yearly fertilizing

This is a shrub every garden should have. It is one of the first flowers of spring. A few days of warm weather in January or February will bring forth the first flowers, which keep opening during each subsequent warm spell. It is excellent for banks, where it will spread as the arching branches root wherever they touch the ground. It may be cut back after bloom each spring, making a bank cover which is about 2 1/2 to 3 feet tall.

KERRIA or EASTER ROSE
Kerria japonica cv. 'Pleniflora'

Size: 6 feet high, 4 to 5 feet wide
Exposure: Moderate shade to full sun
Type of Blossom: Round double, two inches across

Color: Golden yellow
Blossom Time: Mid-spring
Blooming Habit: Flowers on last year's arching branches
When to Prune: After bloom
When to Fertilize: After bloom
Other Features: Green stems are interesting in the winter
Problems: None

The Easter Rose is an outstanding shrub which is used far too infrequently. It will take a lot of shade provided it has some sun each day. The habit of growth is somewhat loose and interesting, with the branches arching outward and downward. The double flowers are set on these branches and it is a beautiful picture when it blooms. My father has a row of these underneath some large *Photinia serrulata*, but where they get the afternoon sun. It seems that every Easter these dainty powderpuff flowers are at their peak.

 LILAC
Syringa sp.

The South is *not* lilac country. Our soil is too acid and our summers too hot and muggy. Yet we can temper our garden environment and work diligently to grow these wonderful plants of the last Spring. They are worth the effort!

The best choice for withstanding our heat in the South is the Persian lilac, *Syringa × persica*, although it does not have the beautiful, large flowers of the common lilac. The common lilac is the best of the large-flowering types to try. The double-flowered and hybrid lilacs seldom perform as well as the specie, *Syringa vulgaris*, and the common cultivar 'Alba.'

Grow all lilacs in morning sun and in beds which have been limed well. Use ground bark as the humus when preparing the soil since it isn't as acid-forming as peat moss. Work perlite into the bed for drainage if the soil is tight and sticky. Keep lilacs well-mulched with pine straw but leave a saucer around the stems.

Cut back the old trunks and stems every few years to keep the plant compact and bushy. Fertilize with bone meal each year right before bloom and with a 5-10-15 fertilizer after bloom.

The main effort is to keep lilacs in rich, well-drained, sweet soil which is cool in the hot afternoon.

Mildew may be a problem; when you see it, treat lilacs with a recommended fungicide.

PERSIAN LILAC
Syringa × persica

Size: 8 to 10 feet high, 4 to 5 feet wide
Exposure: Morning sun, afternoon shade
Type of Blossom: Showy panicles of fragrant flowers

Color: Lavender-blue, white, and rose
Blossom Time: Spring, for several weeks
Blooming Habit: On last year's growth
When to Prune: After bloom
When to Fertilize: Use bone meal as the weather warms and 5-10-15 after bloom
Other Features: Flowers are extremely fragrant
Problems: Mildew and lilac borer
Cultivars: 'Alba,' white; 'Rubra,' rose-red

This is the best of the lilacs for the South. Follow the above general planting instructions very carefully. The specie, which is lavender-blue, is the strongest and best.

COMMON LILAC
Syringa vulgaris

Size: 12 to 15 feet high, 6 to 8 feet wide
Exposure: Full morning sun
Type of Blossom: Large panicles of fragrant flowers
Color: Lavender-blue, white
Blossom Time: Spring
Blooming Habit: Last year's growth off young wood
When to Prune: After bloom
When to Fertilize: Before bloom with bone meal, after bloom with 5-10-15
Other Features: Very fragrant flowers, handsome shrub
Problems: Mildew and lilac borers
Cultivars: 'Alba,' single white

The specie of Common Lilac, which is lavender-blue, is the strongest and best for us to grow although it seldom, if ever, reaches the 20 feet so often seen farther north, nor does it reach the huge 10- to 12-foot spread. The white cultivar, 'Alba,' also does fairly well and is more upright than the specie.

Plant these according to the instructions above. They won't be like the gorgeous specimens seen in the Rochester, New York, parks, but they will be worth having.

MERATIA, WINTERSWEET
Chimonanthus praecox

Size: 10 feet high, 4 to 5 feet across
Exposure: Sun to part shade
Type of Blossom: Small, very fragrant
Color: Yellow with brown markings
Blossom Time: Mid-winter
Blooming Habit: Flowers are formed on last year's growth
When to Prune: After bloom
When to Fertilize: Early spring

Other Features: Extremely fragrant flowers starting about Christmas
Problems: A rather coarse shrub to be used in the background
Cultivars: 'Grandiflora,' larger flowers but with less fragrance

I grew up loving this plant as much as any we had. It connoted Christmas because every year it was in bloom during this wonderful time of the year. Even if the weather were freezing, my mother would break off a few springs of Meratia. On the mantle in the library there was always a Christmas decoration into which she would stick these little branches. With the fire burning in the fireplace, the small flowers would thaw and the fragrance would permeate the room. Even today that fragrance means Christmas to me.

The Meratia is a rather coarse shrub which should not be used in a spot of great importance but should be placed in the background of the garden so that the fragrance of the flowers spreads throughout the area at a time when there is precious little to enjoy in the Southern garden.

The cultivar 'Grandiflora' has been sold as being superior, but the larger flowers lack the permeating aroma of the specie and I would avoid it.

❧ LOST GORDONIA
Franklinia Alatamaha

Size: In ideal situations this may reach 25 feet as a tree, but when grown as a shrub it seldom exceeds 8 or 10 feet
Exposure: Afternoon shade
Type of Blossom: 3-inch slightly-cupped flowers with prominent stamens
Color: White with yellow stamens
Blossom Time: Summer to fall
Blooming Habit: On new shoots
When to Prune: In winter, but very sparsely
When to Fertilize: Spring
Other Features: Red fall color
Problems: Must have acid, high humus, well-drained soil

The rare Lost Gordonia is a specimen shrub or small tree which adds a note of uniqueness to the garden. It *must* be grown in rich, high-humus soil with excellent drainage. However, it must never become dry. Water to keep it evenly moist in dry periods.

Since it is susceptible to Phytopthera root rot, treat the bed with a recommended drench before planting. Once established in the correct type soil, the roots will overcome any subsequent attacks of the ever-present disease.

The Lost Gordonia is not for every garden or gardener; it takes considerable time and effort to establish. It is a unique plant of Southern history, having been discovered on the banks of the Altamaha River in Georgia in the late 1700's by William Bartram on one of his explorations. (Incidentally, the spelling of the river's name changed after Bartram named the plant.) He collected the seed and later started plants in his garden in Philadelphia. The plant has never been found in the wild again.

❧ MOCK ORANGE
❧ Philadelphus × virginalis

Size: 8 to 10 feet high, 5 feet wide
Exposure: Full sun to part shade
Type of Blossom: Large, 2-inch semi-double flowers
Color: White
Blossom Time: Mid to late spring
Blooming Habit: Blossoms form on last year's growth
When to Prune: After bloom
When to Fertilize: After bloom
Other Features: Fragrant flowers; heavy, handsome shrub
Problems: None to worry about
Cultivars: There are several cultivars of doubtful advantage over the specie here in the South

The Mock Orange is a handsome plant which produces large numbers of fragrant, glistening white flowers in the spring. It is prized for the fragrance which adds a great deal to the spring garden.

❧ PEARL BUSH
❧ Exochorda racemosa

Size: 10 to 12 feet high, 5 to 6 feet wide
Exposure: Sun to part shade
Type of Blossom: Slightly cup-shaped, single, 2-inch flowers
Color: White
Blossom Time: Mid to late spring
Blooming Habit: Old wood
When to Prune: After bloom
When to Fertilize: After bloom
Other Features: The small, round buds look like pearls
Problems: The plant may become twiggy; thin it each year to force strong growth

The Pearl Bush is an interesting spring-flowering shrub which should be grown in the background because it becomes large. The real interest is in its white round buds, which resemble pearls. Give the Pearl Bush some attention as described above or it will become rather straggly and unsightly with many dead twigs on the inside of the bush.

❧ DOUBLE-FLOWERED POMEGRANATE
❧ Punica Granatum cv. 'Flore Pleno'

Size: 10 feet, but usually kept lower
Exposure: Sun, but in a protected place
Type of Blossom: Double flowers, 2 to 3 inches across

Color: Orange to red
Blossom Time: Summer
Blooming Habit: Flowers form on new shoots
When to Prune: Winter
When to Fertilize: Spring
Other Features: May produce some fruit which are showy in the late summer to fall
Problems: May be somewhat tender
Cultivars: 'Nana' is a lower-growing cultivar than 'Flore Pleno'

I list the pomegranate with the admonition to protect it during the more severe winters since it is subject to winter kill at about 0° F. or slightly above. It is an ancient and unusual horticultural plant which is attractive in the summer with numerous double orange-red to red flowers. The double-flowering pomegranates seldom produce good fruit but they are more attractive than the fruiting cultivars. They also seem to be hardier.

The best of the fruiting cultivars for the garden is 'Wonderful,' which also has extra petals and is considered a "double." Its fruit is attractive in the fall and is edible. It is listed as hardy to 20° F., but I have seen them take colder weather than that. Still, be careful to protect all pomegranates by planting away from the cold west wind and keeping a mulch over the roots.

❦ JAPANESE FLOWERING QUINCE
Chaenomeles speciosa

Size: 6 feet or more, almost as wide as tall
Exposure: Sun to light shade (blooms best in full sun)
Type of Blossom: Individual flowers, usually single, but some cultivars with extra petals and almost double
Color: White, pink, red, orange-red, and orange
Blossom Time: Early spring
Blooming Habit: Flowers form on last year's wood
When to Prune: After bloom
When to Fertilize: Spring
Other Features: Some cultivars set fruit which make excellent jelly
Problems: Fire blight may occur infrequently
Cultivars: 'Cameo,' double apricot; 'Jet Trail,' low-growing single red; 'Nivalis,' single white; 'Rubra Grandiflora,' large crimson; 'Texas Scarlet,' single red

The Japanese Flowering Quince is another of our winter-blossoming shrubs. It starts flowering with any warming spell and more flowers open as each warm period arrives, even though severe cold might intervene.

It prefers well-drained, sunny soil and does well on banks where few other plants will thrive. Keep this quince thinned out and rejuvenated so that it forces new wood in the late summer and fall. This wood produces the most bloom. Severe pruning may be necessary to restore the plant to a bushy compact form, but expect a disruption of the flowers for a couple of years after such severe pruning.

'Texas Scarlet' Japanese Flowering Quince   Meratia

Double-Flowered Pomegranate

Bridal-Wreath Spiraea

Scotch Broom

The Japanese Flowering Quince does produce a very hard fruit which is excellent for making the best tart fruit jelly I have ever eaten. It is not, however, to be confused with our old-fashioned fruiting quince which is in the genus Cydonia. The fruiting quince, *Cydonia oblonga,* may be seen on occasion and is also a worthwhile plant.

❧ SCOTCH BROOM
Cytisus scoparius

Size: 6 to 8 feet high, 8 feet or more across
Exposure: Full sun to part shade
Type of Blossom: Pea-like flowers
Color: Yellow, red, orange
Blossom Time: Late spring
Blooming Habit: Buds are set on last year's growth
When to Prune: After bloom
When to Fertilize: After bloom
Other Features: Attractive green stems in the winter
Problems: Will not stand poor drainage
Cultivars: Cultivars range in color from yellow to red and orange

The Scotch Broom is not used as often as it should be. The shrub is attractive during all seasons but most attractive when it is in flower in the late spring. The long arching green stems produce large quantities of yellow, orange, or red flowers depending on the cultivar chosen. I prefer the yellow because it is the most showy.

The Scotch Broom will grow in almost any kind of soil provided it is well-drained; it will gradually die away when the soil is tight and sticky. Planted in the right place, it will grow into a very large shrub. Though it is listed as an 8-foot plant, I have seen them growing taller than that naturally, on ditch banks near the old nursery.

❧ SPIRAEA
Spiraea sp.

The genus Spiraea provides some of our most beautiful spring-flowering shrubs. They are rather common plants which are often used improperly. Their best use is as specimen plants which are allowed to grow in their naturally graceful habit. There is nothing as beautiful as the long arching branches of a Spiraea engulfed with huge numbers of white flowers in the spring. Many of the Spiraeas also have attractive fall color.

Spiraeas used as hedges or foundation plants are almost always clipped so severely that the whole beauty of the plant is ruined. When growing Spiraeas, place them where they may grow naturally and leave the pruners behind until the old wood needs removing.

There are a few summer-flowering cultivars which may have a specialized place, such as the rose-red flowering cultivar of *Spiraea bumalda,* 'Anthony Waterer,' and the pink, *Spiraea × Billiardi.* These are all right, I suppose, but they are not my idea of great shrubs to use. The following listings are only the spring-flowering Spiraeas.

SPIRAEA ARGUTA
Spiraea × arguta

Size: 6 feet high, 4 to 6 feet wide
Exposure: Full sun to light shade
Type of Blossom: Clusters of flowers arising along the branches
Color: White
Blossom Time: Spring
Blooming Habit: Buds form on old wood
When to Prune: After bloom
When to Fertilize: After bloom
Other Features: Light, airy foliage
Problems: May need rejuvenation every few years

Spiraea × Arguta is similar to our old favorite, *Spiraea Thunbergii,* but has much heavier clusters of flowers. It will grow under a wide range of conditions. It is sometimes listed as Bridal Bower Spiraea, but few refer to it by that name.

SPIRAEA PRUNIFOLIA
Spiraea prunifolia

Size: 6 feet high, 5 to 6 feet across
Exposure: Sun to light shade
Type of Blossom: Double flowers covering the arching branches
Color: White
Blossom Time: Spring
Blooming Habit: On old wood
When to Prune: After bloom
When to Fertilize: After bloom
Other Features: Long arching branches give a soft effect
Problems: May need rejuvenation from time to time

BRIDAL-WREATH SPIRAEA
Spiraea × Vanhouttei

Size: 6 feet high, 4 to 6 feet across
Exposure: Full sun to light shade
Type of Blossom: Clusters of single flowers on arching branches
Color: White
Blossom Time: Spring

Blooming Habit: Old wood
When to Prune: After bloom
When to Fertilize: After bloom
Other Features: Attractive all summer with its arching branches and fine foliage
Problems: May need rejuvenation from time to time

S. × *Vanhouttei* is the Spiraea most often given the name Bridal-Wreath, though you will find several others given it erroneously.

This is the best of all the spring-flowering Spiraeas for toughness, consistent bloom, and sheer beauty. In the background of a garden, it is one of the most beautiful of our shrubs with its long arching branches covered with white clusters of blossoms, sometimes curving over and sweeping the ground.

❧ SWEET SHRUB
Calycanthus floridus

Size: 8 to 10 feet high
Exposure: Sun to moderate shade
Type of Blossom: Round to oval, 2 inches across
Color: Reddish-brown
Blossom Time: Mid-spring
Blooming Habit: Last year's wood
When to Prune: After bloom
When to Fertilize: After bloom
Other Features: Fragrant blossoms, attractive foliage
Problems: Seeds and suckers freely

The Sweet Shrub is a native in the South and a garden plant since colonial times. It is noted for the numerous intensely fragrant reddish-brown flowers which appear in the mid-spring. It is native to much of the area and may be found growing wild in our woods. Small seedlings are easily transplanted from the wild if taken up during the winter and spring before new leaves appear.

Seeds may also be gathered from the unusual pods seen on the plant in the late summer or early fall. Pick the pods when they are crisp and dry, remove the seeds, and dry them on a paper towel out of the sun. Store them in an old film cartridge holder (be sure to mark the contents) in the crisper of the refrigerator. Plant the seed in early spring in a well-prepared bed. Do not cover them too deeply. The seeds will soon germinate and the young plants should be allowed to grow in the seedling bed through the summer and fall. Transplant to permanent locations as soon as they are dormant in the late fall.

Sweet Shrubs vary tremendously in fragrance. Since many nurserymen propagate their plants from seed, you will discover that not all nursery-grown plants are as fragrant as you wish. To insure the fragrance desired, it is necessary to propagate by cuttings or layers. Layering is the easiest method for the home gardener who wants only a few plants. Find an intensely fragrant plant and layer it in the winter or late summer, using hardened but young wood. Transplant the following spring before new growth starts.

🌿 TAMARISK or SALT CEDAR
Tamarix ramosissima

Size: 15 feet high in tree form, 8 to 10 feet as a pruned shrub
Exposure: Sun
Type of Blossom: Airy panicles of pink blossoms
Color: Pink to rose-pink
Blossom Time: Late spring through summer
Blooming Habit: Panicles form on new twigs from old wood
When to Prune: Winter
When to Fertilize: Spring
Other Features: Well-adapted to dry soil and poor growing conditions
Problems: Should be pruned severely to keep as a shrub
Cultivars: 'Rosea,' listed as a dark rose-pink

Tamarisk or Salt Cedar is one of those wonderful plants which thrives on neglect. With little attention except pruning every year or so, it provides the garden with a light, airy shrub filled with pink blossoms during much of the summer.

🌿 VIBURNUM
Viburnum sp.

The Viburnums provide many excellent plants for the garden. Evergreen Viburnums are widely used farther north and farther south but most are neglected in our area. However, the group which produces large white or pink "snowballs" in the spring are widely grown and admired. Many are intensely fragrant and give the mid-spring garden a delightful aroma.

The Common Snowball, *Viburnum Opulus* cv. 'Sterile,' has large balls of pure white, sterile flowers which are perhaps the showiest but are not fragrant. The Japanese Snowball, *Viburnum plicatum sterile* (*V. plicatum* forma *plicatum*), has smaller pure white globose heads. The Double File Viburnum, *Viburnum plicatum* forma *tomentosum*, has more fertile than sterile flowers. The flowers are set in ranks on the branches rather than in round clusters. It is a beautiful shrub when in bloom.

The Viburnums are easy to grow if you choose the right type for the spot in the garden. Some grow tall while others are more compact. Choose wisely for the area which you have.

All those listed below are easy to grow and take little extra care.

NON-FRAGRANT SPRING-FLOWERING VIBURNUMS

COMMON SNOWBALL
Viburnum Opulus cv. 'Sterile' ('Roseum')

Size: 12 feet high, 8 to 10 feet across
Exposure: Sun to light shade

Sweet Shrub

Sweet Shrub

Common Snowball

Double File Viburnum

Double File Viburnum

Type of Blossom: Large round clusters like snowballs
Color: White
Blossom Time: Spring
Blooming Habit: Flowers form on previous growth
When to Prune: After bloom
When to Fertilize: After bloom
Other Features: Attractive foliage and compact shrub
Problems: Aphids occasionally

The Common Snowball has been grown in the Southern garden for many years. It is one of the more spectacular flowering shrubs in the spring. In the fall the foliage will occasionally turn a beautiful red here as it always does farther north.

JAPANESE SNOWBALL
Viburnum plicatum sterile (V. plicatum forma *plicatum)*

Size: 10 feet high, 8 feet wide
Exposure: Sun to part shade
Type of Blossom: Globose heads of sterile flowers
Color: White
Blossom Time: Mid to late spring
Blooming Habit: Last year's growth
When to Prune: After bloom
When to Fertilize: After bloom
Other Features: Very attractive dense, upright shrub
Problems: Few, if any

I prefer the Japanese over the Common Snowball. The flower clusters are smaller but more numerous and the plant is more attractive.

DOUBLE FILE VIBURNUM
Viburnum plicatum forma *tomentosum*

Size: 8 to 10 feet high, 6 to 8 feet across
Exposure: Sun to moderate shade
Type of Blossom: Fertile and sterile flowers set in a file on the younger wood; sterile flowers showy
Color: White
Blossom Time: Mid to late spring
Blooming Habit: Last year's growth
When to Prune: After blooms but only when needed
When to Fertilize: After bloom
Other Features: Beautiful shrub with branches in layers
Problems: None to worry about

VIBURNUM BURKWOODII
Viburnum × Burkwoodii

Size: Will grow into a small tree of 10 to 12 feet; may be kept as a bushy shrub at 6 to 8 feet
Exposure: Sun to part shade
Type of Blossom: 4-inch round clusters
Color: Pink progressing to white
Blossom Time: Spring
Blooming Habit: Old wood
When to Prune: After bloom
When to Fertilize: After bloom
Other Features: A loose spreading shrub unless pruned; may be almost evergreen
Problems: Tends to grow into a small tree unless pruned

The *Viburnum × Burkwoodii* is a plant which I grew up with in the family garden. Many years later it has been allowed to grow upward and form a multi-trunk small tree which spreads over part of the terrace. What a delight it is to sit underneath in the spring when the fragrant flowers are at their peak! The only drawback might be the loose growth which will spread if left unchecked.

It is one of the earlier fragrant Viburnums to blossom.

VIBURNUM CARLCEPHALUM
Viburnum × carlcephalum

Size: 6 to 8 feet high, 5- to 6-foot spread
Exposure: Sun to light shade
Type of Blossom: Round clusters measuring to 6 inches
Color: Pink buds opening to a white flower
Blossom Time: Spring
Blooming Habit: Old wood
When to Prune: After bloom
When to Fertilize: After bloom
Other Features: Spreading shrub, large flower clusters; very fragrant
Problems: Needs pruning to remain compact

The *Viburnum × carlcephalum* has the largest flower cluster of all the fragrant Viburnums listed here. They are also extremely heavily scented. The shrub is loose and very attractive but may be pruned into a more compact form. I think this is probably the best of all the fragrant Viburnums I have ever seen.

VIBURNUM JUDDII
Viburnum × Juddii

Size: 6 to 8 feet high, 4 to 6 feet across
Exposure: Sun to light shade
Type of Blossom: Round flower clusters
Color: Pink buds open to pure white flowers

Viburnum Burkwoodii

Viburnum Carlcephalum

Viburnum Juddii

White Fringe Tree

Blossom Time: Spring
Blooming Habit: Old wood
When to Prune: After bloom
When to Fertilize: After bloom
Other Features: The most dense and compact of the fragrant Viburnums listed
Problems: Few, if any

Viburnum × Juddii is my choice for a specimen shrub which has the scent of the other fragrant Viburnums but the form of a beautiful specimen plant. It takes less pruning to remain compact.

 WEIGELA, CARDINAL SHRUB
Weigela cv. 'Vanicekii'

Size: 6 feet high, 4 to 5 feet wide
Exposure: Sun to light shade
Type of Blossom: Tubular
Color: Rose-red
Blossom Time: Late spring
Blooming Habit: Short shoots from last year's growth
When to Prune: Immediately after bloom
When to Fertilize: Spring or after bloom
Other Features: Handsome oval to upright shrub
Problems: Old wood should be removed from time to time

The Weigela is an old favorite and fills in between the spring- and summer-flowering shrubs. The Cardinal Shrub has a rich rose-red flower and is probably the showiest of all the Weigelas.

The Weigelas have few problems except that the oldest wood should continually be removed to force the wood each year on which the new shoots will flower.

There are several other colors of Weigela which have some interest: a pink, *Weigela florida* (the specie color), and a white, *Weigela florida* cv. 'Alba.'

WHITE FRINGETREE or GRANCY GRAY BEARD
Chionanthus virginicus

Size: As a shrub, 12 feet high
Exposure: Full sun to moderate shade
Type of Blossom: Silky panicles
Color: White
Blossom Time: Late spring
Blooming Habit: Old wood
When to Prune: After bloom
When to Fertilize: After bloom
Other Features: Dark blue clusters of grape-like fruit in the fall
Problems: May have some scale; use a systemic insecticide

Though the White Fringetree was described in the chapter on trees, it is equally desirable when pruned as a shrub. Nip the young plants below the terminal bud of the main stem and any of the longer branches. Keep the plant's top cut back lightly to force a shrub form.

Though this plant is native and will grow in some shade, the heaviest bloom comes on plants in at least a half-day full sun. It may be used at the edge of the woods if the exposure is any but northern.

The silky, showy white panicles of flowers are extraordinary in the spring, and the summer foliage makes an excellent background. Since the male and female flowers may be set on separate plants, not all plants will produce fruit, but both flowers are equally showy.

It is reported to have scale problems occasionally, but I have never experienced that problem.

 WILLOW
Salix sp.

The willows make up a great group of shrubs for our gardens, being planted for their unusual silky buds which appear in the very early spring, followed by the flower which generally appears before the leaves. The flower is a showy upright catkin. There are also species which have unusual stem formations like the Fan Tail Willow, *Salix sachalinensis* 'Sekka,' with flattened branches, and *Salix Matsudana* 'Tortuosa,' with contorted stems.

But the willows are not problem-free. Willow Aphids and scale will take their toll. Spraying or treating with a systemic fertilizer in the ground will control most of the problems, and the unusual characteristics of these plants make the effort worthwhile.

CORKSCREW WILLOW
Salix Matsudana cv. 'Tortuosa'

Size: 40 feet as a tree, but pruning it as a shrub can keep it under 12 feet
Exposure: Sun to light shade
Type of Blossom: Catkins, but noted for its large buds
Color: Silky buds followed by yellow flowers
Blossom Time: Early spring
Blooming Habit: Last year's growth
When to Prune: After bloom
When to Fertilize: After bloom
Other Features: Grown primarily for its unusual twisted branches
Problems: Usual willow problems of aphids and scale

The Corkscrew or Contorted Willow is generally grown as a large shrub by pruning it severely as a young plant and by encouraging multiple stems from the base. It may also be grown as a tree. The twisted branches give a unique appearance. The buds are not as showy as the Pussy Willow, but the catkins, when in flower in the early spring, are outstanding.

FAN TAIL WILLOW
Salix sachalinensis cv. 'Sekka'

Size: Tree form to 30 feet, shrub form to 12 feet
Exposure: Sun to light shade
Type of Blossom: Catkin preceded by silver buds
Color: Buds are silver, flowers yellow
Blossom Time: Early spring
Blooming Habit: On last year's wood
When to Prune: After bloom, but sparingly when older
When to Fertilize: After bloom
Other Features: The flattened branches are much prized when dried and used in flower arrangements
Problems: Usual willow problems

The Fan Tail Willow is greatly prized by flower arrangers all over the world. The flattened branches may be over 6 inches wide and, when dried, add great interest in an arrangement. In our part of the world it is seldom used as a tree but almost always as a shrub, formed by severe pruning when it is young to force many shoots from the base. Further pruning is seldom needed except to keep it in bounds, letting nature produce the rare and unusually wide flattened branches.

PUSSY WILLOW
Salix discolor

Size: Tree form reaches 25 feet, shrub form under 12 feet
Exposure: Sun to part shade
Type of Blossom: Upright catkin coming from a prominent large, silky bud
Color: The buds are silky-pink, the flowers are yellow
Blossom Time: Early spring
Blooming Habit: Last year's growth
When to Prune: After bloom
When to Fertilize: After bloom
Other Features: Clean upright shrub, rounded in form
Problems: Usual willow problems

The native Pussy Willow, *Salix discolor,* is the toughest and yet showiest of the Pussy Willows for us. Though there are other willows with showy buds, the growth of this one makes it my choice for the South.

Keep the oldest wood pruned out of the Pussy Willow so that the young stems form the majority of the plant. These will produce the best buds and flowers. If the bud-filled twigs are cut when they are first showy and then dried, they will last for many months.

Goat Willow, *Salix caprea,* is also used extensively for a Pussy Willow. The catkins are somewhat larger, and in bloom it is a mite more spectacular. If your nurseryman lists the Goat Willow instead of the native Pussy Willow, *Salix discolor,* do not shy away. It is perfectly suitable and worth having.

A QUICK GUIDE TO OUR SHRUBS' INTERESTING FEATURES

SHRUBS WITH FRAGRANT FLOWERS

Chaste Tree (Summer)
Clerodendrum (Summer)
Winter Honeysuckle (Winter/Early Spring)
Meratia, Wintersweet (Very Early Winter)
Mock Orange (Spring)
Lilacs (Spring)
Fragrant Viburnums (Spring)

SHRUBS WHICH BLOSSOM IN THE SUMMER

Althaea, Rose of Sharon
Butterfly Bush
Chaste Tree
Clerodendrum
Gold Flower, Hypericum
Annabelle Hydrangea
Blue-Pink Hydrangea
Hills of Snow Hydrangea
Oakleaf Hydrangea
Peegee Hydrangea
Double Flowering Pomegranate
Tamarisk

VERY EARLY-FLOWERING SHRUBS (In order of bloom)

Meratia, Wintersweet
Winter Honeysuckle
Flowering Quince
January Jasmine
Forsythia
Pussy Willow
Fan Tail Willow
Corkscrew Willow

SHRUBS FOR DRIED ARRANGEMENTS

Clerodendrum (Fruiting Branches)
Hydrangeas (All)
Common Snowball
Japanese Snowball
Pussy Willow
Fan Tail Willow
Corkscrew Willow

FLOWERING SHRUBS WHICH FORCE WELL INSIDE

January Jasmine
Forsythia
Meratia, Wintersweet
Flowering Quince
Pussy Willow

FLOWERING SHRUBS WITH SHOWY FRUIT

Clerodendrum
Winter Honeysuckle
Double Flowering Pomegranate
Flowering Quince
White Fringetree (Female Plants Only)

'Nivalis' Japanese
Flowering Quince

Atlanta Rose Society's display garden at the Atlanta Botanical Garden

ROSES FOR THE SOUTH

The rose is the perfect flowering shrub. No other shrub in the garden will bloom for five to six months. No other can be used as a bedding, background, specimen, cutting garden, hedge, or even a climbing plant. There are wild roses in Chile, the fruit of which are harvested for the enormous quantities of Vitamin C. There are greenhouse roses which are forced for year-round cutting and sale and there are miniature post roses which may be grown inside the house. The genus Rosa is most versatile. Of course, not every individual rose type or cultivar accomplishes all of the above functions; actually there is a different species or cultivar for each of the functions listed. As a whole, it is a remarkable group of plants.

The blossom of the rose is its most striking feature. There are few flowers on any plant which can be as magnificent as those on a well-grown hybrid tea rose. There are few shrubs with the mass of flowers which a well-grown floribunda has.

Historically, the rose has been with the gardener for hundreds, perhaps thousands, of years. Wars have even been named for it, and I would suspect that quite a few verbal or physical conflicts have occurred over whose rose was the most beautiful. Its beauty has inspired the gardener and still does. The poet, the playwright, the composer, and the artist have all tried to capture its remarkable qualities.

Roses do have thorns! What is beautiful is not always easy to obtain, and the proper culture of the rose is of absolute importance so that the gardener can produce something to write or sing about.

My grandfather was a rosarian; so was my father, and so am I. I mentioned the Meratia as being a nostalgic shrub for me because my mother would bring in the blossoms to scent the house at Christmas. I also remember many warmer Christmases when my father would cut an Etoile de Hollande rose from the garden for the Christmas table. One of the highlights of my life was my choice of one of Mike Dering's huge red seedlings to name the Harry G. Hastings Rose in honor of my grandfather. Of course it was red, for he always said, "All roses are beautiful as long as they are red."

I've budded roses in the nursery as a 13-year old, I've packed and shipped them to places all over this part of the country, and I've grown them here at Sweet Apple. I think I have a right to be opinionated about them.

What is the status of the rose as a Southern garden plant? I believe it is not so good these days. Roses have been oversold, the victims of popularity, a need for new models, and a lot of hype. Where is the "Rose of the Century" which came out, say, ten years ago? I can't even remember its name, much less find it in many nurseries.

I am constantly asked why there is so much more Blackspot disease these days. There really isn't. Our modern roses are just not bred for innate resistance to Blackspot or any other disease; when not sprayed constantly, they look pretty pitiful. Now we are supposed to have fungicides to protect them, so why bother breeding resistance or propagating older varieties which were not devastated by the onslaughts of disease? Nurserymen seem to want to concentrate on size, color, and something new these days. This makes a rigid spray program imperative and therefore more work for the rose gardener. The Southern gardener needs a beautiful new Blackspot-resistant rose far more than this country needs a "nickel cigar."

Let's face it: The South is a different rose world from California, Oregon, Ohio, or New England. We need roses which withstand a long growing season, high heat and humidity, clay soil, and rampant diseases. We need *Southern roses*, not roses for other parts of the country where conditions are a lot different.

These words are written for the average gardener and not for the rose hobbyists whose great expertise allows them to grow beautiful roses which are basically born and bred for some other place. The rest of you, who just want a few beautiful roses to admire in the garden or to cut and bring inside to brighten your life, are the object of the following advice about growing roses in the South.

CLASSES OF ROSES

Garden roses are divided into several general classes. Your choice of the class of rose which you will plant depends on your needs and your desires.

Hybrid Tea Rose

Floribunda Rose

Grandiflora Rose

Hybrid Tea Roses are the real "monthly" roses of the garden. The plants are generally upright. The canes are heavy and most of the blossoms will be formed individually at the end of a new shoot. The flowers may be large and heavily doubled with sixty or more petals.

Floribunda Roses are the shrub roses with many shoots forming a more oval-shaped bush. The flowers are usually set in clusters of from three to five at the end of a new shoot. The terminal and the lateral buds usually open in unison, giving a large display all at once. The plants have heavy foliage when grown well, and make an excellent hedge or background group.

Grandiflora Roses are supposed to be crosses between Floribundas and Hybrid Teas, bred to produce a taller, heavier, more upright plant than the Hybrid Tea but with larger flowers than the Floribunda. The flowers are generally set in clusters of three at the end of a new shoot. The terminal bud opens before the laterals. Though the flowers may approach the size of a Hybrid Tea, most often they are slightly smaller. They are generally better growing and less prone to die-back and disease problems.

Climbing Hybrid Tea Roses are really long-caned bush roses. Instead of being only three to five feet tall, the canes may be as much as eight to ten feet. They may be pinned against a wall, fence, or fan trellis or used as a pillar against a post or narrow, upright structure.

Kordesii Climbers are a rather new and distinct group of climbers, more vigorous than the Climbing Hybrid Teas and more floriferous. Like the Climbing Hybrid Teas, they are recurrent bloomers and will flower as long as new wood is being set. The Kordesii Climbers are easier to grow on a fence or wall because the branches are not as rigid and upright as the Climbing Hybrid Teas. Many are very disease-resistant and require less spraying.

The above is a listing only of the groups most often seen in catalogs and nurseries. There are many other worthwhile ones, including many we call "old fashioned roses" and of course the increasingly popular miniatures which may be grown in pots, tubs, planter boxes, or even as borders.

We will discuss the specific cultivars for your garden later. Other decisions and actions need to be taken first.

Climbing Hybrid Tea Rose

GROWING ROSES IN THE SOUTHERN GARDEN

Roses are plants of sunny spots, first and foremost. You can meet other requirements with good techniques, but the rose area of the garden *must* have at least six hours of full sun per day. They are plants which need rich but well-drained soil. Heavy soil is not an impediment if it has plenty of humus and good drainage. Roses are heavy feeders and should be given an even supply of nutrients during their growing season. Most modern roses require constant rejuvenation through proper and timely pruning. Finally, roses need protection from insects and diseases.

Choosing the Site for Roses

1. Choose an open area of the garden which is as free from shade as possible. Remember, they must have at least six hours of full sun per day during the growing season.
2. Stay away from low, soggy, and poorly-drained areas.
3. Choose as rich soil as possible.
4. Choose an area with good air movement to keep down fungus attacks.

Preparing the Rose Area for Planting

Always plant roses in beds, even climbers and Floribunda roses for hedges. Here is how to do it:

1. Work the soil as deeply as possible. The experts dig out the soil to 36 inches and put 6 inches of gravel in the bottom for drainage. We regular gardeners should break up the soil with a mattock and till it as deeply as the tiller will go.
2. Unless you are going to build the bed by removing the soil, adding gravel, and then amending the soil to be put back in the bed, you should crown the bed; that is, raise it in the center about a foot higher than at the edges. This will help the drainage tremendously.
3. Now amend the soil well with peat moss, ground bark, perlite for drainage, and manure. A good beginning point for a 100-square-foot bed is:
   One 6-cubic-foot bale of peat moss
   One 3-cubic-foot bag of ground bark
   One 3-cubic-foot bag of perlite
   20 pounds of limestone (for most soils)
   50 pounds of cattle manure (dehydrated, not composted, if you can find it)

   Till these materials into the bed until they are thoroughly and evenly incorporated into the whole root zone. Feel the soil. If it crumbles nicely, you have added enough. If it still feels slick between your fingers, add more ground bark.
4. Be sure there is enough bulk to raise the center of the bed 12 inches above the edges. If there is not, be sure to add more soil and amendments. Crowning the bed is of great importance.
5. Make a V-shaped ditch around the bed so that excess water from the bed will move into this ditch and away from the bed.

Work the soil thoroughly, adding required amendments.

Rake the bed and pull soil to a crown.

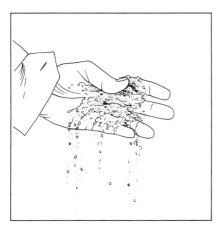

Feel the soil to be sure it's loose and friable.

Planting Roses

I prefer planting bare-root roses in the very late fall or as soon as you can get them. Packaged roses are also fine, provided they are not waxed, and provided they have been kept in a cold place before you purchase them. Waxing, per se, does not harm a rose. However, the reason for waxing is to prevent the canes from drying out in warm stores. It is this warmth which is bad for roses. The roots begin to grow and the canes fill with sap, and then the plant goes through a tremendous shock when it is put outside. Mail-order rose plants are acceptable because they generally meet my requirements.

Have your bed ready when you get the plants. You want to put them in the ground as soon as possible after they arrive or after you pick them up.

After you receive your plants or bring them home from the nursery, follow these planting steps:

1. Remove the plants from the package and put the roots in a bucket of water. Let them soak for several hours (overnight is best) before taking them to the garden to plant.
2. Look at the roots when you unwrap the package. Prune off any broken ones and cut away any broken or spindly shoots. A good new rose plant will have three heavy canes the size of your finger which are at least 12 inches long.
3. After soaking, dig a hole which will comfortably accommodate the roots without bending.
4. Look at the way the roots come from the base of the plant. They spread outward and downward at an angle. Notice the open area in the center of the roots where none seem to be growing.
5. Find the graft union. This will be a swollen area just below where the canes start from the main trunk. A well-grown plant will have this union no more than 3 or 4 inches above the roots. Avoid "high shank roses," those with the bud union 6 or more inches above the roots.
6. Planting depth in the South is very important, and it is different from what is recommended for farther north and farther south. In the South, plant roses with the graft union (swollen area) right on top of the ground. Do not cover the graft union with soil when planting.
7. Now, with the loose soil, make a cone in the bottom of the hole, pointed end up. Make the cone high enough so that you can place the roots on the cone and the graft union will be right on top of the ground when the hole is filled with soil. Snuggle the plant down on the cone so the roots lie on top, slanted down and out.
8. Fill the hole with loose soil. Press the soil tightly around the roots to eliminate any air pockets. Make a saucer around each plant to hold water.
9. After all your new roses are planted, soak each one slowly to settle the soil around the roots.
10. Mulch the bed with pine-straw but leave the saucer open. Do not mulch around the canes.

Caring for Roses through the Year

NEW ROSES

Your bed of roses will remain dormant until spring. If the weather dips to below 10° F., it will help to draw pine-straw up against the canes for protection against the cold. As soon as the weather moderates, pull the pine-straw back as it was.

In late February, pull the pine-straw back and cultivate the bed lightly with a long-handled hand cultivator. Apply a combination fertilizer and systemic insecticide. Place this dry material in a circle around each plant at the outer edge of the original hole you dug when planting. Use the manufacturer's recommendation. Now pull the mulch back over the bed, leaving a saucer around the center of each plant.

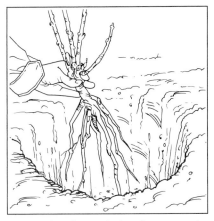

Be sure the planting hole is large enough to accommodate the roots without bending.

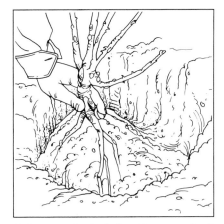

Make a cone in the hole with prepared soil and place the plant on top so that the roots press against the soil with no air-pockets.

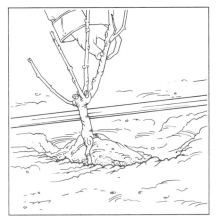

Be sure the graft union is above the surface of the soil.

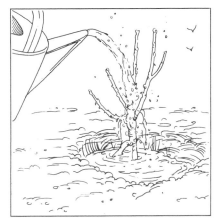

Pack prepared soil tightly around the roots. When the hole is half filled, water thoroughly to settle the soil and drive out air-pockets.

Fill the hole. DO NOT COVER THE GRAFT.

Apply a good fresh mulch like pine-straw.

Check each plant for die-back of the canes. This problem will show up as brown tips. Cut off all brown tips now. If the plant is beginning to put out buds, cut the canes back to a healthy growing bud near the tip of the cane.

OLD ROSES

After the first year and each year thereafter, treat roses in the following way:

1. In January, use a dormant spray of lime sulfur. Spray the canes, branches, and even old hanging leaves. Spray the top of the old mulch. This kills many of the overwintering spores of rose diseases.
2. In late February or very early March, start your major rose work:
   a. Prune your roses. (See "How to Prune Roses" below.)
   b. Remove all the old mulch and plant litter. Do not re-use the mulch because it is full of disease spores and insect eggs.
   c. Cultivate the bed lightly.
   d. Apply dehydrated cow or sheep manure if you can find it in large bags.
   e. Apply a combination rose fertilizer and systemic insecticide in a circle around the plants. Make a 4- to 6-inch band under the outer reach of the pruned canes.
   f. Place a fresh new mulch over the bed, leaving a saucer around each plant.

How to Prune Roses

All roses which blossom through the summer will set their flowers on wood grown during this blossoming time. The theory of pruning roses *in the South* is to prune the plants in late February or early March very severely so that large amounts of heavy new growth will come and produce an abundance of flowers through the season.

It is important to understand the reason for pruning in the South in late February or early March rather than in the fall or winter as authorities in other areas *wrongly* recommend for us. In the South, early pruning can be disastrous. Our winter weather patterns are very different from those in other parts of the country. In general, our winters are rather mild with daytime temperatures in the mid-50's and 60's except when a real "Arctic Express" flows over the Great Plains and down the Mississippi Valley. The jet stream picks up these fronts and pushes them across the country. When the jet stream is flowing far South, we have terrific drops in temperature. At these times, the temperature may reach as low as zero over much of our area.

The combination of mild temperatures on most days and these deep freezes causes severe problems for plants. Roses are one group which may suffer badly. By altering his pruning methods, however, the gardener can prevent most of the trouble.

Inspect plant and decide how to prune.

Remove all dead wood and canes which have begun to have rough bark.

Try to leave 3 to 5 good canes on each plant.

Head back the canes which are left. Prune these to 12 to 15 inches.

The warm days will force new growth on roses. If you prune the plants severely in the fall or winter, there are just a few growth buds left. These sprout very quickly, perhaps pushing out four or five inches in just a few days. When the "Arctic Express" arrives, these shoots may be killed, making repruning necessary and reducing the size of the plant.

Rosarians in the South have found that the better procedure is to leave the plants alone until these cold snaps are over, usually about the end of February. The new growth may be forced out on unpruned plants but it will be on the upper parts of the canes. If there is winter damage, it will not matter since these areas will be removed later during regular pruning.

Hybrid Tea and **Grandiflora Roses** should be pruned in the following way:

1. Examine the plant and choose three to five of the best canes which are coming out from close to the graft union. These canes will form the

structure of the pruned plant. The best canes to leave are those which are one or two years old, are as large as your thumb, and are 15 or more inches long. They should be a clean green; they should not have brown or purple splotches.

2. Starting at the bottom, near the graft union, first remove all dead and weak canes. Then remove all old canes, especially those with corky bark. Remove all diseased canes. Try to leave at least three good canes spaced evenly around the plant. If there are not three good canes, leave two. Never leave a bad cane on the plant. A healthy bush will grow from two or even one cane; it just takes more time and more attention.

3. Now cut these canes back to about 15 inches.

4. Make all the cuts about 1/2 inch above a bud (in other words, above a leaf scar where a latent bud is). Make the cut on a slant with the high side above the bud or leaf scar so a raindrop can't rest on the wood and rot it.

5. Seal all cuts with a dab of wood glue like Elmer's. I prefer this to the black asphalt-base materials.

6. Not all of the buds to which you have pruned will grow. After growth has started, check the canes to see which buds have become new shoots. Cut back to these developing shoots. The stem above the developing shoot will die back to the shoot and should be removed. Be sure to seal these cuts also.

Floribunda Roses are pruned at the same time and basically in a similar way, with the following exceptions:

1. Since Floribunda roses are more shrub-like, you should leave five to seven canes.

2. Floribunda roses are pruned back only about two-thirds or to about 20 inches.

Borer damage when a cane was not sealed

Climbing Hybrid Tea Roses are pruned similarly to bush Hybrid Teas and at the same time, with the following exception: Thin the plant as with bush Hybrid Teas, but *do not* cut back these one- or two-year-old canes. They will be the structure to tie on the fence or trellis.

Spring-blooming climbers are best thinned in the winter to remove all the old, non-productive wood. Restrict your thinning to this type of cane. Leave all other canes because they will produce the blossoms.

These basic principles will cover most rose pruning for the average gardener. There are other types of roses which you might grow, and the method of pruning them may vary from the above principles. How you should prune the plant will be determined by the time of its bloom and what type of wood produces the flowers. Generally, if the type blossoms on the current season's growth (new shoots), prune as described above. If the type blossoms on last year's growth, do major structural pruning and thinning in late February or early March, and light thinning and maintenance pruning later, after blossoming has finished.

Summer Grooming and Flower Cutting

Summertime, when your roses are producing huge numbers of beautiful flowers, is the time to enjoy them. The plants will need attention, however, as the flowering season progresses. Cutting the flowers is a type of pruning and will encourage more flower shoots. Always cut a flower stem above a set of five leaves instead of the first set of leaves under the flower stalk, which are only three leaflets.

Do not be afraid to do summer grooming any time a problem arises. Remove any dead stalk as soon as possible. Cut back canes which are dying back or developing purple or brown areas below the affected area. Treat all cuts, except when cutting a flower, with wood glue to prevent borers or rot from developing.

Canker should be removed when grooming roses.

Aphids on a floribunda rose

Japanese Beetles ruining a rose

Blackspot, our worst disease

Keeping Your Roses Healthy

Roses need to be kept growing healthily and luxuriantly. Fertilize them every six to eight weeks until early September with the material used in the spring. Water them, by soaking, when the weather is very dry. Control weeds with a heavy mulch but never allow it to touch the base of the canes or the main stem. Remove spindly, weak growth and die-back whenever you see it. If you keep the plant growing healthily, you will avoid many insect and disease problems. But if they should begin to show up, attend to them promptly.

Rose varieties are innately different in their response to insects and diseases. Older varieties seem to have more inbred resistance than the new ones do. Light-pinks, whites, and yellows are much more susceptible to thrip damage than the darker colors. Yellows and whites seem to be much more susceptible to Blackspot than reds. A conversation with a rosarian or attendance at a meeting of your local rose society will give you a lot of information on the ability of the various cultivars to withstand insects and diseases. Start with the hardiest cultivars. It keeps a new rosarian from quitting in disgust.

Aphids, thrips, spider mites, chafers, bud worms, and Japanese beetles all attack the rose. Using a systemic insecticide in the ground will eliminate many aphids and spider mites, but will not affect thrips, bud worms, chafers, or Japanese beetles, in most cases. You will need to keep a sprayer ready to control them. Check with your County Extension Agent for the material recommended in your area.

Blackspot and Mildew are the two most devastating diseases of roses. In our part of the world, Blackspot is the worst problem. Healthy, strong-growing roses have less problem with Blackspot than weak, spindly plants. If you keep your plants growing well, it is much easier to control Blackspot. Fungicides are preventatives, in most cases, and not curatives. Once an infection occurs, remove those leaves and take them away. Start a spray program with a recommended material immediately to protect the rest of the plant from infection.

Obtaining New Rose Plants

The most common way to obtain a new rose plant is to purchase it from a nursery or from a mail-order catalog. The widest selections are usually from a mail-order company specializing in roses. Many nurseries and other plant suppliers also have excellent plants from which to choose. In my opinion, the practice of offering only container-grown roses in the spring is not good. My years of experience have taught me that roses do far better when planted in the late fall, after the first hard freezes, and during the winter. Spring planting, especially after blossoms appear, is way too late to have the plant become well-established and perform properly the first season. Bare-root plants are excellent choices when planting in the fall and winter, and they are generally less expensive than container-grown plants.

Purchasing a rose is not the only way of getting a new plant. Many roses are easily propagated from cuttings taken in the late fall or winter. Remember, though, that roses which are protected by plant patent laws (most of the newer ones) may not be propagated legally. Since I prefer the older, hardier, and more disease-resistant varieties which are either no longer patented or never were, making cuttings is a practical and easy way to obtain plants from friends. Not all roses, however, grow well on their own roots. That is the reason so many are grafted upon a wild-rose root stock. Many do grow well on their own roots, and these are the ones which are easily propagated by cuttings.

HOW TO MAKE ROSE CUTTINGS

Wait until the new wood is hard and woody. Then follow these steps:

1. Make a few long cuttings from the current season's growth. These may be as long as 2 or 3 feet. The wood should be about the size of your finger down to the size of a pencil.

2. Cut them into approximately 6-inch lengths. Make the bottom cut on a slant, with the highest part about $1/4$ inch below a leaf scar. Make the top cut about $1/4$ inch above a leaf scar. If the lengths vary now, don't worry about it. Wrap the cuttings in a wet paper towel or cloth and put in the vegetable crisper in the refrigerator until you are ready to root.
3. Roses are best rooted in a sandy loam soil, peat moss and sand, or pure vermiculite or perlite. This should be in a bed in the open. A cold frame is an excellent place to root roses.
4. As soon as the cuttings are made and the weather is cool, stick them in the medium about 1 inch deep. The use of a rooting hormone will hasten the rooting process and help a better root system to develop.

It will take several months for the roots to appear and be sufficiently large for transplanting. I would suggest potting them when the roots are an inch long and there are a good number of them ready. As soon as the leaves begin to form on the cuttings, set the new plants in the garden.

WHICH ROSES ARE BEST?

Differences of opinion are what get rid of poor farm land, make a horse race interesting, and sell many different types of roses. It is like entering a briar thicket to try to recommend a group of roses to a group of gardeners. I am old enough and stubborn enough to enter the briars, so here goes!

THE TWELVE BEST OF ALL BUSH ROSES

ROSE	CLASS	COLOR
CHRYSLER IMPERIAL	HT	Red
EUROPEANA	Flor.	Red
FASHION	Flor.	Coral-Pink
FRAGRANT CLOUD	HT	Orange-Red
HONEY FAVORITE	HT	Light Pink
KING'S RANSOM	HT	Yellow
MISTER LINCOLN	HT	Red
PASCALI	HT	White
PEACE	HT	Yellow, Tinge of Pink
QUEEN ELIZABETH	Grand.	Pink
TIFFANY	HT	Pink, Yellow Base
TROPICANA	HT	Orange-Red

KEY:
HT—Hybrid Tea   HP—Hybrid Perpetual
Flor.—Floribunda   OF—Old-Fashioned
Grand.—Grandiflora   Poly.—Polyantha

NOTE: I chose the Harry G. Hastings, HT (Red) specifically for the South. I think it is one of the twelve best, but I am definitely prejudiced. Since it is hard to find now, I add it as a footnote to the "Best" list.

THE BEST CLIMBERS

ROSE	CLASS	COLOR
BLAZE	HW	Bright Red Clusters
CL. CECILE BRUNNER	Poly.	Pink Miniature
CL. CRIMSON GLORY	HT	Red
CL. ETOILE DE HOLLAND	HT	Red
DORTMUND, KORDESII CLIMBER	HT	Red, White Petal Base
GOLDEN SHOWERS	HT	Yellow
NEW DAWN	HW	Pink
CL. PEACE	HT	Yellow, Tinge of Pink
CL. QUEEN ELIZABETH	Grand.	Pink

KEY:

HT—Hybrid Tea	HP—Hybrid Perpetual
Flor.—Floribunda	HW—Hybrid Wichuraiana
Grand.—Grandiflora	OF—Old-Fashioned
	Poly.—Polyantha

NOTE: Lady Banksia, Rosa Banksiae cv. 'Lutea,' is a thornless, almost evergreen spring-flowering rose from China. The flowers are double yellow, 1 inch across. In the parts of the South where it will survive the cold, it is well worth having.

There are hundreds and hundreds of rose cultivars listed in catalogs and sold in nurseries. Each year there are dozens of new ones introduced. There are "winners" of various selection committees like the All-America Rose Selections. It can be extremely confusing for us common gardeners.

The best advice I can give is to beware of new roses until they are *proven in the South*. Most of the yearly selections are based on a number of test grounds throughout the entire country. The scores are averaged, and though the Southern test results may be low, they may be averaged up and a new "winner" may appear which doesn't perform well in our area of the country.

Many of the American Rose Society's local chapters in the South have gardens in conjunction with botanical gardens, public gardens, and city parks. These are the best places to inspect rose varieties to find which do best. Most of these gardens have both old and new roses and they are an excellent place for you to compare one against another.

I have given you my "Best" list above. On page 305 is a more general list of varieties which I have had experience with and feel would be a good starting point for the average gardener.

Harry G. Hastings

Eclipse

Chrysler Imperial

Queen Elizabeth

Tropicana

Climbing Cecile Brunner

A GOOD BASIC LIST OF BUSH ROSES FOR THE SOUTH

NAME	CLASS	COLOR
CECILE BRUNNER	Poly.	Small Pink Flowers
CHARLOTTE ARMSTRONG	HT	Rose-Pink
CHRYSLER IMPERIAL	HT	Red
CRIMSON GLORY	HT	Red
DAINTY BESS	HT	Pink, Single
ECLIPSE	HT	Yellow
ETOILE DE HOLLANDE	HT	Red
EUROPEANA	Flor.	Red
FASHION	Flor.	Coral-Pink
FRAGRANT CLOUD	HT	Orange-Red
FRAU KARL DRUSCHKI	HP	White
HAPPY	Dwarf Poly.	Red
HARRY G. HASTINGS	HT	Red
HONEY FAVORITE	HT.	Light Pink
ICEBERG	Flor.	White
JOHN S. ARMSTRONG	Grand.	Red
KAISERIN AUGUSTE VIKTORIA	HT	White
KING'S RANSOM	HT	Yellow
MAMAN COCHET	OF	Silvery-Pink
MICHELE MEILLAND	HT	Pink
MISTER LINCOLN	HT	Red
MONTEZUMA	Grand.	Orange-Red
PASCALI	HT	White
PAUL NEYRON	HP	Pink
PEACE	HT	Yellow, Tinge of Pink
QUEEN ELIZABETH	Grand.	Pink
REDGOLD	Flor.	Red and Gold
SPARTAN	Flor.	Orange-Red
SUTTER'S GOLD	HT	Yellow
TALISMAN	HT	Red and Gold
THE FAIRY	Flor.	Pink
TIFFANY	HT	Pink, Yellow Base
TROPICANA	HT	Orange-Red

KEY:

HT—Hybrid Tea
Flor.—Floribunda
Grand.—Grandiflora

HP—Hybrid Perpetual
OF—Old-Fashioned
Poly.—Polyantha

CHAPTER 7

SOUTHERN LAWNS

A plane arriving in England generally flies very low on its approach to London's Heathrow Airport to get under the almost constant cloud cover. This low approach introduces the first-time visitor to the extraordinary sight of a seemingly continuous, emerald green landscape. What a difference when flying into Cairo, where the desert sand gives a landscape of gold, or into New York, where everything seems to be planted in buildings or strewn with rubbish! From the air, at least, England looks like a dream of the perfect garden; there is something about grass which is tranquil, unifying, and perfectly natural. I have been to Japan and seen their swept sand gardens, which seem unnatural to me. In my way of thinking, a place needs grass to qualify as a garden.

My first visit to England many years ago astounded me. The whole country, at least from the air, seemed to be one great lawn with groups of trees, lines of streams, and glittering lakes, all placed by some supreme landscape designer. On the ground you are overwhelmed with lawns like those in paintings or picture books. The turf is thick, the color is emerald green, and it is almost always neatly trimmed. Since that day, a trip to London for me always includes a walk through Hyde Park, not on the paths but across the playing fields. This restores my faith in the gardening adventure, for there truly is some place where beautiful lawns are not a problem to have.

307

Nowhere else does grass grow as it does in England.

Don't despair if you have had problems getting grass to grow. Think of the Egyptian who cherishes a tiny plot of green amongst all the surrounding sand. England and Ireland are the exceptions when it comes to growing grass. Most of us in the rest of the world cannot do nearly as well.

We all try, wherever we are, to have an oasis of green, thick turf around our homes. Grass is an integral part of the beauty we aspire to, and though the South is no England and grass does have its problems, Egypt is worse off than we are. The next time you think your lawn is dying out, remember that there are places where even a sprig or two of green is an achievement.

Growing a lawn is the major gardening experience for most of us. In fact, it may be the only gardening experience for many a golfer or fisherman or other outdoor enthusiast. More money is spent on lawns, I would

The Sahara Desert—There *is* someplace worse off than we are!

guess, and more money wasted than in any other gardening effort. There are as many theories about lawnmaking as there are birds in the sky. Experts abound and it is said that the professional life expectancy of a golf course greenskeeper is at zero if a green is unplayable during the course's annual tournament, because every golfer in the club is an expert who could have prevented the disaster if only he had been consulted.

Though lawnmaking in the South has its problems, the problems are basically no different than in growing any other group of plants. Grasses are plants which must grow in an environment in which they receive what they need to survive. When these needs are not met, the turf is poor. When these needs are met, the turf is as we want it: rich green, thick, and luxuriant. This cannot be accomplished by scattering seed over soil which is closely kin to concrete.

Growing a beautiful lawn is a combination of a number of gardening factors, many of which we have discussed when growing other plants:

1. Choose the right grass for the situation.
2. Plant at the correct time of the year.
3. Prepare the soil properly.
4. Apply the right growth nutrients.
5. Seed or sod the lawn correctly.
6. Keep the grass growing with a good fertilizer program.
7. Cut correctly (it's just like pruning correctly).
8. Control attacks of insects and diseases.

There are several real and practical differences between growing a lawn and growing other plants in your garden. There is usually more lawn than any other growing area. Lawn areas are seldom chosen for being the best place to grow grass. Usually, everything else is placed in its best spot and grass is assigned to the rest. Generally, lawn areas are the most visible of all the home landscape and should be kept looking good all the time. And, since lawns are such a large part of the garden, they take more time than we are sometimes willing to spend.

Don't be discouraged if you have had a failure in the past. It is possible to grow a good lawn in the South, and it is worth the effort. Fly over England and you will be convinced that the following procedures and practices are worthwhile.

So far, the perfect grass for the South has eluded us. Somewhere it exists, I guess, but until it is found, we have to work with what we have. It is important to understand the limitations of each of our grasses. You may sacrifice one quality for another which is more important to you. I cannot give you the name of a perfect grass for your lawn; nobody can, despite the never-ending claims of the perfect lawn grass for sale.

LAWN GRASSES

The lawn grasses we grow are divided into two main groups: warm-season grasses and cool-season grasses. Building a beautiful lawn starts with deciding which grass you are going to use.

You will notice that many of these grasses are listed as being started from sod. I have used sod as a general word covering all vegetative plantings. In the nursery you will find blocks of grass which may be purchased and laid solid to form an instant lawn. These may also be pulled apart and sprigged in freshly-prepared soil.

Sometimes your nurseryman will offer sprigs for sale. These are just as worthwhile and save the effort of pulling the blocks apart. Recently, nurseries have also been offering plugs. Most of these are 4-inch squares of sod which have been established in cell trays. They provide the homeowner with an easy way to start a lawn by plugging, without the hard chore of chopping thick turf into small squares.

The way you start your lawn vegetatively is largely up to you and depends on the effort and money you want to spend. The least expensive way is to buy blocks of sod which have been cut with large machines at the sod nurseries. If you wish to purchase sprigs, plugs, or some other variation to save yourself time and effort, watch the economics or you may find yourself spending a great deal more money than you meant to.

Common Bermuda Grass and Centipede Grass may also be seeded. This is the best way to establish a Common Bermuda Grass lawn, for the seed germinates quickly and the new seedlings grow rapidly and soon are spreading. The seed, however, is very small and special techniques are needed to broadcast it evenly. Centipede Grass also makes seed and may be started in the same manner. However, the seed are expensive and slow to germinate, which may allow heavy weed-grass or broadleaf weed infestations prior to coming up. The seeds are very small, like Bermuda Grass seed, and must be handled and distributed carefully.

In the South all the cool-season grasses are planted from seed with the possible exception of Bluegrass which on rare occasions may be found in the sod form. However, to be practical, plan to start your cool-season lawn from seed. It is less expensive, and since these grasses germinate rather quickly, a new green lawn is not that far off anyway.

Until the perfect grass for the South is found, we have to work with what we have.

SOUTHERN LAWN GRASSES

COMMON NAME	CLASS	HOW TO START	GROWTH HABIT	TEXTURE	EXPOSURE
COMMON BERMUDA GRASS	Warm-Season	Sod or Seed	Rhizomes and Stolons	Medium	Sun
TIFGREEN BERMUDA GRASS	Warm-Season	Sod	Rhizomes and Runners	Fine	Sun
TIFWAY BERMUDA GRASS	Warm-Season	Sod	Rhizomes and Runners	Very Fine	Sun
CENTIPEDE GRASS	Warm-Season	Sod or Seed	Runners	Medium	Sun to Part Shade
TALL FESCUE	Cool-Season	Seed	Expanding Clumps	Medium	Sun to Part Shade
CREEPING RED FESCUE	Cool-Season	Seed	Expanding Clumps	Fine	Light to Moderate Shade
CHEWING FESCUE	Cool-Season	Seed	Expanding Clumps	Fine	Light to Moderate Shade
KENTUCKY BLUEGRASS	Cool-Season	Seed	Rhizomes	Fine	Part Shade
ST. AUGUSTINE GRASS	Warm-Season	Sod	Runners	Coarse	Sun to Moderate Shade
MEYER ZOYSIA GRASS	Warm-Season	Sod	Runners	Medium	Sun to Part Shade
EMERALD ZOYSIA GRASS	Warm-Season	Sod	Runners	Fine	Sun to Moderate Shade

ALL ABOUT SOUTHERN GRASSES

Warm-Season Grasses

The Southern warm-season or summer grasses are ideal for us. They are tough, they are heat-resistant, they grow well in our soils, and they have truly lasting qualities. They come back each year with renewed vigor and become thicker with age.

But they are not green in the winter. Frost will brown the tops and new green will not appear until the weather is warm. Practically speaking, these grasses are green from mid-April or early-May until frost, a period of around 190 to 200 days. Thus, the lawn is green about 55% of the time. This makes these grasses less than acceptable to many homeowners.

There are advantages, though; while these grasses are green, they are in heavy growth. This heavy growth coincides with warm weather, the time when our use of the lawn is the greatest.

🌿 BERMUDA GRASS

Bermuda Grass is one of our best and toughest lawn grasses. It grows well in the heat of summer, will take a wide range of soil conditions, including pH, and is moderately drought-resistant while still maintaining good color and growth. It may be mowed relatively closely (1 $1/2$ to 2 inches) and withstands heavy traffic. The texture is medium, the color a good green. Bermuda Grass must be grown in the sun. Common Bermuda Grass spreads by both underground rhyzomes and above-ground runners or stolons. It will rapidly spread from lawns into rich, loose flower beds and vegetable areas where it may become a pest unless removed quickly.

🌿 HYBRID BERMUDA GRASSES

A number of very fine hybrids of Bermuda Grass have been developed mainly by the grass research and breeding program of Dr. Glenn W. Burton at the Georgia Coastal Plains Experiment Station.

There are two which are widely used as turf for the home lawn, Tifgreen (Tifton 319) and Tifway (Tifton 419).

Tifgreen is a low-growing, rapidly-spreading hybrid with a good green color, fine texture, good disease-resistance, and good cold-tolerance. It withstands some traffic but must be maintained properly for good results.

Tifway has a darker green color and will take more traffic than Tifgreen. Like Tifgreen, it spreads rapidly when the soil is properly prepared and must be cared for or the results will be disappointing.

The Hybrid Bermuda Grasses spread just like Common Bermuda and must be watched when flower beds or vegetable areas are adjacent. Since they do not produce viable seed, reseeding in other areas is not a problem. They should be grown only in the sun.

Tifgreen Bermuda Grass

Centipede Grass

St. Augustine Grass

Kentucky 31 Fescue Grass

Emerald Zoysia Grass

CENTIPEDE GRASS

Centipede is coarser than Bermuda Grass, can stand more neglect, and is tougher when growing well. It will take some shade. It requires a low pH of between 4.5 and 5.5 and should never be limed. It should not be over-fertilized, especially with high-phosphate fertilizers. Thatch will build up in old Centipede lawns, resulting in a rather dirty appearance.

Centipede is easier to control when adjacent to garden areas since it spreads only by runners on top of the ground. If you keep these clipped, you will have no further problems.

ST. AUGUSTINE GRASS

This thick, coarse grass is grown through much of the lower South but has its hardiness problems beyond the Coastal Plains. However, where it will grow, it is ideal for high-traffic areas and areas which are too shady for Centipede. St. Augustine spreads by runners on top of the ground. It establishes a thick new turf very rapidly from sod.

You must watch for Chinch Bugs, which can damage a St. Augustine lawn rapidly. There is also a viral disease which causes the grass plants to decline.

ZOYSIA GRASS

The Zoysia Grasses grown in the South make some of our best lawns. The color is attractive, the turf very thick, the texture excellent; and when properly maintained it is tough and can take heavy traffic.

Zoysia spreads slowly and makes such a thick turf that it is hard to cut with a rotary mower. Overseeding for green in the winter is almost impossible because of the thick turf.

These are high-maintenance grasses and even though they make our best lawns, they do so only when given the proper care.

Emerald Zoysia is probably our most beautiful turf grass. It has dark green color, makes a very thick turf, and has extremely fine texture. It will tolerate some shade, though it grows thinly when there is too little light. Heavy thatching causes problems with Emerald Zoysia and the thick turf makes rotary mowing impossible. However, it is the best grass for the highly-maintained lawn.

Meyer Zoysia is my choice of all the Zoysias because it spreads more rapidly, is more resistant to traffic, and seems to require less maintenance since it does not have the thatch problems of Emerald Zoysia. The texture is coarser than Emerald and the color is not as rich green.

Evergreen Cool-Season Grasses

The lack of green on warm-season grasses in the winter causes us to search for "evergreen" grasses which will give the lawn a beautiful year-round appearance.

The grasses chosen are not ideal as lawn grasses in the South, for each has some special drawback which must be dealt with before a beautiful lawn can be established. The failure to deal with each of these drawbacks is what causes problems for many homeowners.

In general the cool-season grasses have two excellent periods of growth, fall and spring. In the winter they grow slowly and in the summer they have a very hard time. Remember, when the daytime temperatures are from 55° F. to 75° F., cool season grasses are growing best. When the weather is frosty or freezing they grow slowly but retain their good color, at least until the temperature reaches 15° F. or so. During the summer when the temperature is above 80° F. and especially when it is also dry, these grasses grow slowly and often lose their rich green color. Often, the combination of heat and dry weather will cause such weakened growth that the turf thins and weeds encroach.

The critical period for these grasses is during the time when the lawn is used the most. Couple weak growth with high use and the beautiful turf of the fall, winter, and spring may become less than what you wish.

These comments are directed at most of the South. In the higher elevations where the summer nights are cool and the rains more frequent, the cool-season grasses grow well and should be the type used for most lawns. Where they can be grown, they are beautiful—almost, but not quite, like England.

The major cool-season grasses are listed below. These can be grown satisfactorily except in the lower part of our region where they should not be seriously considered. The major cool-season grass and the one most widely used is Tall Fescue (Kentucky 31). The others mentioned are strictly special use grasses, as you will see.

TALL FESCUE (KENTUCKY 31)

Tall Fescue is the most often used grass for home lawns in much of the South. It is evergreen, deep-rooted, and moderately drought resistant. It is, however, a pasture grass converted to lawn use. This fact should be seriously noted, for ignoring it causes much grief to the homeowner. It is also called Rough Fescue because the blades feel rough when rubbed one way and smooth when rubbed the other. It was introduced as a deep-rooted winter pasture grass, a use for which it is ideally suited even though the roughness of the blade is less appealing to animals, who will eat any other grass first.

Though not completely ideal as a lawn grass, Tall Fescue may be adapted to turf areas if properly handled. Since it is naturally a tall-growing grass plant and has a high, fleshy crown or base, it must be cut tall or the plant will "stool" or make a clump and leave the center exposed. Hot sun, especially during dry periods, will burn this fleshy crown and the plant will suffer badly. Thinning out of Tall Fescue lawns is often the result of too-close mowing. The ideal height to cut Tall Fescue is at 3 to 4 inches.

The growth cycle of Tall Fescue is also important to understand. Its major growth period starts in the fall as the temperature cools to 75° F. Fertilizing should be done at this time to give the plant what it needs to begin its new season of growth. This is also the best time to seed a new Tall Fescue lawn or rejuvenate a weakened one.

The active growth continues through the winter when the weather is mild and becomes heavy once again as the weather moderates in the spring. Fertilizer should be added in the early spring to encourage this second period of active growth. This is the alternate time for seeding or reseeding, but it is definitely a secondary time and should be avoided except for patching or thickening of areas which have suffered during the winter. New lawns started in the spring begin with a definite disadvantage because there is not enough time to grow a deep-rooted, drought-resistant root system before the hot summer arrives. Seeding or reseeding after early April is almost always a waste of time and money.

Tall Fescue slows its growth as the weather gets warmer and above 75° F. In the late spring it naturally goes to seed, and at that time it is at its weakest growth point.

Tall Fescue should be kept watered, cut tall, and never heavily fertilized during the summer. Weeds should be carefully controlled, and any insect or disease problems should be promptly corrected.

Recently, new Tall Fescues which are referred to as **Turf Type Tall Fescue Grasses** have begun to appear. These are reputed to be deeper rooted, more compact, and to withstand cutting better. I have seen only a few of these growing, and they do seem to live up to their "press" even though their use has not been general enough, at this writing, to warrant my enthusiastic endorsement. They are certainly better than the Tall Fescue for the refined lawn, but the choice as to which to use seems more a function of which ones are available in the seed outlet than anything else. **Mojave** and **Falcon** are two I have seen which seem to have much merit.

CREEPING RED AND CHEWING FESCUE

There are also other fescues with limited use which should be considered. The main two are Creeping Red Fescue, which is neither red nor does it creep, and Chewing Fescue. These are specialty grasses, beautiful in color and texture and excellent for shaded areas where there is moist, well-drained soil and where extra water may be given in the hottest, driest parts of the summer. They are not for general use as their heat and drought tolerance is low.

They should be planted, fertilized, and maintained on the same schedule as Tall Fescue. They should be cut, however, much lower at about 2 inches.

KENTUCKY BLUEGRASS

Kentucky Bluegrass and its strains like Merion, Fylking, and Adelphi are perhaps our most beautiful lawn grasses. Where they grow well, usually much farther north, they are outstanding and form some of the best lawns. In the South these grasses should be used only in the upper piedmont and in the mountains. They will grow in shady areas quite well and in the sun when given enough extra moisture in dry weather. There is no better grass than Kentucky Bluegrass where it will grow, but adapting it to your specific location may be difficult.

Planting and maintaining follows the same schedule as Tall Fescue.

SELECTING THE RIGHT GRASS FOR YOUR LAWN

It would be so wonderful if there were just one very superior type of grass for the South. Unfortunately, as you have seen from the above descriptions of the various grasses which can be grown, there are many choices. To have a lawn you must choose which is best for your location, for your life-style, and for the appearance of the landscape which you are developing.

Some lawns are relatively easy to maintain, others take a lot of attention. Some grow well when it is cool, while others grow best when it is hot. The time of greatest use will be a factor in the choice of which one to plant.

I admonish you to make the choice wisely, without too much attention to "miracles" which may be advertised. Your County Extension Agent should have bulletins which will help. Also, what is growing well in your area should be considered. A reliable nursery or seed supplier is also an excellent source of information.

As you start making the choice, ask yourself the following questions and discuss the answers with the expert you have chosen to help:

- How much sun and shade does the lawn area receive?
- When will be the time of most use?
- How much time will you be willing to give to the lawn's maintenance?
- How important is it to have a most beautiful lawn?
- Does a brown winter lawn bother you?
- How much money and effort do you want to expend when starting the lawn?

After these questions are answered look at the grass selection chart and choose the grass which you think is best for you.

A Kentucky 31 Fescue lawn

GRASS SELECTION BY CHARACTERISTICS

	MAINTENANCE			TEXTURE			LIGHT				PLANTING FORM		OVERSEED/ WINTER GREEN	THICK TURF
	LOW	HIGH	HIGHEST	FINE	COARSE	MEDIUM	SUNNY	LIGHT SHADE	MOD. SHADE	SHADE-TOLERANT	SEED	SOD		
Common Bermuda	x					x	x				x			
Tifgreen Bermuda			x	x			x					x	x	x
Tifway Bermuda			x	x			x					x		x
Chewing Fescue		x	x	x					x	x	x			
Creeping Red Fescue		x	x	x					x	x	x			
Tall Fescue (Kentucky 31)		x			x		x	x			x			
Emerald Zoysia		x	x	x			x	x	x			x		x
Meyer Zoysia	x					x	x	x				x	x	x
Centipede	x					x	x	x	x	x	x	x	x	x
Kentucky Bluegrass		x	x			x		x	x		x			
St. Augustine			x*		x		x	x	x	x		x		x

*Has Chinch Bug and Decline Virus problems, and lacks cold tolerance

WHEN TO PLANT

The seasons for planting new lawns depend entirely on the type of grasses you are using. These times may vary, depending on altitude and earliness of the season. In the fall, start planting as soon as the nights begin to be cool and there is moisture in the ground. In the spring, start as soon as the weather begins to warm.

Warm-Season grasses can be planted from either seed or sod. If planting from **seed**, follow these planting times:
- Common Bermuda Grass—Early May until early July
- Centipede Grass—Mid-April until mid-June

If planting from **sod** (vegetatively), always plant after danger of frost, and follow these planting times:
- All Bermuda Grasses—Early May until first of August
- Centipede Grass—Early May until first of August
- St. Augustine Grass—Early May until first of August
- Zoysia Grasses—After frost until early August

Cool-season grasses all have the same planting dates since they are all being planted from seed. Fall is the best time to plant these grasses. They can be planted from September 1 until frost. In the spring, planting of cool-season grasses should occur from early March until mid-April.

PLANTING THE NEW LAWN

SOIL PREPARATION

Grasses are plants with specific requirements for growth. Soil preparation is just as important in establishing a new lawn as it is in having good vegetables or beautiful flowers. Good soil preparation is hard work, and shortcuts will result in poor performance. If a previous lawn in that same area has died out or become weed-infested, scattering more seed will not make the lawn spring back to life. As soon as poor growing weather arrives, the lawn will be back in the same shape and all the seed and fertilizer will have been wasted.

Breaking the Ground

Traffic, poor soil management, and natural depletion of grasses will cause the soil to be hard and become baked in heat. To start a new lawn, work the soil deeply and thoroughly with a plow or tiller. The deeper it is worked, the better the growth will be and the longer your lawn will stay beautiful. The soil should be broken at least 8 inches deep, but deeper if possible.

Adding Humus

Lawns are like all other growing areas in the South: they need humus to loosen the clay and to increase drainage. Peat moss, ground bark, vermiculite, and perlite are all excellent materials to use. If you can find old-fashioned dehydrated (not composted) cow manure, it is excellent to use with the humus material.

To enrich one thousand square feet of heavy clay soil, you should add:
- One 6-cubic-foot bale of peat moss
- Three 3-cubic-foot bags of ground bark
- Three 3-cubic-foot bags of perlite
- Add three 3-cubic-foot bags of vermiculite if the soil tends to be very dry
- 100 pounds of *dehydrated* cattle manure

Apply these materials evenly over the broken-up soil and till again so that they are thoroughly incorporated into the root zone of the plants. This layer should be at least 6 inches deep.

Lime and Fertilizer

Grasses need ample nutrients to grow well. The fertilizer you need for starting new grass plants will be different from what you will need year after year once the lawn is established. I have found the best formula for starting a new lawn to be a 12-4-8 with approximately 50% of the nitrogen (6 units of the 12) as a slow-release type, usually Uramite. Beware of using a 10-10-10 fertilizer when starting a new lawn. These are generally high in quick-acting nitrogen, and they will make your lawn grow too succulently and rapidly in the beginning, resulting in nitrogen deficiency later, especially if planting is done in the early spring (cool-season grasses) when rainfall is great.

Most grasses grow best in the 6.0 pH range. Thus, lime should be added to many of our soils. It is very important to have a soil test made if at all possible. For an area of one thousand square feet add:
- 10 to 15 pounds of a 12-4-8 fertilizer
- 50 pounds of pelletized dolomitic limestone
  (Do not use limestone on Centipede Grass.)

Distribute the lime and fertilizer evenly over the new lawn. Rake it into the top 2 or 3 inches with a sharp-tooth garden rake (bow rake).

Now you are ready to seed or sod the lawn.

SEEDING A NEW LAWN

Larger seeds, especially of Fescue and Bluegrass, are easily sown by hand or in a fertilizer/seed distributor. Be sure to apply the right amount of seed and distribute them evenly. Overseeding can be as bad as underseeding and a lot more expensive. The proper seeding rates per thousand square feet are:
- Bermuda Grass—2 lbs.
- Bluegrass—3 to 5 lbs.
- Centipede Grass—$1/4$ to $1/2$ lbs.
- All Fescues—5 to 8 lbs.

To prevent skips, it is wise to spread half of the seed lengthwise and half crosswise. After distributing the seed, rake them into the ground with the garden rake to be sure that they are covered.

The procedure for planting very small seeds of grasses such as Bermuda Grass and Centipede is the same except that it is helpful to mix the seed thoroughly with an equal amount of dry sand. This allows the seed to be much more evenly distributed. Do not rake the small seed heavily because they should not be covered deeply.

Once you have planted the seed, it is wise to cover the newly-seeded area lightly with clean wheat or oat straw. This prevents a crust from forming and helps germination. After applying the straw, water the lawn area well to settle the seed and start the germination process.

SODDING A NEW LAWN

The steps for sodding are the same as for seeding, up to the point of planting. Once the seed bed is made and the fertilizer and lime added (except with Centipede, add no lime), the procedures differ.

Most homeowners are more successful with solid or strip-sodding or plugging rather than sprigging, which requires a special machine to cut the sprigs into the ground. The first two methods may seem more expensive, but in the long run the results outweigh the slight increase in cost.

The main consideration when strip-sodding or plugging is to be sure that the roots are covered well and that the top is not. It is like planting any growing plant. Planting too deeply is worse than planting too shallowly.

Here are a few helpful hints for sodding correctly:
- Do not plant too deeply.
- Plant strips across the slope so that ruts will not form.
- Plug in a triangular manner.
- Be sure that when you are finished, you have set the strips, sod, or plugs thoroughly in the ground.

It is hard to determine the right amount of sod for an area; it depends entirely on how wide you make the strips or how big you cut the plugs and how you space them. Space the pre-cut, pre-grown plugs on 1-foot centers for fastest coverage. Space 2- to 3-inch strips in rows which are 12 to 18 inches apart.

OVERSEEDING WITH ANNUAL RYEGRASS

Southerners have always wanted evergreen lawns. Before the widespread use of Tall Fescue as a lawn grass, the only possible way was to overseed the dormant warm-season grasses with Ryegrass. This is a satisfactory way to deal with a brown lawn in the winter if the turf will support the second grass.

You can overseed Common Bermuda Grass, Meyer Zoysia, and properly-handled Centipede with annual Ryegrass. The other warm-season grasses which have been discussed make such a thick turf that the Ryegrass cannot get its roots to the ground.

The time to overseed Ryegrass is in mid to late September or early October, before the first frost. Cut the lawn closer than normal and sow the Ryegrass at a rate of about 10 pounds per thousand square feet. Water the lawn thoroughly to take the seed to the ground. Fertilize with a half-application of a regular lawn fertilizer.

Keep the lawn mowed normally throughout the winter. In the spring, fertilize the dual lawn at the recommended (normal) rate for growing the warm-season grass but about two weeks earlier than normal.

The transition period, that is, the time when the warm-season grass is beginning to grow and the Ryegrass is beginning to die, is of major importance. The Ryegrass must not be allowed to grow tall. If the lawn is not cut properly, the Ryegrass will shade the warm-season grass excessively and weaken the plants as they break dormancy. This may cause thinning of your permanent grass or even result in dead patches.

Never overplant cool-season grasses with Ryegrass. This will only weaken your permanent lawn because the Ryegrass will compete for space, nutrients, and water with the permanent cool-season grass, which is actively growing at the same time.

CUTTING YOUR NEW GRASS

Cut newly seeded lawns as soon as the seedling grass reaches its normal cutting height (see chart on page 325 for correct heights). Catch the clippings so they do not mat over the young, tender grass seedlings. Cutting helps to toughen the young grass plants and make the running types begin to spread. Be sure to cut young grass when it is dry so the mower wheels will not mat down the seedlings.

WATERING YOUR NEW LAWN

Newly germinating grass seedlings have very small roots, and dry weather can take its toll. Spreading wheat or oat straw will help insulate the soil and prevent the surface from drying out and the young roots from dying. In long, dry periods, apply additional water. See the remarks on regular watering practice for maintaining a beautiful lawn.

RENOVATING AN OLD LAWN

Old lawns are tiresome at best. We seldom inherit a beautiful lawn; all too often our own lawns decline and look awful. What should be done?

As I said, a lawn which has declined will not spring back to life for long by just throwing out seed and fertilizing a bit. The twice-yearly ritual of "seed strowing" goes on each spring and fall in the South. This may be great for the seed industry, but it's bad for the home owner's pocketbook, his temperament, and the beauty of the home. Little is accomplished.

A lawn which needs
renovating

Moss indicates poor
surface drainage and
acid soil.

When a lawn declines, there is always a good reason. If a healthy grass plant cannot survive, how on earth can a weak young seedling? The problem almost always is in the degeneration of the soil, unless an external force such as winter cold, summer drought, some insect, or disease destroys the healthy plants. Thus, when grass becomes weak and unhealthy, you should look at the soil for the answer.

What you have to decide now is whether to revive the lawn or whether to start over as described above. The best test is to get down on your hands and knees and look at one square foot of the lawn. If there are four or more live plants of Fescue or two or more live plants of Bermuda Grass, Centipede, St. Augustine, or Zoysia in that one square foot, the lawn should be worth saving. If there are fewer than that, you need to start a whole new lawn.

Most lawns degenerate because of compaction and bad soil structure. This comes about over the years because of excessive traffic, improper or too little fertilizing, and a failure to keep the lawn properly aerated. The steps to regeneration are as follows:

Plug-type aerator

1. Aerate the lawn area with a plug-type aerator. Run the aerator lengthwise and then crosswise.
2. Lime the area (except in the case of Centipede).
3. Fertilize with an organic fertilizer such as dehydrated cattle manure.
4. Also, fertilize with a starter fertilizer like the 12-4-8 described above.
5. Reseed the lawn. (Reseed cool-season grasses in the fall.)
6. Re-plug or strip vegetatively-propagated grasses like Zoysia in the late spring.
7. Top-dress particularly bad lawns also with ground bark or peat moss. Be careful that you do not cover the plants of Zoysia, Fescue, or Bluegrass.
8. Water the lawn area as soon as you have finished all the above steps.
9. Start a regular maintenance program so that your lawn will not degenerate again.

Note: Treat lawn areas which have been infested with weeds before you take the above steps. Your County Extension Agent or nurseryman will have information as to the best materials to use on your own particular weeds.

MAINTAINING A BEAUTIFUL LAWN

REGULAR FERTILIZING

Supplying adequate nutrients to your lawn is an absolute necessity to keep it growing well and producing a thick turf. A healthy lawn will generally need about five pounds of nitrogen per thousand square feet per year during the time the grass is actively growing. An exception is Centipede Grass, which needs about half that amount. Supply this amount in two or three applications, depending on the type of fertilizer used. You can apply slow-release nitrogen formulas only twice during the season; apply quick-release formulas at least three times.

Too-close cutting, or scalping, will cause grass to die out.

Most grasses respond best to fertilizers with a 3-1-2 ratio. Centipede may be harmed by excessive phosphate in the soil, so avoid high-phosphate fertilizers like 10-10-10.

MOWING CORRECTLY

Improperly-cut lawns may degenerate rapidly. Some grasses which are cut too closely will thin and die out. Grasses which are allowed to grow too much between cuttings, especially Bermuda Grass, will be unsightly after each cutting and may be weakened. A sharp mower blade is also extremely important. The blade should cut the grass, not break it. Ragged cuts will brown and make the lawn unattractive.

The great majority of lawn owners use rotary mowers. There are very few reel-type mowers on the market and they are very expensive. Some grasses, like Emerald Zoysia, may be so thick that mowing with a rotary mower is difficult. If you keep the blades sharp and mow frequently, you should be able to cut most Emerald Zoysia lawns satisfactorily with a rotary mower.

RECOMMENDED CUTTING HEIGHTS	
Common Bermuda Grass	2 inches
Hybrid Bermuda Grass	1 to 1 1/2 inches
Centipede Grass	1 1/2 to 2 inches
Tall Fescue	3 to 3 1/2 inches
Fine Fescues	1 1/2 to 2 inches
Kentucky Bluegrass	2 to 2 1/2 inches
St. Augustine Grass	2 to 2 1/2 inches
Zoysia (all types)	1 to 2 inches

The frequency of mowing is most important, and is determined entirely by the speed of growth. Cut lawns frequently enough to remove only about one-fourth of the height at any one cutting. This keeps the plant growing low to the ground and prevents "stemming" (a tall stalk developing with a tuft of leaves of top). Cutting into this stalk area will remove the green and leave the lawn brown until new leaves appear. This occurs with Bermuda Grass which is not cut often enough.

Cool-season grasses will grow slowly during the summer. In hot, dry weather you should mow less frequently (it probably isn't really needed anyway). Cut Tall Fescue higher in the summer to leave as much cover over the fleshy crown as possible. Cutting at 3 1/2 to 4 inches in the summer is helpful if your mower can be raised that high.

If a lawn is cut at the proper frequency, the clippings do not need to be caught and removed. Clippings are seldom the cause of the build-up of thatch, which will be discussed later. Returning the green material to the ground does return nutrients and is part of the soil's cycle. But never leave clippings which are matted over the grass because they can cause serious problems.

DETHATCHING

Thatch is an accumulation of dead grass plant parts which builds up in the lawn. It is usually made of old stems and grass blades which have died naturally. Grasses like Zoysia, Centipede, St. Augustine, and the Hybrid Bermudas can build enormous amounts of thatch each year. Mowing properly will help keep thatching low, but you should dethatch these thick turf grasses each spring right before the new growing season. Machines designed for this purpose are called verticut or dethatcher machines and may be rented. Years of thatch accumulation may result in serious insect and disease problems as well as reduced vigor of the plants.

Dethatcher

Thatch build-up in a lawn

WATERING

One of the favorite American pastimes is lawn-watering. Sitting on the front steps with a hose and watering the lawn may be therapeutic for the lawn owner, but it is definitely bad for the lawn; in fact, it might even be disastrous.

Lawns need huge amounts of moisture, about 1 inch of rainfall or its equivalent per week during growing periods. Lawns under trees need even more; we must remember how much water a tree takes from the soil. Watering during a dry period is helpful and may be essential. A good rule is to water when there hasn't been an inch of rain in two weeks.

Light watering wets only the surface and brings the roots upward until they are within a few inches of the surface. When the water is withheld or when the weather is extremely hot, the topsoil dries out and the roots suffer.

An impulse sprinkler is the best type to use on a lawn.

Each time you water, you should supply at least $1/2$ inch. A good way to determine if you are giving the right amount is to place a pound coffee can or some other wide straight-sided can halfway between the sprinkler and the extremity of the water fall. Accumulate at least $1/2$ inch of water in the can before you move the sprinkler. If the water should start to puddle on the ground, turn off the sprinkler until the water is absorbed. Turn on the sprinkler and let it run again until the half-inch of water has been accumulated. Water again in three or four days if no rainfall occurs.

Always water during the morning or mid-afternoon so that the grass goes into the evening with its blades dry. Late afternoon or evening watering invites attacks of insects and disease because both are more active under humid or damp conditions in the cool, still evening.

THE USE OF TOPSOIL

It is an old practice to buy topsoil to spread over a lawn area prior to starting a new lawn or from time to time as a top-dressing over declining lawns. Topsoil may be helpful in some instances. If you need soil to smooth out depressions or to replace washed-away soil, use topsoil simply because it is probably better than the soil in your yard.

The mere placing of topsoil over a lawn area which is to be seeded in no way alleviates the need for further soil preparation. In fact, it may do more harm than good unless the old soil is plowed or tilled first and the topsoil worked into the top layers of the old soil. Otherwise the roots will stay in the topsoil and not penetrate the lower soil areas; and then in dry periods, when the surface areas dry out, the plants will suffer.

Top-dress only when it is necessary to smooth the lawn. Never top-dress so heavily that the grass tops are covered. Top-dressing may be particularly disastrous on Zoysia and the Fescues.

I prefer to spend my money on materials to make topsoil out of my old soil. Peat moss, ground bark, cow manure, and perlite are better investments than topsoil in almost all cases. If you build your own topsoil with good materials and deep plowing or tilling, in the long run the results will be better.

INSECT AND DISEASE PROBLEMS

Lawns are subject to pest problems. A healthy, vigorous lawn is your best defense. At times there may be attacks of diseases like Dollar Spot and Brown Patch and perhaps others. Diseases form regular patterns of die-out. A Brown Patch attack is seen as a browning of parts of the lawn. These spots will be regular and will make an expanding patch or circle. Your local chemical supplier or County Extension Agent will give you the best control for your area. Always treat the patch, giving particular emphasis to the area which lies adjacent and outside the dying grass patch.

Insects make brown patches also but these will expand irregularly. A dry application of an insecticide or spraying the lawn with a recommended chemical will control the infestation.

Take action to control diseases as soon as you see them.

Japanese Beetle Grubs may destroy a lawn without any indication that they are attacking, since they feed underground on the roots of grass plants. The lawn gets thinner and thinner and may even disappear after a few years of the attacks. The grubs feed on the roots of the grass and, unseen, can ruin a beautiful lawn. These crescent-shaped grubs will be in the ground much of the year. Treatment is done with a dry chemical like Oftanol or Diazinon. These materials are most effective when applied in the fall before the ground begins to cool and the spring after the ground has warmed. Treatment with Milky Spore is a permanent control but it is expensive.

Army Worms can be seen! They will march through a lawn and eat it up before your eyes. Prepare to treat as soon as they are reported in your area. One or two days may mean a destroyed lawn. Contact your local nurseryman or County Extension Agent for the best control measures for these terrible creatures.

WEEDS

"Weeds have ruined my lawn. What can I do?" Over and over I hear that plaintive cry. Though there are chemicals which will control most of our serious weed problems, we should use them only as a last resort. The best way to control weeds is by maintaining the health and vigor of the lawn, not by spraying.

Someone once described a weed as any plant which is out of place. Some of our lawn weeds may be satisfactory plants elsewhere but they are unsatisfactory in a lawn. I should emphasize that weeds don't kill grass; they merely grow in areas where the grass is growing poorly. The right grass planted and grown well in the right environment will grow just as strongly as a weed. It is when the wrong grass is planted in an area, or when soil conditions are poor, or when grass is growing unhealthily, that we have serious weed problems in the lawn.

I have tried to give you all the alternative choices of lawn grasses for the South. I have tried to show how to keep your lawn growing well. Following these suggestions will do more than anything else to prevent your lawn being taken over by weeds.

This doesn't mean that you will never see a weed again; it just means that your weed problems should be minimal.

Let us look now at the types of weed problems which you may face and what you can do about them. There are two major groups of weeds: (1) annual weeds, which grow from a seed, make a plant, and die in one season (these are the easiest to control); and (2) perennial weeds, which grow initially from a seed to a mature plant in a season, but do not die completely. They return the next season from the dormant plant. Perennial weeds are the hardest to control.

Now let us break down these classes into more easily-identified weed problems.

Weed Grasses

Any unwanted grass becomes a weed. Common Bermuda Grass in a hybrid Bermuda Grass lawn must be considered a weed grass and should be removed.

The worst weed grasses, however, are those which come from seed, such as Crabgrass, Goosegrass, Crowsfoot Grass, and Dallis Grass. Nutgrass is the nemesis of many Southern lawns. It is not a grass but a sedge, and it is one exception to the rule that well-grown grasses prevent weed infestations in lawns. Perhaps the old adage *is* correct: "The only way to control Nutgrass is to move."

Fortunately, many of our weed grasses are annuals, with the exception of Nutgrass, which is a perennial. You can obtain good control of these annual weed grasses through the use of pre-emergence weed and grass preventers.

Crabgrass

Nutgrass

Dandelion

Ground Ivy and Wild Lespedeza

Violets

Common Clover

Wild Garlic (Wild Onion)

Narrowleaf Plantain

Annual Weeds

Dandelion (a botanical perennial which often acts like an annual), Wild Mustard, Pepperweed, spurges, Henbit, Vetch, and many more, depending on your particular location, are annuals which have a very difficult time becoming established in a thick, heavy turf. You can virtually eliminate these if you use a pre-emergence weed and grass preventer in the spring and maintain a thick, healthy turf.

Perennial Weeds

Nutgrass (Nutsedge), Ground Ivy, Violets, the clovers, Lespedeza, Wild Onion (Wild Garlic), Chickweed, and Purslain are perennials and must be removed by digging them out or by repeated applications of chemicals which will selectively kill them. A thick, healthy turf will retard or even prevent the initial infestations, but if they become established, you will need a drastic means of removal.

WEED CONTROL

The first step toward weed control is to keep the lawn grasses growing well. This first and foremost rule cannot be overemphasized.

An annual application of one of the pre-emergence weed and grass preventers, often referred to simply as Crabgrass preventers, is step number two. These dry materials should be applied *before* the weed or weed grass seed germinate. A good guide to the time of application is to apply when Forsythia is in bloom.

Warning: Never apply these materials to lawns which are going to be reseeded within six months.

You must remove perennial weeds which have become established in a lawn by digging them out or by spraying them with a chemical specifically recommended for the control of that particular weed.

Chemical control is difficult when these weeds have been allowed to grow for some time during the current growing season. Best control is obtained when they are growing freshly in the spring.

Advice and Help

I have been trying to help people with weed problems for years and find it one of the most difficult jobs I ever face. Since what looks like Chickweed to you may actually be Purslain, the best method is to take a sample of the weed to someone who knows, rather than trying to describe it over the phone or in a letter.

Dig the weed or weed grass with some roots and plenty of top. Put it in a plastic bag and close the bag tightly. Take it as soon as possible to your garden supply dealer or County Extension Agent. Follow their recommendations carefully.

Using Chemical Weed Controls

This is only the first volume of my three-volume series and I want you to be healthy when the next two volumes appear. **Apply chemicals carefully and safely. Protect yourself, your family, your pets and your other plants. Follow these rules:**

1. Use *only* the chemicals recommended.
2. Mix at the recommended strength. A little may be good; too much may kill other plants close by or be harmful to you and your pets.
3. Protect yourself from breathing the material or getting it on your skin:
   Use a face mask.
   Wear a long-sleeved shirt.
   Wear rubber gloves.
4. Spray when the air is still to prevent vapor or mist from drifting onto nearby plants.
5. Never spray the ground near the following:
   Azalea
   Boxwood
   Dogwood
   Holly
   Magnolia
6. Never spray the top of the ground where you see plant roots under the mulch.
7. *Never* use a weed killer in a sprayer used for fungicides and insecticides. Buy two sprayers and save your other plants.

INDEX

INDEX

Elm:
    Chinese, 69, 75
Elmer's glue, 298
England, 4, 157, 169, 307, 308
Espaliering trees, 136–137
Euonymus: *Euonymus*, 196–197
    Boxleaf, 198
    Fortunei Euonymus Group: *E.*
        Fortunei,196
        Colorata: *E. Fortunei* cv. 'Colorata,'
            197
        Emerald Gaity: *E. Fortunei* cv.
            'Emerald Gaity,' 197, 198
        Sarcoxie: *E. Fortunei* cv. 'Sarcoxie,'
            197
    Japanese: *E. japonica*, 197
    Manhattan: *E. kiautschovica* cv.
        'Manhattan,' 199
    Southern: *E. kiautschovica* (formerly *E.*
        patens), 197, 198
Evaporation, 66
Evergreen(s):
    bare-root planting, 55
    best trees; heights (table), 84
    broadleaf, 14, 188, 219, 228
    coniferous, 188, 220, 228
    rhododendrons, 251–252
Exochorda racemosa, see Pearl Bush

Fagus, see Beech
Fall, 25, 73–74, 87
Farouk, King, 1
Fertilizer(s):
    forms, 37–38
    formulas, 49
    liquid, 50
    major nutrients, 37
    organics and inorganics, 32, 37
    soluble, 49
    spikes, 50
    spreaders, 49, 50
Fescue:
    characteristics (chart), 318, 328
    Chewing, 311, 318
    Creeping Red, 311, 318
    Tall (Kentucky 31), 311, 313, 315, 317,
        318, 325
    Turf Type, 316
Fiacre, Saint, 8
Figs, 55
Finland, 27
Firethorn: *Pyracantha*, 216–217
Flat Head Borer, 158
Florida, 29
Floweracres, Georgia, 1, 2, 8, 11
Flowering cherry, *see* Cherry: flowering

Flowering shrubs, 256–258
    blossoms, 257
    deciduous, 188, 256–258
    pruned as trees, 174
    pruning, 258
Flowering trees, 145–177
    blooming dates and season, 147
    blossoms on new growth, 175
    blossoms on old wood, 175
    color of blossoms, 149
    growth habits, 149
    growth rate, 149
    height and breadth, 149
    insect/disease problems, 149
    maintenance, 175
    mulching, 177
    planting, 175
    problems, 176–177
    pruning, 176
    purpose, 146
    selecting, 147–149
    shade trees and, 66
    street plantings, 135
    summer-flowering, 169ff
    weed control chemicals, 177
Forsythia: *Forsythia* × *intermedia*, 15, 263,
    287
    Spring Glory, 257, 264
Fossils, 102
Franklinia, 62
Franklinia Alatamaha, see Lost Gordonia
Fraxinus, see Ash
Frost, 21

Galle, Fred, 232
Garden:
    definition, 8
    location as factor, 22
    nature of, 8–10
Gardenia: *Gardenia jasminoides*, 24, 184,
    199–200, 219
    August Beauty: *G. jasminoides* cv.
        'August Beauty,' 200
    Creeping: *G. jasminoides* cv. 'Radicans,'
        201
    Mystery: *G. jasminoides* cv. 'Mystery,'
        200
Gardening:
    art of, 29
    creativity, 10–14
    failure in, 7
    faith in, 6
    fun in, 8
    landscaping and, 9–10
    schedules in, 26
    Southern heritage, 3, 4

high temperatures, 28
planting zones, 24
Temple of Solomon, 97
Tennessee, 95
Thatch, 326
Thuja, see Arborvitae
Tomatoes, 27, 41
Tools, 42–49
   caution on, 50–51
   hand, 46
   long-handled, 44–45
Topsoil, 3, 34, 328
Trace elements, 38
Tree(s):
   air conditioning and, 65, 66
   problem trees, avoiding, 143
   Southern landscapes, 14
Tree of Heaven, 68
Tsuga canadensis, see Hemlock
Tulip Poplar, *see* Poplar: Yellow or Tulip

Unter den Linden, 108
Urban Forestry Unit (state), 143

Vegetable garden, 12
Viburnum: *Viburnum*, 279
   Burkwoodii: *V.* × *Burkwoodii*, 282, 283
   Carlcephalum: *V.* × *carlcephalum*, 282, 283
   Double File: *V. plicatum* forma *tomentosum*, 280, 281
   Fragrant, 287
   Juddii: *V.* × *Juddii*, 282, 283
   see also Snowball
Violets, 331
Vitamin C., 288
Vitex Agnus-castus, see Chaste Tree

Walnut:
   Black: *Juglans nigra*, 81, 84, 86, 132
Water breaker, 48
Watering equipment, 47–48
Waxing, 293
Weather, 20–22

gardeners' dealing with, 22
protecting plants, 22
sayings, 20–21
see also Cold weather; Temperature
Weed trimmer, 43, 150
Weeds, 329–330
   annual, 332
   chemicals; care, 333
   control, 332–333
   perennial, 332
Weigela, see Cardinal Shrub
West Nobaria, Egypt, 5, 10
White Fringe Tree, *see* Grancy Gray Beard
White Judas Tree, *see* Judas Tree: White
Willow: *Salix*, 285
   Corkscrew: *S. Matsudana* cv. 'Tortuosa,' 285, 287
   Fan Tail: *S. sachalinensis* cv. 'Sekka,' 286, 287
   Goat: *S. caprea*, 286, 287
   Pussy: *S. discolor*, 286, 287
   Weeping: *S. babylonica*, 72, 81, 82, 85, 88, 133
Wind, 69
Windsor Castle, England, 26
Winter, 66
   of 1984–85, 25
Wintersweet, *see* Meratia
Witch Hazel: *Hamamelis virginiana*, 169, 174

Yellow Poplar, *see* Poplar: Yellow or Tulip
Yew, 220, 225, 226
   Plum: *Cephalotaxus Harringtonia* var. *drupacea*, 227
   Southern: *Podocarpus macrophyllus*, 227
   Taxus × *media*, 227
Yucca filamentosa, see Adam's Needle
Yucca: *Yucca*, 218

Zone temperature map, 23, 24
Zoysia grass, 314, 319, 325, 326, 328
   Emerald, 311, 313, 318
   Meyer, 311, 318